Children's Book Publishing in Britain Since 1945

This book is dedicated to the memory of Edward Blishen and Kaye Webb, both unforgettably delightful people who also worked tirelessly for children and their books.

Children's Book Publishing in Britain Since 1945

Edited by

Kimberley Reynolds and Nicholas Tucker

SCOLAR PRESS

Published by
Scolar Press
Gower House
Croft Road
Aldershot
Hants GU11 3HR
England

Ashgate Publishing Company
Old Post Road
Brookfield
Vermont 05036–9704
USA

British Library Cataloguing-in-Publication data.

Children's book publishing in Britain since 1945
1. Children's literature – Publishing – Great Britain – History – 20th century
I. Reynolds, Kimberley II. Tucker, Nicholas
070.5'083'0941

Library of Congress Cataloging-in-Publication data.

Children's book publishing in Britain since 1945/edited by Kimberley Reynolds and Nicholas Tucker.
Includes bibliographical references.
ISBN 1–85928–236–9 (acid-free paper)
1. Children's literature—Publishing—Great Britain—History—20th century.   I. Reynolds, Kimberley.   II. Tucker, Nicholas.
Z326.C48   1997
070.5'0941'0904—dc21   97–19546
                    CIP

ISBN 1 85928 236 9

Printed on acid-free paper
Typeset in Sabon by Intype London Ltd and printed in Great Britain by Biddles Limited, Guildford

Contents

Acknowledgements

The editors and contributors would like to thank the many people who generously gave their time and shared their knowledge (and sometimes their libraries, correspondence and lunches) with us while this book was in preparation. It has only been possible to include a small proportion of the information, stories and insights they offered here, although with the support of the Arts Council of England many of the interviews have been recorded and are available in the form of transcripts in an 'Oral Archive of Children's Publishing' at Roehampton Institute, London.

Special thanks to Liz Attenborough, Nina Bawden, Paul Binding, Edward Blishen, Laura Cecil, Aidan Chambers, Nancy Chambers, Margaret Clark, Eileen Colwell, Michael Dawson, Philippa Dickinson, David Fickling, Klaus Flugge, Joanna Goldsworthy, Ron Heapy, C. Walter Hodges, Marni Hodgkin, Miriam Hodgson, Shirley Hughes, Tony Lacey, Robert Leeson, David Lloyd, Julia MacRae, Anne McNeil, Gwen Marsh, Elaine Moss, Iona Opie, Philippa Pearce, Caroline Roberts, Pam Royds, Rosemary Stones, Renu Sabherwal, Anne Sarrag, Judy Taylor, Geoffrey Trease, John Rowe Townsend, Jill Paton Walsh, Kaye Webb, and Jane Winterbottom.

The editors are grateful to Angela Macpherson of Bags of Books in Lewes, East Sussex for her generous loan of artwork for the cover.

Responsibility for any inaccuracies in the text rests with the editors, who are still learning about the period, personalities and achievements in children's publishing after 1945.

Sadly, since we began this project Edward Blishen and Kaye Webb have died.

Contributors

Nicholas Tucker lectures on developmental psychology and children's literature at the University of Sussex. He is author of five books about children, childhood and reading, including *The Child and the Book; a literary and psychological exploration*, published by the Cambridge University Press in 1981 and reissued in their Canto Classic series in 1990. He has also written six books for children, broadcasts frequently and reviews widely in the national press.

Kimberley Reynolds is Reader in Children's Literature and Director of the National Centre for Research in Children's Literature at Roehampton Institute, London. Recent publications include *Children's Literature in the 1890s and 1990s* and *Victorian Heroines: Representations of femininity in nineteenth-century literature and art*. She is currently working with Gillian Avery on a collection of essays about images of the death of children.

Keith Barker is a librarian at Westhill College, Birmingham. He is Review Editor of *The School Librarian*, and past editor of *Youth Library Review*. He is the author of *In the Realms of Gold* (Julia MacRae) and of monographs on Gillian Cross and Dick King-Smith (School Library Association), editor of *Information books for children* (Ashgate) and *Graphic Account* (Youth Libraries Group) and compiler of *Bridging the Gap* (Book Trust/British Council). In 1994 he was chair of the Youth Libraries Group and therefore chair of the panel which selected the Carnegie and Kate Greenaway medals that year.

Judith Graham is a Principal Lecturer in Education at Roehampton Institute, London. Before this post she taught at the University of Greenwich and at the London Institute of Education. She is the author of a book on illustration in children's books *Pictures on the Page* (NATE 1990), and has written and lectured on this topic and on aspects of literacy, language and children's literature.

Geoff Fox is Senior Lecturer in English and Drama at the School of Education,

Exeter University. He is well-known as a conference speaker and writer on children's books, and has taught literature in North America and Australia as well as in the UK. He has been editor of *Children's Literature in Education* since its first issue in 1970.

Philip Pullman taught in middle schools in Oxford for twelve years, and then lectured in English and Children's Literature at Westminster College, Oxford for ten years until 1996. He has written on graphic novels and visual literacy, and published several children's books. The latest of these, *Northern Lights* (Point, 1995) won the *Guardian* Children's Fiction Award and the Carnegie Medal.

Susanne Greenhalgh is Senior Lecturer in Drama at Roehampton Institute, London, where she is also active in the Women's Studies Programme which she helped to found. She has written about a wide range of subjects, including growing up female, women terrorists, and seventeenth-century witch trials.

Preface

It is easy to take children's books for granted – a tour of any High Street in Britain will find them for sale in all kinds of formats, across a huge spectrum of prices, and in a wide range of outlets. There are books for babies and young adults; books for boys, for girls and for readers of both sexes; books which reflect the life experiences of children from ethnic minorities, children with diseases, and children with disabilities; books for young readers who want to confront problems and for those who want to escape from them; books which set out to teach and those which set out to entertain; books which have been read by generations of young people and books reflecting current trends and preoccupations.

At no time before has there been such diversity in children's publishing, but because books are so abundant and available few people stop to think about how they come into being. There is nothing natural about the children's book scene today; it is a product of historical circumstance, ideology, and market forces. Neither are children's books neutral. We live in a text-based society, and the books we give young people to read (whether these are traditional printed texts or those which employ new technologies and media) play an important role in acculturating them.

The history of publishing for children is long, distinguished and complex. Among other things, it encompasses the histories of childhood, of printing, of illustration, of librarianship, and of reading. Studying books produced specifically for young readers reveals a great deal about what a society values, fears and aspires to at any given moment. Some work has been done on these aspects of the early history of publishing for children, and recently a number of studies of the 'golden age' of children's literature (roughly from Lewis Carroll to A.A. Milne) have appeared. To date, however, little work has been done on children's publishing in the second half of this century, and the need for such work is urgent. The urgency stems in part from changes in the structure of publishing: at the end of the twentieth century it is usual to find many imprints which once belonged to individual publishing houses now appearing under the same corporate umbrella. With each move and merger individuals disappear, and documents (including manuscripts, illustrated letters and artwork) are lost, destroyed and otherwise dispersed. It therefore becomes increasingly difficult to locate detailed information about anything – from economics to changes in ethos and intention. A further impetus to begin the process of documenting contemporary children's publishing is provided by the speed of technological change. The widespread use of word processors, computers and electronic mail means that there are diminishing numbers of letters, manuscripts and other forms of 'hard copy' to save and consult.

Fortunately, many of the individuals who shaped the children's publishing industry in the years since 1945 are alive and active today. They represent a living archive; in many cases their memories are the only sources which can be consulted for information about publishing decisions, practices, ideals and issues. In the course of writing this book we have visited many of the editors, publishers, writers and illustrators involved in creating the modern children's book industry. Their generosity, vision, enthusiasm for their work and respect for each other is impressive, and working with them has been both an education and a pleasure. In the following pages we have tried to tell their story, using their own words as often as possible. In the process significant changes in working conditions – especially as these relate to the place of children's divisions in corporate hierarchies – come to the fore.

As the study moves forward in time it becomes clear that the higher financial profiles of successful children's imprints within large publishing houses have frequently been attended by loss of autonomy, changes in ethos, and, latterly, a tendency to 'asset strip' children's lists in search of characters which can be merchandised. Far from being able to use such successes to support innovative and responsible publishing, many of today's editors watch in dismay as characters from books are moved into independent profit centres and turned into products whose sales are often so much in excess of fiction that they threaten the very existence of the format for which they were originally conceived. Indeed, so hard does the marketing tail wag the publishing dog that the very nature of creating fictional characters is beginning to change. Books are now produced from other products: one of Reed's best-selling books in 1996 was based on the doll Barbie, and HarperCollins is in the process of bringing out books based on televised adaptations of Enid Blyton novels. Such books keep retailers and accountants happy, but possibly do so at the risk of killing the golden goose. It will be interesting to see whether the reading experiences of those youngsters brought up on a diet of such book-products – which currently sell extremely well – will produce a new generation of readers.

Changes in the marketing of books have affected every aspect of children's publishing. Today the success of a book is often attributed to the marketing department, which can influence the very nature of the list. Editors are under pressure to produce books that sell and in quantities which are unprecedented. The demand to find co-editions is insatiable, and no matter how fine a book is, unless it is marked out as a UK prizewinner, it will not be published without a substantial commitment from publishers based in other countries. The result is a vicious circle which effectively marginalizes those who create books – editors, writers and illustrators. Today, even once an editor has decided to bring out a particular title s/he may be required by the company to drop the book, for reasons which have nothing to do with its literary merit.

Another change in the conditions under which most children's books are produced at the end of the twentieth century is the amount of time available to shape individual books. We were repeatedly told about the protracted discussions between writers and editors which produced some of the great books of the last fifty years. In an unpublished, unedited, autobiographical fragment, the late Robert Westall recalled what it was like to work with Marni Hodgkin, one of the editors who contributed substantially to developing children's publishing in the post-war period (see Chapter 2). He described an office over-flowing with paper and manuscripts, each one of which was read by Marni Hodgkin or her assistant, where single discussions could last five hours, and which offered writers time, interest and support at all times of the day.

> if the physical space was cramped ... the atmosphere was immense, august and grand. ... One seemed to breathe the very air of Mount Parnassus, if not Mount Olympus. ... Ideas and friendship was [*sic*] all; money, marketing, sales were never mentioned. Of course, elsewhere in the building there were ... people who saw to those sorts of things properly; but we had a mutual wish never to discuss them; it got in the way of the real task. Once, purely because somebody else asked me, I asked them [Marni and her assistant] how many copies of *The Machine-gunners* I had sold. Marni and Di looked at each other, rather perplexed, as if I'd suddenly asked the price of cod at Billingsgate Market. Di got a children's exercise book out of her drawer, ran her finger down a list of scrawled figures, and told me. Then we all breathed a sigh of relief and got back to business. ...
>
> What I remember her for most, though, is a terrible rigorous honesty even in her own despite. Like when I got two simultaneous offers for the paperback rights to *The Machine-gunners*. One was from the world-famous Penguin Books and the other was from her own Macmillan paperback house. She wrote, scrupulously laying out the pros and cons of both offers, and ended up 'with Macmillan, you will get more money in obscurity. With Penguin, you will get the kudos and fame. Now I leave you to make your own mind up ...' On such foundations whole worlds can stand.

Unfortunately, there are few accounts such as Westall's, and a paucity of information about the history of contemporary children's publishing. Over the years, however, several key figures from the post-war children's publishing scene have written about their work for the specialist children's literature journal, *Signal*, and their accounts form a valuable resource. *This* study, however, is the first sustained attempt to construct the story of modern children's book publishing in Britain. It is only a beginning, and in no sense claims to be complete. A second volume is planned, and the work of interviewing those who make children's books continues. For this volume we have brought together contributions from individuals who have developed their enthusiasm for and expertise in specific areas of children's literature over a number of years. Although the subjects covered have been chosen because they highlight what we believe are important issues in the development of modern children's publishing, they inevitably reflect our interests and preoccupations. There is more work to be done from many points of view, but we hope that this attempt to identify and organize material about children's publishing in the important years since 1945 will support and inspire others working in this field.

Kimberley Reynolds and Nicholas Tucker

1 Setting the Scene

Nicholas Tucker

The year 1945 was a crucial one in British history. The six-year war that came to an end saw many social and political changes, with more still to come. But while radical legislation helped transform social policy, cultural life and the values that informed it often went on very much as before. There were a number of reasons for such enduring conservatism. A war in which many civilians suffered badly was not seen by any branch of opinion as a good time for rocking the political boat at home, socially or otherwise. Much of British war-time propaganda, therefore, had concentrated on celebrating shared values dating from the past rather than looking to the future. In this world of universal food and energy shortages, travel restrictions and common danger, it was natural to look backwards for contrasting and consoling images of a time before total warfare.

This was particularly true of the small world of children's literature. Comics and a few novels did take up immediate war themes, just as they had done during the First World War, but accompanying contemporary social issues were portrayed at a very over-simplified, nationalist level. More subtle political analysis of happenings both at home and abroad simply did not happen in children's literature. Nor were many criticisms of Britain heard in terms of its still existing class barriers and the economic inequality that accompanied them. Pre-war silence about such topics in the world of children's books and general popular entertainment continued largely as before.

Voices from abroad, in terms of American or Commonwealth children's writers, were not a significant factor at this early stage. An initially debt-ridden post-war Britain had enough trouble financing its own children's literature, let alone buying in material or translations from abroad. The American influence upon British publishing was in time to become an important one, and more is said about this in Chapter 2. But in 1945 British children's literature and publishing remained strongly parochial. As such, it makes sense to study it as an entity in its own right, both in this chapter and in the bulk of those that follow.

With little modern British children's fiction published as possible competition, it was not surprising that sales of A.A. Milne's children's stories – already very popular – greatly increased during the war. Modern best-sellers that also looked to the past, like Richmal Crompton's William books, with their full complements of cooks, gardeners and maids, were as sought after as ever. Immensely popular writers like Enid Blyton and W.E. Johns continued to write stories reflecting a world of middle-class prejudice against selected foreigners, half-castes and gypsies. Home-grown villains as often as not continued to be portrayed as surly working-class characters, generally with designs on other people's property. This was how children's books had always been, and there was as yet little pressure for change.

Damage caused in bombing raids to publishers' stocks and printing plates also meant that up to twenty million children's books suddenly disappeared altogether, often with no hope of re-publication. This led to shortages of well-known nineteenth-century titles such as Charles Kingsley's *The Water-Babies* and Louisa M. Alcott's *Little Women*. At the same time, paper rationing during the war and for some time afterwards was strictly enforced. In these circumstances, it made commercial sense to allocate what resources there were to those authors who had always sold best. This meant that tried and tested conservative writers such as Crompton, Blyton and Johns took up a disproportionate percentage of children's book sales up to and after 1945. In Blyton's case, some of the fifty-three different publishers with whom she had dealings made over the bulk of their paper quotas to her books.[1]

Keen child readers who could not get hold of these best-sellers were often forced back to long-past children's literature wherever they could find it. My older brother and I, aged six and four when the war started, made constant use in the next six years of our grandfather's ancient bound copies of the *Boy's Own Paper*. One of my friends was reading Walter Scott's *Ivanhoe* in 1945. Like child readers in previous centuries when more appropriate contemporary literature was also scarce, one soon learned to track down what little there was by way of child-centred entertainment and then make the best of it.

Children's comics continued to thrive, but again in a non-innovatory manner. Weekly comic-strips in Britain regularly featured up to 20 per cent of recycled material; hardly strong encouragement for any radical new approaches. The popular *Dandy* and *Beano* comics, produced by the publishing firm D.C. Thomson in Dundee, had always been somewhat backward-looking, featuring teachers wearing gowns and mortar-boards who handed out daily canings or the dunce's cap long after such practices were beginning to diminish or disappear from British schools. Such anachronisms were part of the traditional knock-about humour so popular in these comics. But they also symbolised a general unwillingness to portray the modern world.

Disagreeable contemporary happenings like the war itself could hardly be ignored altogether in children's literature, although the popular Rupert Bear comic strip in the *Daily Express* did its best here, hardly ever referring to wartime conditions between 1939 and 1945. There were comic-strips elsewhere featuring Nazi characters forever getting the worst of the situation, such as *Addie and Hermy, the Nasty Nazis*, appearing in the *Dandy*, and *Musso the Wop – He's a Big-a-da Flop!*, coming out in the *Beano*. But these strips both closed by 1942. After that, comic Nazis tended to make more fleeting appearances in other regular comic-strips often still happy to feature pre-war characters living in an unchanging world. In the *Beano's* strip *Lord Snooty and his pals*, originating in 1938 and running for years afterwards until comparatively recently, characters still wore Eton collars and were surrounded by traditional British comic-strip icons like irascible old colonels with gouty feet.

After the war older text comics such as *Champion, Hotspur* and *Rover* carried on with the super-patriotic anti-German stories that had done them so well for the previous six years. But school stories were still usually set in the public boarding schools that most of their young readers would never have known save from children's fiction. There was some glimmering of a new social awareness here, in that the schoolboy heroes in such stories were no longer exclusively drawn from the upper classes. A few were now working-class boys who had somehow managed to win a place without having to pay fees. As such, they were often pictured making a stand against excessive snobbery while still ultimately endorsing the good old school and at least most of what it had always stood for. It was some time before state day schools were seen as suitable vehicles for stories; a prejudice also repeated in the school settings chosen by British films of the time such as the Boulting Brother's *The Guinea Pig* (1949), or loving remakes of classics like *Vice Versa* (1947) and *Tom Brown's Schooldays* (1951). All this was in tune with still existing pre-war cultural values, where middle or upper-class characters of whatever age regularly played a disproportionately large part in popular entertainment.

A people's war and the period afterwards would seem a strange time to continue this pattern, yet there was very little grumbling at any popular level about the regular re-appearance of these time-bound conservative clichés. One effect of the war's home propaganda was to minimize class differences in the public imagination in favour of an image of Britain where everyone was pictured as working contentedly together. Whatever the truth of this particular image, and however comforting it proved at the time, it also helped put to the back of the public mind the class differences that still continued to exist. In this atmosphere, authors and film-makers were free to carry on using largely the same social clichés as before without much risk of criticism, all apparently in the interest of preserving a notion of national unity.

Politicians of all persuasions in the war-time coalition government also threw their weight behind an image of a united Britain. This was not as hard for left-wing politicians as might have been imagined. While Britain had a strong Labour movement, it never followed a clear Marxist agenda. Analysis of Britain in terms of class was therefore less common on the left than arguments about more specific issues such as low pay, poor housing conditions and unemployment. While there was a strong feeling that such social wrongs should be put right, arguments for a more fundamental shake-up of British society rarely amounted to a great deal in orthodox Labour circles. Abolishing the monarchy, House of Lords and the public schools were not popular issues on the left, never making it into Labour's manifesto at any time up to and well beyond 1945.

It is therefore not surprising to find twentieth-century children's literature also in a generally quiescent state so far as political issues were concerned. George Orwell argued before the war for a socialist children's literature possibly backed up by the Trade Union Council, but this was little more than an after-thought and never got anywhere[2]. The pre-war Left Book Club published only one collection of stories aimed at children. As a young man Geoffrey Trease wrote a pair of Marxist adventure stories: *Bows Against the Barons* and *Comrades for the Charter*, both published by Martin Lawrence in 1934. These never proved hugely successful, and after the war Trease reissued his earlier adventure stories stripped of Marxist ideology in tune with his own later renunciation of communism.

This lack of political engagement was nothing new in children's literature. But the type and extent of worldly innocence it represented made it increasingly difficult for adults to find anything they occasionally wanted to read in children's literature. This was a reversal of the situation found at the turn of the century, when Robert Louis Stevenson, Frances Hodgson Burnett, Kenneth Grahame and many other children's writers had once been read and appreciated by all ages. But reading habits had begun to change after the First World War. Adult readers began to lose the habit of enjoying books written around a formula that children also liked.

Deprived of this additional adult readership, twentieth-century children's books reacted by writing down to their readers more than before. The single most successful children's writer in inter-war Britain was A.A. Milne. His particular vision of childhood was loved by some but much derided by satirists writing for an adult market, such as P.G. Wodehouse and Dorothy Parker. Contemporary school stories, adventure yarns and animal tales written for children also became more firmly separated from adult fiction, featuring younger heroes and heroines who were no longer seen to grow up to adulthood as their story proceeded. Such books were generally much shorter than their nineteenth-century counterparts, and frequently preserved the page illustrations which were beginning to disappear from adult fiction. Arthur Ransome was writing and illustrating longer novels for children, but with no real intention of reaching a mass adult audience as well.

A few books continued to span the child–adult divide. Richmal Crompton's William stories appeared in adult magazines before publication in book form, and some popular adult writers still appealed to older children, too. One such was Sapper, the pseudonym adopted by Cyril McNeile, who from 1920 onwards wrote highly successful adventure stories featuring Bulldog Drummond, an intrepid ex-army officer. W.E. Johns' undemanding, juvenile Biggles stories, starring a heroic British aviator, also commanded some adult readers, including young airmen who fought in the Battle of Britain. But, increasingly, adult and child readers were occupying different camps. While many adult novels were reaching out towards new sophistication, sometimes eschewing the happy endings and moral tidiness common in former times, twentieth-century children's books in their turn tended to become more exclusively child-centred.

Enid Blyton's huge success from the 1930s onwards was perhaps the final factor in turning the children's adventure story firmly away from any remaining adult interest. Her use of a repetitive formula whereby child characters regularly won all before them in an evidently unreal universe had little to offer mature readers. But most children adored these stories at the time and many still do today. Yet Enid Blyton was rarely an author that children took with them into late adolescence and adulthood in the way that sometimes used to happen with writers such as Robert Louis Stevenson and Louisa M. Alcott. Just as Blyton was often the most-loved of all children's authors, so was she often mocked by the very same readers once they felt they had truly left their childhood behind them.

Popular fantasy and comedy writing for children were hardly any more demanding in the immediate post-war period. Amiable, comically muddled adult characters like Hugh Lofting's Doctor Dolittle or Norman Hunter's Professor Branestawm continued to offer charming, uncomplicated entertainment but only to the very young. Fairy story collections were also by now increasingly infantilised, dropping the sophisticated art-work and more complex texts of some Victorian editions in favour of child-centred simplicity throughout. The enduring success of Disney's film version of *Snow White* was another factor in the general reorientation of fairy tales towards the overall sentimentality now thought to reflect the needs and understanding of the young.

This type of development in children's fiction was symptomatic of the more indulgent adult attitudes towards the young found in inter-war Britain and continuing up to our own day. For middle-class mothers in particular, freed from the poverty, miserable housing and large families that still continued to haunt many working-class parents, a growing appreciation of the importance of baby care and some understanding of child psychology during all this time gradually became part of what society came to expect from them. Nannies or nursery maids were no longer always seen as sufficient for bringing up a child, even had most middle-class parents still been able to afford them. Instead, mothers themselves with their often smaller families came to feel it was their duty to bring up children according to the 'enlightened' methods laid down by various experts. Active involvement in the community or time frequently passed in the company of close friends was now something that women were largely expected to forego, at least until their children were at school. Publishers both endorsed this new spirit of maternalism while also providing for it with a succession of picture books depicting mother and child spending time lovingly together. This assumption of an omni-present mother forever showering affection on her child has persisted in children's literature ever since.

This expectation of close, continuous parental involvement did not necessarily stop at early childhood. The assumptions that bracketed mothers and infants so permanently together as an entirely natural and self-sufficient dyad also came to extend to older children. Part of the attention they too could now often count on from parents would include reading-aloud sessions before bed-time. Mothers anxious to impart a feeling of loving affection and closeness to their children did not always take to the depictions of violence found in some former nineteenth-century adventure stories for the young. Nor did many of them continue to relish the occasional morbidity found in classics like *Jane Eyre* or *Tom Brown's School Days*. More mindful of what child experts had to say about the possibly dire effects of upsetting children with unsuitable material, many mothers preferred to play safe in their reading sessions. Often more to their taste were those milder children's stories beginning to appear in twentieth-century Britain, short on painful truths or moral fervour but long on child-centred entertainment set in a bland, passionless world where everything eventually falls comfortably into place.

The Second World War arguably reinforced family life by first disrupting it. Fathers away from home longed to be re-united with their families. Mothers separated from their children by the evacuation or by taking on exhausting jobs during the day, also fantasised about getting back to normal while sometimes enjoying their new freedom. There was a marked increase in the birth-rate by the end of the war as fathers returned home and scores of mothers left work. In harmony with this return to normality, children's books published after 1945 continued very much as before. With a general shortage of reading matter, most new books were soon snapped up, providing publishers with a further disincentive for trying anything new. Despite political change, those chiefly responsible for writing, publishing and distributing children's books continued in the same vein. Inheritors of a middle-class literary culture which suited their own needs very well, they were largely content to hand on to others the same torch that was once passed to them.

The 1944 Education Act put little pressure on publishers to produce more books reflecting the social diversity of British children. Book provision for recreational reading in unselective schools was still virtually non-existent. In the grammar schools, libraries usually chose to follow the socially superior public schools in the provision of books, often of the improving variety: essays, belles-lettres, memoirs and autobiography all written from a safe, frequently nineteenth-century vantage point. Self-advancement was the watchword here rather than easy enjoyment, with particularly weighty titles often reserved for prize days at the end of the school year. I was one of a number of pupils at my grammar school to be presented with George Borrows's dated autobiographical ramble, *Wild Wales*, in 1953, ninety-six years after it was first published. This book is unread now and was still fairly unreadable forty years ago, but this never stopped it from taking its place with a number of other 'safe' titles every year as suitable awards for sixteen-year-old pupils.

The provision of fiction in lessons and school libraries was hardly any more exciting. While comics with their classless readership would routinely be condemned or even confiscated by irate parents or teachers, classics from the past, almost invariably written from a decidedly establishment point of view, continued to be thought most suitable. These were the books, according to Geoffrey Trease,[3] which continually took the side of the cavaliers against the roundheads, or which pictured the French Revolution chiefly in terms of the number of aristocrats guillotined on the scaffold. But since it was largely middle-class parents who bought books at the time, it was hardly surprising that such books tended to take a less than revolutionary line when it came to dealing with social issues either past or present.

It followed, therefore, that the stories set in modern times available to school libraries in 1945 were still largely of the type that rarely got far away from the imaginary lives and activities of comfortably off young people having fun on their holidays. As was also the case with novels written for adults around this time, few children's stories existed devoted entirely to descriptions of working-class life. One such was Eve Garnett's *The Family from One End Street*, published in 1937 and appearing in Puffin Books in 1941. The picture it conveyed, however affectionate, was always one of amiable caricature, with the Ruggles family fundamentally content in their lowly position in life if only there were a little more ready money to purchase new shoes. No awkward questions here, although this still did not prevent the story from widespread translation in the USSR. Communist beggars cannot be choosers, however, and British books describing working-class life in 1937 in any detail at all were such an exception it would have been pointless waiting for anything more radical to turn up in publishers' lists.

This dearth of fiction featuring ordinary children with ordinary emotions eventually produced a reaction from authors themselves, sometimes prompted by the reading needs of their own children. Nina Bawden writes in her autobiography about being

> depressed by the books my sons were reading which seemed dull to me, chiefly because the characters were wooden, and uninvolved in any kind of reality I recognised. I think I wanted to give my children something that would encourage them to feel they could make a difference to what happened in the world, show them fictional children who were people like themselves, bright and gutsy and determined, able to think, to reason, to hold a moral view.[4]

Her first children's book, *The Secret Passage*, appeared in 1963 after innumerable rejections from other publishers. After that,

> I might not have written a second novel for children, if children had not sent me the kind of letters that surprised and delighted me. What had interested them in my story was what I had hoped would interest them. Not the plot, although they seemed to find it exciting enough, but the emotions, the feelings, of the characters. 'I didn't know', they wrote, 'that other people felt like that.'[5]

Two years before, John Rowe Townsend's *Gumble's Yard* set a new standard for writing about more unprivileged children in a sympathetic and realistic way. For him, the children's books of the time seemed

> Terribly harmless and hygienic and middle-class, carefully calculated never to give a child a nightmare or a complex. . . . . the father would be a professional man, and they'd go to boarding school and go on holiday to Switzerland, and . . . do all the things that rather OK, upper middle-class children are supposed to do. And so actually what set me partly to writing was the feeling that, for a great majority of children in this country, life wasn't anything like that . . . It was just a feeling that the whole thing was simply on a different plane from life for most children as they would know it.[6]

Until writers like Townsend and Bawden had started writing, even if state school libraries had wanted to stock books describing the everyday lives of ordinary children in a way that avoided both cliché or caricature, they would not have known where to look. While no children's authors went out of their way to be systematically anti working-class, in many of their books this class simply did not exist outside minor supporting roles such as servants, helpful artisans or occasionally uncouth villains. He who pays the publisher calls the stories, and it is hardly surprising that middle-class book purchasers wanted stories reflecting their mode of life or that of those wealthier than themselves. In this way, it was hoped their children could be provided with suitable social aspirations while also enjoying a good story.

Demand for a wider range of books might have been expected from the Public Library system. But this too was both permanently strapped for cash while also firmly cast in the direction of self-improvement, often preferring classics of the past to children's best-sellers of the present. Although membership had long been free, this was a right much less taken up by potential readers from the manual working class, sometimes for obvious reasons. The children's writer Robert Leeson, describing his life in the 1930s, remembers how 'My mother got a ticket for the library in the next town – there wasn't a library in our own place – and because she was a council tenant she had to get somebody to vouch for us to get a library ticket.'[7]

Children from a working-class background who did use libraries would therefore be a minority in their own community where reading for pleasure was not usually seen as a particularly valued skill in either sex. As Leeson recalls, 'To most of the people on our estate, I should think reading, except the occasional comic, was an alien exercise. It wasn't for us.'[8] Boys who read a lot might even be seen as effeminate; girls who did the same could be suspected of not fully pulling their weight in the domestic chores seen as their lot in life.

The British working class after the war was roughly double the size of the middle class. Working-class child readers, although proportionately fewer, still numbered about the same as middle-class child readers. But they were seldom made to feel at home in a library system stocked with books reflecting a largely middle-class social background. Nor was the reading environment noticeably inviting. Eileen Colwell, who established a pioneering children's library in Hendon between the wars, remembered 'no good libraries at any time during my childhood and youth, least of all at school. It was possible theoretically to provide separate children's rooms . . . but few followed this example for reasons of expense and through pure indifference to the needs of children.'[9]

It was some time after 1945 that this dismal picture started to show any real improvement. The placid world of post-war publishing for children chose to spend its energies arguing over different issues, such as the amount and supposed poor quality of Enid Blyton's writing and its alleged bad effects on young readers. The gravest charge here was her limited vocabulary: a serious crime in the eyes of parents who wanted their children to gain practical advantage in the English language while also enjoying themselves with a book. But this concern apart, middle-class parents still generally liked seeing their children reading, albeit respectable books, and so building up and perfecting the literacy skills necessary for them in their educational and social advancement. Library visiting was therefore generally encouraged, sometimes as part of a family event. Only the occasional book-worms, thought to read too much, were seen as something of a problem, although comics or other 'low' literature bought direct by young readers were sometimes accused of exerting a bad influence.

A reading child was a quiet child, and parents also appreciated the role books could play in keeping otherwise unruly children tamed for hours on end. In Richmal Crompton's William stories his long-suffering and censorious father is never shown objecting to his son's reading matter. This is despite the fact that this always consisted of adventure stories specialising in gory detail, sometimes read out aloud to his parents, despite their protests. Just keeping William out of mischief was felt to be compensation enough. But while William's parents did not care for the detail of his books, they and their real life counterparts were never uneasy about the conservative depiction of gender roles or ethnic or class stereotypes found in all children's adventure stories pre- or immediately post-war. It was only the small circulation communist newspaper *Daily Worker*, later *Morning Star*, that kept up a consistent attack on the narrow social conformism found in so much British children's fiction at the time.

As for children themselves, with almost no competition from television at the time, many of them turned to fiction for their main imaginative entertainment. For really keen readers, it was not so much a question of finding a particularly suitable book – any story that was not too boring would do in order to provide the cherished temporary escape from reality. Middle-class children found themselves better catered for here in terms of a sense of shared identity with the stories they were reading. Working-class children in search of good reading might take longer to realise that, however much they loved their favourite books, they still came to them more as outsiders.

This point is made by Robert Leeson about his own childhood reading:

'Fantasy stories were distinctly class-oriented, and the working-class child had to indulge in two flights of fantasy . . . one to get into the characters, and the second to get into the adventure. That seemed to me to be a big effort and a colossal waste of time.'[10] But he did find one book that spoke to him as the sort of child he felt he was: 'When I came across a book like Tom Holland's *Slings Road: A School Story for Boys* (1931), in which I felt I was represented in the book, it gave an added and a very special pleasure. So that I do think that I would stress the . . . sense in which if you do not appear in the literary world of your society, you don't exist.'[11]

Voices were raised during the post-war period questioning the power of radio to divert children from suitable hobbies such as reading. But like many other fits of moral panic about the malign influence of various media on the young, this fear was very exaggerated. Radio was indeed popular, but again particularly with middle-class audiences. In times of peace Radio Luxembourg's commercial station constantly attracted more listeners, many from the British working class. By contrast, BBC programmes aimed specifically at children were usually middle-class in tone, with presenters who either came directly from private school teaching or who sounded as if they had. BBC's famous *Children's Hour* also reflected the conservative reading tastes of the time in its radio adaptations. Stories chosen included classics written by Kenneth Grahame, A.A. Milne, John Masefield and E. Nesbit. Modern fare was well represented too, with some plays written for radio later appearing in book form. But these again tended to be safe choices, such as Anthony Buckeridge's popular Jennings stories, set in a boarding preparatory school in the countryside. As Susanne Greenhalgh discusses in chapter 7, more socially challenging choices of literature for the radio were rare indeed.

This conservative cultural background that generally informed children's book publishing continued to operate for some years to come. Those who worked for publishers tended to share the values common at the time while often having a particular enthusiasm for reading for its own sake. Providing children with attractive books which also reflected a positive, optimistic view of childhood was seen as particularly important. For some editors this represented a chance to offer children the type of book not available when they were young. Such books had above all to be well written, breaking away from the clichés and mechanical plots formerly so often found in hurriedly produced books and comics for the young. After that, the 'good' book had to satisfy the editor on more amorphous grounds of taste and general suitability. For Eleanor Graham, first editor of the enormously influential Puffin Story Book series, defining such books had proved a persistent problem during her years as a children's bookseller in London. 'Mothers, aunts, and the rest came in with only the haziest ideas of what to choose – but it had always to be a *"good"* book. I got so tired of that word.'[12]

In the same article Graham admits that 'the whole matter of "good" books for children haunted me through the great part of my working days.'[13] But some idea of the criteria she used can be deduced from those working with her once she became Puffin editor. Margaret Clark, one of her young staff in the Puffin years, recalls how she and her fellow 'dogsbodies' privately 'attacked Eleanor Graham's choice of books, with arguments that grow familiar with experience: she was unmarried, had no children (a necessary corollary in those days), she worked in an ivory tower, surrounding herself with a mystique that separated her from the realism she claimed for her books, she was obdurate in declining books that did not meet her critical standards, despite their popularity with children'.[14] Margaret Clark distances herself from these youthful criticisms in the same article, drawing attention instead to Graham's distinguished record as a pioneering figure in children's literature. But the critical points she once made still contain a measure of truth. The high standards Graham expected of her authors also coincided with a vision of the best literature as serving an educated élite among children.

The fact that so many of the books she liked embodied particular, middle-class backgrounds and attitudes would have been seen by her as a necessary advantage rather than any sort of problem. Such attitudes in literature were considered standard for all who aspired to a good life. Should working-class children also read such books, it was supposed that they too might as a result find their aspirations rising accordingly; something also seen as a good thing in its own right.

Writing over twenty years later in 1974, Graham to some extent modifies this position when she states her belief that 'Any child, even from the most ignorant and wretched home, is possessed of the same spark that lights the mind – yes, and spirit – to the appreciation of the wonder and the beauty of good poetry. And it was strange, how hotly and indignantly that was denied.'[15] But in her efforts at the time to raise the standards of children's books by always insisting on quality above everything else, she also played a part in focusing Puffin Books's attention and energy on the needs of the selective reader coming from more critically aware, book-buying homes.

Graham wrote in a previous article that she was 'frequently urged to get some Blyton on our list, but I never did. It was not intended for that kind of public.'[16] In similar vein, Barbara Ker Wilson coming to Bodley Head in 1956 as a young editor of children's books, was 'dismayed to discover five early Blyton titles on the list, and set about selling them off to William Collins's Glasgow publishing offices, where they were received with delight. (In a similar move, OUP had sold off W.E. Johns's Biggles titles to Hodder & Stoughton.)'[17] While the intention of both publishers was to uphold literary standards, the effect was also to limit the appeal of their books to a more educated audience. Middle-class children also often enjoyed Blyton and Biggles books, but their parents and teachers required that more demanding fare was also always available for them, either as suitable birthday or Christmas presents or else as approved choices from the public library system. This was not just in order to fulfil ideas of self-improvement; it was also using the choice of a certain type of literature and the language, values and modes of address principally associated with it as one way of defining membership of a particular social class.

As for children different from the norm, such as the disabled or the generally dispossessed, these were largely invisible in children's fiction. It was still commonly thought that one important if unstated aim of children's fiction was to set appropriate role models for young readers. Books dwelling on less fortunate children or very different child characters would therefore have been seen as pointless, unable to suggest any suitable examples for emulation. Describing society's outcasts in fiction, however well done, was also too reminiscent for some of the Victorian type of moralising in fiction from which parents and teachers were now keen to move.

Setting good examples to children had always been seen as the responsibility of everyone closely involved with the young, including those writing children's books. Failure to do this was thought highly undesirable, leading to the possibility of direct imitation of inappropriate behaviour by inexperienced young readers. This particular view of child psychology is a long-standing one, still heard today in arguments about the supposedly noxious effects of violent films and videos on the young. Anecdotes about such ill-advised imitation of art into life have always been around. In performances of J.M. Barrie's *Peter Pan*, mention is made of Peter having to apply special fairy dust to the Darling children before they could attempt to fly like him. Without this piece of stage-craft, it was feared that some children in the audience might go home and try flying from an open window for themselves. This was not an entirely idle anxiety; Barrie was asked by the London Ambulance Service to add this line, 'so many children having gone home and tried it from their beds and needing surgical attention'.[18]

There is obviously more to the whole argument about whether children always imitate the literature they come across, yet in 1945 the science of reader or viewer response had still hardly advanced beyond this type of anecdotal evidence. Much more emphasis was given to descriptions of what children read rather than paying attention to what each one of them might bring internally to any particular book. It was also easier to blame some books, comics or films for influencing the mass of children in a particular way, rather than to look at other more pervasive social or individual factors in children's lives that might also help explain their attitudes and behaviour. When the relationship between child and culture is seen in these simple terms, undesirable films or reading matter would naturally be considered as a bad influence on a young audience: a point made in the parliamentary debates about banning Horror Comics in 1955. In such a climate, it was understandable that books, radio, films and comics aimed at children at the time all tended to play reasonably safe most of the time.

Changes 1960 onwards

One particularly important agent for the immense changes in children's literature that eventually started to occur in the 1960s was the growth of children's libraries. As early as 1945 new regulations required the establishment of libraries in schools. Such changes were slow to come, but gathered pace over the years. By 1964 there was a 30 per cent increase in overall expenditure on public libraries, with children's needs often foremost in mind.[19] With their enlarged budgets and improved facilities, children's librarians became an important force for publishers to bear in mind. Many of the best-equipped children's libraries were in inner-city areas, reflecting the controlling local Labour Party's traditional commitment to higher spending in education.

The librarians concerned could not help but notice that the huge majority of books in stock still reflected broadly middle-class backgrounds. While this would once have been seen as part of the natural order of things, some librarians in the 1960s began to question this picture. In a less class-conscious and prejudiced cultural climate, celebrating working-class lifestyles for their own sakes soon came to seem a legitimate aim for children's literature. Publishers and writers duly followed suit, with school stories in particular changing from favourite boarding-school settings to the state, day schools of most of today's children's fiction. Geoffrey Trease had begun this process in 1949 with his story *No Boats on Bannermere*, featuring a group of ordinary children attending a state-run grammar school. E.W. Hildick took things further in his Jim Starling stories, first published in 1957, all set in Cement Street Secondary Modern School.

Inner-city librarians and teachers also became conscious that young readers from the new ethnic minorities also had little to read reflecting their own experiences. After trying her hand at selling children's books in an East London Saturday street market, Elaine Moss concluded in 1974 that 'the desperate need for picture books with black or Asian children in them is evident every minute of the day. Britain has been very slow off the mark in this respect.'[20] Those black characters that did appear in children's fiction were often patronizing stereotypes left over from former colonial attitudes. Once again publishers responded with new books reflecting new attitudes. Pioneering movements like Anne Woods' *Federation of Children's Book Groups* encouraged book purchasing across all social classes, with some success. School bookshops helped distribute these books to a wider audience than before.

Another important influence for change was the new insistence on the changing role of girls and women in fiction as in life. Previous attitudes in picture books often meant that boys were shown taking most of the action while girls tended to be relegated to supporting domestic roles. In reading primers like the *Janet and John* series, produced by the London firm of James Nisbet from 1949 onwards and by 1968 estimated to be in use in over 80 per cent of British primary schools, fathers always seemed to take the active role while mothers busied themselves domestically either washing up, cooking or ironing in the background. The new women of the 1970s wanted something better than this, and gradually, often against considerable opposition, began to get some of their way. The 1980s also saw new demands for widening children's literature's catchment area even further, for example by including more disabled characters in stories. The battle to make children's books more truly representative of all the nation's children still goes on.

These new social pressures eventually led to fundamental changes in publishers' attitudes towards children's literature. In 1945 editors would be expected to do little more than reach back into their childhood memories or else talk to their own children and their friends in order to acquire some rough mental map of the type of readers they had in mind. The pervading image of the child reader was therefore essentially middle-class, catered for by only moderately updated versions of the type of school, adventure or animal stories established earlier this century. This brand of certainty was seriously challenged during the 1960s and beyond. Consciousness of a widening children's market made up of individuals coming from very different backgrounds finally destroyed the former, unitary image of the child reader as essentially white, middle-class and privately educated. The influential Plowden Report into Primary Education in 1967 was scathing about existing reading primers. It considered 'their middle-class world represented by the text and illustrations often alien to children'.[21] At the same time, competition among children's publishers became fiercer once it was realised that children's books could also be money-spinners at a time when profit margins elsewhere were sometimes becoming severely squeezed.

But the books they then came to publish faced new, important rivals for children's attention from other sources. Widespread television viewing by children in the 1960s and beyond was the most important challenge confronting children's publishers at the time and increasingly so as more electronic equipment continued to come on the market. Faced by this opposition, quality publishers' allegiance to the 'good' book became rather more tenuous. In 1964 Judy Taylor, children's books editor at Bodley Head, had no compunction about turning down Roald Dahl's *James and the Giant Peach*. Interviewed later by Dahl's biographer, she stressed that 'as an editor, one has to like a book oneself. I could see that Dahl would be popular with children, but publishing for them has to involve more than that.'[22]

Tables were soon to turn once publishers began contemplating previously unknown cash-flow problems. Kaye Webb was appointed as Puffin supremo by Allen Lane in 1961 as a corrective to what he saw as the 'fuddy-duddy' approach of her predecessor, Eleanor Graham.[23] But Kaye Webb also had difficulty living with some of the publishing decisions foisted on her primarily for financial reasons, as in the case of another Dahl title. 'I really was secretly very glad that I was resigning just before they did *George's Marvellous Medicine*. I thought "I really can't bear it, that beastly book!" But on the other hand, if I had said no he wouldn't have let me have any of the others.'[24]

It was not so much that standards in children's book publishing necessarily began to decline; there had always been a great deal of poor material produced for this market. But quality publishers had always sought to associate themselves with the best authors, including those who wrote for children. 'Best' in this sense did not necessarily mean those writers who also made a lot of money. In fiction it was more a case of looking for books which broadly met canons of good taste, fine style, subtle characterisation and vivid imagination. But as finances became squeezed and the demand for accessible literature for a wider social group of children grew, the whole concept of what a 'good' book for children consisted of began to change. Literature as a source of desirable role-models conveyed through characters always talking to each other in standard English began to give way to fiction containing characters who were more earthy and often less idealised than before. Controversies about the desirability of best-sellers like Blyton and Dahl, who did not always appear to set high literary or moral standards in their books, became less important at a time when there seemed a real question whether some television-obsessed children would ever willingly pick up a book written for them at all.

Another important factor in this new atmosphere was the dramatic growth of paperback editions for children. For years Puffin Books had been the market leaders in this area of publishing, successfully battling it out against other publishers, unwilling to sub-lease their best titles, and against librarians, who disliked the less durable paperback for both practical and aesthetic reasons. But, with more spending money around in the 1960s, paperback purchases grew quickly, with more publishers eager to get in on the act. The self-improving tone of so many Puffin Books, typified by revivals of titles like Mrs Molesworth's *The Cuckoo Clock* (1977) gave way to fiction that was more lively and contemporary. This was important, since children's books could not afford to look unduly staid compared with their new media rivals. In particular, children had now begun to view a good deal of adult material on television, leading to a gradual but inevitable erosion of what was once considered suitable material for the young.

In response, children's books also began to take on once-controversial themes unknown to previous generations of readers. Many of the social problems formerly unspoken about in front of children started appearing in the works of some children's authors. Homosexuality, child abuse, incest, rape, drug-taking, alcoholism: it was all there in the older ranges of children's literature during and after the 1970s. The language of children's books also began to change. Swear-words and rude jokes as well as slang and what was once seen as slipshod, ungrammatical speech could now sometimes be found in print, however upsetting to those parents who still looked to literature to set higher standards for their children. But the 'Piss off!' so objected to by some parent-purchasers in Richard Adams' epic *Watership Down*, first published in 1972 and later appearing as a Puffin book, did nothing to hinder its vast sales. Roald Dahl, meanwhile, became a millionaire by providing books which, among other things, contained moments of scatological humour irresistible to children.

Parents were not always happy with this new literary frankness, although toleration of the same type of thing on television or film was usually much greater. Children's books for most adults still broadly stood for something different and better than ordinary reality – a reversion to the older norms by which stories were once expected to set high standards for children by chiefly concerning themselves with idealised child characters. Yet, given that literacy skills remained as important as ever for academic success, the parents of the 1960s mainly had to accept the new types of book their children were reading, even though they may not always have approved of everything within them. No one ever complained about child book-worms in the 1970s; the fear now was that children might ruin their eyes not by reading but by watching too much television.

Television itself was also changing radically over the years in the direction of more outspokenness. The growing stress on hedonism for its own sake found in British culture and the decline of moral censorship, signalled by the publication against opposition of *Lady Chatterley's Lover* in 1959, gradually helped make Britain a very different place. In tune with these cultural changes, children's books became more concerned with themes of individual fulfilment, with less emphasis given to the importance of community-based values such as duty, loyalty and always doing the right thing by others. The self-improving children's book of old, with its painstaking attention to accuracy in matters of educational detail, became less valued for its own sake. The historical novel for children also began to lose popularity, with young readers generally preferring stories set in the present or, in the case of science fiction, well into the future.

The decline of deference and the growth of satire in British culture also helped erode the establishment values once generally reflected by traditional casts of characters in children's fiction. Adults, previously respected as part of the social status quo, now as often as not found themselves on the wrong side of juvenile ridicule. Parents and teachers, once the butt of humour only in comic-strips and a few novels, frequently saw themselves sent up or at least generally criticised in all types of children's literature. Respect for elders now had to be well and truly earned in children's books; the total parent-worship found in nineteenth-century novels like *Little Women* or *The Swiss Family Robinson* was over. Nor did other traditional values always do well in this new, more critically-minded mood. Environmental concerns and a general fear of warfare once nuclear weapons came on the scene gradually turned children's literature away from its former celebration of fighting in favour of more pacific attitudes. Widely accepted principles, such as always telling the truth, remaining honest, and showing kindness and respect to the old, were now challenged by numbers of new writers keen to point out that defining moral behaviour could sometimes be a far more complex business than the mere following of absolute rules.

Those children's books that an editor in 1945 would have both recognized and welcomed also continued to appear. But in other ways the safe, socially limited, uncontroversial children's book of former times began to show its age and lose readership. It owed its existence to a time when editors and publishers regularly imposed a particular image of childhood upon a mass readership even when this bore little resemblance to what was going on in contemporary childhood. But in the more self-critical and democratically aware 1960s there was less room for those more solemn stories consisting largely of middle-class children behaving responsibly and resourcefully in a world devoid of poverty or suffering. Danger in these more traditional children's stories largely came from outside in the shape of easily spotted villains. Fictional families, meanwhile, usually remained strong and united, with the moral order, if sometimes temporarily disturbed, still generally re-established by the end.

By the 1960s it was becoming evident that, with a swiftly rising divorce rate, danger to children often started from within the family. The essential stability of the world outside could also no longer be taken for granted. Campaigns for nuclear disarmament, protests about environmental damage, and grim visions of the future of a terminally over-populated planet helped children and parents face up to the fact that all was not necessarily for the best in the best of all possible worlds. Both generations looked to fiction to explore some of these themes, and different authors variously obliged. Descriptions of ordinary squabbles between siblings were remarkably few in immediately post-war children's fiction, especially when there was an interesting adventure in the offing. This optimistic image suited parents at the end of the war and for around the next two decades, anxious for their children to grow up with positive role-models in mind. By the 1960s parents and children were ready for a greater degree of truth-telling about what can sometimes go on in the domestic scene. The existence of jealousy between children at a very young age was no longer considered a taboo subject for picture-books. Fierce sibling rivalry at a later stage was no longer ducked as a possible topic. Quarrels between parents also featured, or disputes between parents and particular children.

In former, traditional, fiction sexual interest between children was non-existent or minimal. The 1960s, however, saw an explosion in sexual awareness among all generations. Information picture-books designed to accompany the newly compulsory sex lessons held in school began to name parts and state facts in a more robust and easily digested way. Stories written for adolescents started to recognize the existence of sexual feeling as right and desirable. A few authors such as Judy Blume, Aidan Chambers and David Rees went further, describing actual adolescent sexual encounters with sympathy rather than shock. The increasing treatment of parental divorce also highlighted the role of sexuality in adult lives; hitherto a taboo subject in children's literature. Warnings about sexual abuse and AIDS left little to an imagination previously starved of sexual knowledge in any reasonable amount of detail. Gone were the days when popular cultural definitions of childhood always included an assumed ignorance of sexuality, whether in children themselves or as manifested in anyone else. This particular vision of childhood innocence, however far from the actual truth, also once dictated what sort of material should and should not appear in children's literature. Such literature could in a sense be defined by what it did not choose to describe. The new children's literature now felt it could discuss anything in front of the children – including a range of sexual topics once unthinkable for a young audience.

Children in the 1960s and beyond, therefore, soon came to know a great deal more than they used to about previously forbidden topics. This new sophistication made some former books for children seem somewhat quaint and ripe for satire. Fairy tales, single-sex stories set in public schools, and Enid Blyton's adventure tales all at some time attracted the attention of satirists in print or on television. Modern children's writers themselves would occasionally contrast the new realities they were now describing with what they saw as the customary evasions or moments of sentimentality often found in older post-war books for the young. In Nina Bawden's fine, searing children's novel *Squib*, for example, young Kate is convinced her mother will adopt the sad little boy who gives the book its title. Instead, 'Her mother bent over her and stroked her hair. She said, "Darling, I really am sorry. I can see it would be nice; like a story. But in real life there aren't any right true happy endings. You have to get used to things as they are."'[25]

It would, however, be grossly unfair to mock or minimise all the achievements of the early post-war editors who took children's literature into the 1960s and then often stayed on to help instigate the massive changes that began to take place. People of their time, they inevitably shared some of the normal prejudices of their age and class. Yet their insistence on quality for children led to some excellent writing in the early days after the war in books generally produced to as high a standard as was possible during times of acute paper and print shortages. As editors, they played an important part in the construction of British society's general ideals during that time where children were concerned of, and the books they published were a major source of imaginary entertainment. The authors they commissioned were often particularly influential in putting across a description of what adults felt childhood ought to consist of, whether it was always like that or not. This was no mean achievement; it took the arrival of mass television and other social and cultural influences to change this picture towards one containing greater realism.

The time is now well past when British children's publishers had the field to themselves in order to get across a national, somewhat idealised version of childhood that was particularly meaningful and agreeable to them and to their readers. Those responsible for the pre-television, post-war expansion of the children's books where this image was largely dominant were very often women working in comparative obscurity and seldom highly rewarded for their skills. The story of how they created the children's books that they did, and the great success they encountered over a number of years, is a comparatively neglected one well worth telling.

References

1. Sheila Ray (1982), *The Blyton Phenomenon: The Controversy Surrounding the World's Most Successful Children's Writer* (London: André Deutsch), p.26.
2. Geoffrey Trease (1974), *Laughter at the Door: A Continued Autobiography* (London: Macmillan), p.26.
3. Geoffrey Trease (1964), *Tales Out of School: A Survey of Children's Fiction* (London: Heinemann), p.104.
4. Nina Bawden (1994), *In My Own Time: Almost an Autobiography* (London: Virago), p.154.
5. Ibid., p.156.
6. Interview with John Rowe Townsend, 2 May 1995.
7. Interview with Robert Leeson, 12 July 1995.
8. Ibid.
9. Eileen Colwell (1974), 'At the beginning', *Signal* no. 13, p.30.
10. Interview with Robert Leeson.
11. Ibid.
12. Eleanor Graham (1972), 'The Bumpus years', *Signal* no. 9, p.98.
13. Ibid., p.108.
14. Margaret Clark (1990), 'Lessons in publishing', *Signal* no. 61, p.46.
15. Eleanor Graham (1974), 'At the beginning', *Signal* no. 9, p.103.
16. Eleanor Graham (1973), 'The Puffin years', *Signal* no. 12, p.122.
17. Barbara Ker Wilson (1995), 'Grace abounding', *Signal* no. 78, p.78.
18. Andrew Birkin (1979), *J.M. Barrie and the Lost Boys* (London: Constable), p.162.
19. Alec Ellis (1971), *Library Services for Young People in England and Wales 1830–1970* (London: Pergamon), p.102.
20. Elaine Moss (1974), 'A mirror in the market place', *Signal* no. 15, p.113.
21. *Children and their Primary Schools: A Report of the Central Advisory Council for Education*, vol. 1, 1967, p.213.
22. Jeremy Treglown, (1994), *Roald Dahl: A Biography* (London: Faber & Faber), p.148.
23. J.E. Morpurgo (1979), *Allen Lane: King Penguin* (London: Hutchinson), p.310.
24. Interview with Kaye Webb, 7 February 1995.
25. Nina Bawden (1971), *Squib* (London: Gollancz), p.123.

2   Publishing Practices and the Practicalities of Publishing

Kimberley Reynolds

The niche in the world of contemporary British publishing which is concerned specifically with producing books for children had effectively to be recreated in the post-war period. The nature of children's publishing is inevitably shaped by the conditions within the publishing industry as a whole – its structures, hierarchies, values and assumptions. This chapter is primarily concerned with how these conditions affect the kinds of books produced for young readers – who makes books, for whom and why? The answers to these questions are inextricably linked to the status and profitability of children's book publishing; equally important is the idea of the potential child reader. All three aspects have undergone significant changes in the past fifty years; with the expansion of electronic publishing they are under pressure again.

Setting the scene

In the nineteenth century, British publishers led the world in producing books for young readers. Using each new technological breakthrough – from steam presses to cheaper paper – they made books of all qualities, prices and appearances; at the same time, extensive lists covering most of the genres read today and targeted at specific groups of readers (determined on the basis of age, sex and/or class) were constructed. By the first decades of the twentieth century the 'classic' canon of children's literature was established: from *Pilgrim's Progress* (first published in 1678 but regularly reprinted until this century and adapted specifically for children in the nineteenth century) to *Peter Pan* (1904) and *Winnie-the-Pooh* (1926). A publishing cycle which included annual volumes of periodicals, miscellanies, 'bumper' books, and some early series fiction was in place, and a large number of publishers were actively competing in the flourishing children's trade.[1]

By the end of the Second World War, however, the children's publishing industry in Britain was far less buoyant. There is not space here to go into all of the contributory factors which brought about this transition, and certainly some landmark authors and illustrators were active between 1920 and 1945 (among them Mable Lucy Attwell, Cecily Mary Barker, Enid Blyton, Angela Brazil, Richmal Crompton, A.A. Milne, Arthur Ransome, Noel Streatfeild, and Margaret Tarrant). Indeed, Allen Lane, founder of Penguin Books, tried out a number of imprints for children during this period, culminating in the hugely successful Puffin books under the editorship of Eleanor Graham.[2] However, the production of quality books for young readers was not a primary, or indeed, a comfortable activity in most publishing houses. It is worth thinking in some detail about the circumstances those producing them faced and changes in the way publishing for children was perceived in the years immediately following the Second World War as compared with the situation which prevailed at the beginning of the century.

In a seminal article on the relationship between children's literature and that produced for adults, Felicity Hughes (1978) argues that, in effect, children's literature became déclassé – regarded as if it were done by those who could not write any better for those who could not read any better – at the *fin de siècle*. Prior to this time, a huge proportion of what we now consider 'children's literature' was also read by adults: Hesba Stretton received letters from sailors at sea describing how they had wept over *Jessica's First Prayer*;[3] *Tom Brown's Schooldays* had a strong adult following,[4] and there were many texts, among them *Robinson Crusoe*, *Pilgrim's Progress*, and *Gulliver's Travels*, which could span the whole of a reader's life. Conversely, much of what is now considered too difficult for children, for instance, the works of Dickens, Scott, and Tennyson, was widely enjoyed by many of them.

Hughes argues persuasively that it was at the prompting of writers – among them Henry James – who were concerned with making the novel into a 'serious' art form, that texts whose primary audience was likely to be either women or children were taken out of the mainstream and turned into low-status, popular literature. The effect on those who wrote and published books for children was dramatic and enduring; not least because the linking of two groups – women and children – rendered marginal under the aggressive patriarchy of the late-Victorian and Edwardian periods, led to reductions in status, remuneration and, inevitably, interest. With some notable exceptions (among them de la Mare, Kipling and Tolkien), writers who prided themselves on or were known for the literary merit of their work either steered away from writing for children, or, as in the cases of J.M. Barrie and A.A. Milne, became apologetic and resentful when their children's plays and books were more successful than those they produced for their peers.

This is not to say that no good books for children were published at this time, or that publishing for children was unprofitable – Enid Blyton produced much of her work in the 1930s and 1940s and succeeded in amassing considerable profits for herself and her many publishers. What it does mean is that the sense that it was a fine and exciting thing to produce books for young readers, including those which were of high artistic and literary merit, was largely dissipated by the end of the last war. John Rowe Townsend describes the situation:

> it could be said, as a crude generalization, that the Victorian–Edwardian heyday ended in 1914, and that children's literature picked itself up uncertainly in the twenties and thirties, only to be knocked down again in 1939. The Second World War and the years immediately after it were hard times once more, but in the early to middle fifties a new generation of writers began to emerge; and during the next two decades the amount of talent going into children's books, and the number of good books appearing on the children's list, increased remarkably.[5]

To get a full sense of the precarious nature of British children's publishing during the war years, it is useful to compare the situation in Britain with that in the United States which, throughout the same period, had been building a thriving children's book scene (of course the US publishing industry did not suffer from the many restraints imposed on their British counterparts in this period). For example, there were many highly successful children's lists in major companies, among them Simon & Schuster (perhaps best known for their successful Little Golden Books series, begun in 1942); Viking (where May Massee, generally regarded as the best American children's editor in the business,[6] trained the young Marni Hodgkin who, on moving to the UK in the 1940s, was responsible for the Hart-Davis and Macmillan lists), and Random House, famous for its 'Dr Seuss' series, launched in 1940. In addition to flourishing and far-seeing children's departments, the children's book industry in the US saw the emergence of new specialist publishers such as Franklin Watts who, with his wife, Helen Hoke Watts, did much to revitalize British children's publishing in the 1960s.[7] There were also periodicals, such as the influential *Horn Book* magazine (founded in 1924) devoted to children's books, and, in 1945, the Children's Book Council (CBC), a special organization dedicated to growth and professionalism in children's book publishing, was formed.

By contrast, at the end of the Second World War in Britain there was not a single specialist publisher for children (although Warne was by this time earning a considerable part of its income from the sales of Beatrix Potter books and products); specialist children's editors were just emerging; periodicals and newspapers rarely covered children's books; and no organization was concerned specifically with promoting quality children's literature and its dissemination. Between the end of the 1940s and the 1960s this situation changed dramatically.

Behind the scene: children's publishing 1945–1970

The underlying difference in the evolution of the modern children's publishing industries in the UK and US was one of status and intention. According to

Robin Denniston, Children's Editor at Collins (1953–1959), before the 1950s, what would today be regarded as 'quality' children's literature was not considered a separate branch of publishing from the mainstream work of the firm:

> Authors like Ransome wrote for children because that was the natural way for them to write, and publishers published the books because they published what the author wrote, because they liked and admired them, and made money out of them; and because they had the inner confidence that what they liked and invested in would find a market of others with similar tastes.[8]

During the 1950s British publishers began consciously to establish children's lists and to appoint staff with responsibility for working only in this area. The consequences of this division have been wide-ranging and enduring. Arguably the most important impact of the separation and professionalization of children's publishing in the post-war period was the formation of a complex paradox at its heart: despite the profitability of children's books, they, and the people who produced them, were in many ways invisible within the companies which owned them. For instance, although most of the best-known publishing houses and the various imprints they now encompass have frequently needed to depend substantially on the lucrative and reliable children's lists they established or acquired in the post-war period, very little public recognition has been given to those who were responsible for managing them, or, indeed, to the books themselves.

The marginalization of the children's divisions of publishing houses becomes immediately apparent in a study of publishing histories; their lack of status within the institutions which both gave life to and lived off them is mirrored perfectly in these celebratory accounts of the publishing industry and the figures behind it. Rarely will the history of an individual publishing firm devote more than a few pages to the work of the children's divisions and their editors. For instance, in 1995 Penguin celebrated sixty years of publishing and followed its own tradition of marking significant anniversaries with a book celebrating its history. Neither *Sixty Penguin Years*, nor any of the other histories of Penguin and its founder, for instance, Steve Hare's *Allen Lane and the Penguin Editors 1935–1970* (1995); *Fifty Penguin Years* (1985), or J.E. Morpurgo's *Allen Lane: King Penguin* (1979), offers more than a passing glance at Penguin's highly successful and innovative children's division, Puffin, although, particularly during the difficult 1970s, Puffin's earnings regularly exceeded those from the sales of adult books.[9] The same pattern is found in other publishing histories: *Gollancz: The story of a publishing house 1928–1978* (1978), sums up the contribution of its children's division in two-and-a-half pages; *The Oxford University Press: An Informal History* (1978) in five, and *William Heinemann: A Century of Publishing 1890–1990* covers the contribution of this company to children's publishing in four pages plus some scattered references. The history produced in honour of the Bodley Head's centenary, *The Bodley Head 1887–1987* (1987), devotes an entire chapter to 'Publishing for Children'; however, it is notable that this is among the shortest chapters in the book and claims to cover the whole of children's publishing while the rest of the volume is concerned with documenting individuals and changes involved with books produced for adults.

This paradox: that for much of the post-war period, children's books have contributed substantially to publishers' incomes, but have consistently been made to appear insignificant in the companies themselves, needs to be kept in mind when thinking about the development of the children's publishing industry, for it has been both a source of frustration and of emancipation. Two successful children's publishers involved in revitalizing British publishing for children describe the situation thus:

> *Pam Royds (André Deutsch's Children's Editor, 1964–1991, when Deutsch sold its children's list to Scholastic. She is now Scholastic's Consultant Editor, Fiction):*
>
> When I started I would say that almost all the children's lists were part of general publishing houses, and this had both good things about it and bad. The good thing was that you were part of a publishing house and you shared the excitement of a big adult success and that sort of thing. The bad side of it was that you were Cinderella, and nobody noticed that you existed. . . . every now and then you got frightfully cross because nobody acknowledged what you were doing – André [Deutsch] once referred jokingly to it as my hobby![10]
>
> *Kaye Webb (Puffin Editor, 1961–1979).*
>
> They [the children's books] just didn't exist as far as anybody was concerned. . . . I only wanted to be on the Board of Directors because nobody was speaking up for Puffin. . . . I don't think there was *anybody* who was interested in them. They were all frightfully glad about the figures, but I don't think there was anybody . . . to support them.[11]

Given that for much of the post-war period children's divisions were denied status, resources and influence in the publishing houses which owned them, it is worth asking why they were set up and maintained, and, indeed, given the long history of publishing for children in Great Britain, why the tradition of specialist children's lists and/or publishers had effectively disappeared in the early years of the twentieth century.

Prices, profits and prestige

Problems with the status of children's literature as a separate branch of publishing go some way towards explaining the dismissive attitude to those involved exclusively with making books for young readers. One consequence of the movement to separate 'serious' fiction from that read by women and children was that a 'serious' career in publishing was 'supposed' to be about high culture – new editions of *The Bostonians*, not new stories by Lucy Boston. However, it is a fact of capitalism that a sector of the market which is not only doing well but also offers prospects for expansion is almost never dismantled. In the case of children's books, these pressures worked to create both new problems and new opportunities.

One of the most important problems for children's publishers is price. As long as 'books for children' were essentially part of the publishing mainstream, there was little need for price differentials between children's and adults' reading. The creation of separate markets for children's and adults' literature, coupled with the decline in the status of children's books, effectively created a ceiling to what people were prepared to pay for them. Moreover, whereas in the nineteenth century publishers could sell copies of the same text to different groups of readers at different prices by printing them in editions of different quality, by the early twentieth century fewer editions were produced, and for books aimed at the juvenile market these were almost inevitably at lower prices.[12] This meant that it was necessary to sell many more children's books to make the same profit as their adult counterparts. Sir Stanley Unwin's classic study of the publishing industry, *The Truth About Publishing* (1960; revised for its eighth edition in 1976), describes the problem of the price ceiling; a problem which, despite his predictions, continues to preoccupy children's publishers today:

> ... up to 1939, 7s 6d (37.5p) was generally recognised as the top price at which any 'juvenile' could be expected to have a substantial sale. There were, of course, exceptions, but, generally speaking, it was fatal at that time, to publish a book intended for children at even such a slightly increased price as 8s 6d (42.5p).[13]

Although children's books cost at least as much and, because of the use of illustrative material and larger type faces, often more than adult books to produce, the market is not prepared to pay as much for children's books as for those intended for an adult audience. While Unwin suggests that the situation was improving after 1939 (his arguments, which hinge on the greater discrimination of parents and their increased desire to provide mental food for their children, suggest he is thinking of the climate out of which the 1944 Education Act grew), this has never been the case. As the end of the twentieth century approaches, the market still resists attempts towards parity in the pricing of adults' and children's books. In 1995 Liz Attenborough, then on the Board of Directors at Penguin with responsibility for the children's division (Puffin, Hamish Hamilton Children's Books, Viking and Blackie), described the problems this creates for children's book publishers:

> I think it's quite important to realise in the whole economics of children's publishing that there is less money sloshing around than there is in adult publishing. We can do the same number of co-edition rights deals as our adult equivalents, the same number of transactions, but we all get less money from it. Authors get less money, although they are probably getting the same percentage [as writers for adults], it's the same percentage of a lower selling price. Publishers are making less, book-sellers are making less on every transaction, but each book takes up the same amount of space on their shelves with the same rent and rates as an adult book. So ... children's books have to work trebly hard to earn their place.[14]

An additional factor which can make selling children's books less attractive to publishers is the different sales patterns between children's and adults' books. A publisher bringing out a new adult text will expect it to start earning immediately, the bulk of the sales being made in the first six months; children's books take much longer to become established. Although ultimately they may become good, steady earners, publishers have to wait considerably longer for children's books to cover their costs and start making a profit. This means that, traditionally, large backlists have had to be maintained, and books kept in storage over long periods of time, adding considerably to the costs involved in selling children's books. This problem was particularly acute for children's publishers before the 1980s, when in order both to meet long-term demand and to keep the unit price low it was necessary to have large print runs – frequently of 10,000 copies or more.

It is now possible to have much shorter print runs and to reprint more frequently; however, the costs of warehousing have increased dramatically and it is no longer considered sensible practice to keep large stocks of titles which have not made an initial impact. The result is many more children's titles, much more rapid turnover of these titles, and fewer opportunities for books to become established. Reflecting on this trend, Judy Taylor (retired Director of the Bodley Head, where she was for many years the Children's Editor) observes,

> That must be the most distressing thing for a children's book editor today, because we all know how long it takes for a children's book to become known and established. I suspect that present-day publishers would say, 'Oh, well, it's all right because it'll come out in paperback very soon.' But that means that the child is denied the hardback, and if you love and want a book, you want it in the most robust and nice form.[15]

Despite the problems inherent in publishing which is aimed specifically at children, in the years following the Second World War publishers actively set about creating children's lists. It is possible to understand this as part of the post-war emphasis on the child as representative of the future and his or her resulting need for education and nurture. However, it seems also to have been more than that. The publishers who began children's lists in the 1950s appear to have been motivated by a mixture of altruism (publishing for children was a Good Thing because it gave pleasure and helped to instil appropriate values during a time when society was recovering from the effects and disruptions of war); rivalry (if one publisher had a children's list others would too); business acumen (the child reader of today will become the adult reader of tomorrow), and even domestic pragmatism (sometimes books were 'tried out' on children, and in a few cases children's lists became the responsibility of family members).[16]

By the 1960s, no motives other than those strictly related to business were needed. The Labour Government poured money into school and public libraries, making it possible for specialist librarians to develop children's collections and child-friendly environments.[17] This influx of Government money was frequently complemented by large orders for British books from the United States, where federal funds were also being pumped into public and school libraries as part of Lyndon Johnson's attempt to construct the 'Great Society'.[18] Judy Taylor recalls the sense of excitement and possibility which characterized children's book publishing in the 1960s:

> Those were the days . . . when you could sell children's books in vast quantities. . . . There was a lot of government money about for schools and libraries. It was a real heyday! . . . We used to print ten thousand copies of a picture book without any hesitation.[19]

Because children's books were earning such huge sums (sometimes as much as 70 percent of a company's income[20]) during the 1960s, it was possible for editors to insist on excellence in design and materials. Lavish full-colour books by first-class illustrators, among them Edward Ardizzone, Raymond Briggs, Shirley Hughes, Ezra Jack Keats, Charles Keeping, Gerald Rose, Maurice Sendak and Brian Wildsmith (see Chapter 4), were produced in increasing numbers. The general rate of increase can be seen in the Puffin list: between 1941 and 1961 it grew by a maximum of twelve titles per year, whereas between 1961 and 1965 the number of titles was increased by 50 per cent overall.[21]

The new and initially affluent children's libraries supported children's publishers enthusiastically. Indeed, the influence of children's librarians on the financial success of children's publishing during the formative years of the 1960s cannot be overestimated; subsequently they also exercised considerable influence over the content, appearance, and value systems which underpin much of late twentieth-century publishing for young people.

Women editors and publishers: money, quality and the image of childhood 1945–1970

Publishers' lack of respect for children's books, coupled with their sense that they ought to be producing them, created unprecedented opportunities for women. Publishing, like most other post-war businesses, was male-dominated. The few women who were employed by the firms, with virtually no exceptions, worked as typists, receptionists and telephonists.[22] There were no career pathways for them; certainly no opportunity to become editors or directors. However, because the editing of children's books was thought of as effectively unskilled and certainly inferior work, very few established figures (invariably men) were interested in taking on the task of creating and managing children's lists. There were some notable exceptions to this, foremost among them Patrick Hardy at Viking, and John Bell, ably followed by Frank Eyre, at Oxford University Press; in general, however, this was a female-dominated branch of publishing, and one which was not associated with quality or expertise. Margaret Clark, who worked first for Puffin and later for Bodley

Head, was reminded of and moved to correct this early attitude when editing an edition of *Signal*:

> When ferreting through the pages of Allen Lane's biography . . . I was taken aback
> by the words 'desiccated spinsters' used of those who were editing children's books
> at the time [1940] when Allen Lane was looking for someone to start a children's
> list for him. But the phrase . . . typifies the attitude that then prevailed towards this
> branch of publishing. . . . The truth is that in the 1940s and 1950s children's book
> editors, of whatever sex, *had* to have a very strong belief in what they were doing,
> and a positive and lively view of their work, in an era when children's books had
> not become the big business they are now.[23]

Given their casual approach to children's books, it is not surprising that even publishers who embraced the idea of developing a children's list seemed not to have felt it necessary to give much thought to who was going to run them. Most children's editors from the 1950s to the present day have been women, and most of them were appointed opportunistically or even by default. Kaye Webb (Puffin), was offered her job at a party; Pam Royds (André Deutsch) because her children were at school with the children of someone who worked at Deutsch;[24] Gwen Marsh (J.M. Dent), Margaret Clark (Puffin and Bodley Head) and Liz Attenborough (Puffin) were secretaries; Judy Taylor (Bodley Head) was a 'maid of all work', and Philippa Dickinson (Transworld) was spotted doing a good job as an office junior working on the Puffin Club, a post she had been given to fill in the gap between A-levels and university because her father (Peter Dickinson) was a Puffin author.

Notable exceptions to this rule were Marni Hodgkin and Grace Hogarth, both of whom *were* trained as specialist children's editors in the United States, and Kathleen Lines, who, though she had no editorial expertise, had a thorough grounding in children's literature obtained while serving under Lillian Smith in the Toronto Public Library, which houses the prestigious Osborne Collection of historic children's books. Each of these influential early editors was responsible for training others, who entered the field via many of the same routes; indeed, Grace Hogarth was so well known for this that her protégées (male and female alike) were dubbed 'Grace's Girls'. Thus, a small group comprised almost entirely of women who were not British began to professionalize the field; gradually they began to scale company hierarchies in ways previously impassable to female employees. For the first wave, however, large salaries, corporate success, promotion and recognition were not goals they sought. All emphasize that they enjoyed their work, found it immensely satisfying, and through it laid down the relationships, skills and mental ballast which now sustains them in later life.

The fact that so many children's lists were eventually run by women had many positive aspects. Their general sense of invisibility and marginality in their own companies created both a unique sense of rapport and collaboration between children's editors and the opportunity for almost complete autonomy in the company. The benefits of this situation were not always recognized at the time. Marni Hodgkin summed up the frustrations it engendered in her

1984 Sidney Robbins Memorial Lecture: 'At Macmillan's twelve years of explaining to my fellow editors every Wednesday morning [she, not they, had insisted that she attend the weekly editorial meetings and present her books as did all the company's "real" editors] why such and such a book was a good thing and why another was unsuitable for our list, made no dent at all on their conviction that children's books were something quite other than "real" books.'[25]

While Marni Hodgkin laments the failure of children's books to be taken seriously, with the advantage of hindsight many of her contemporaries recognize that precisely because the books they produced were trivialized, as editors they had extraordinary amounts of freedom, which they used to the full. Kaye Webb makes this point repeatedly: 'He [Allen Lane] just didn't interfere at all. . . . As long as I was making money, nobody was going to interfere with me. . . . I didn't have any interference.'[26]

It was the same in other companies. Pam Royds remembers, 'I had marvellous freedom to build up the list insofar as I could, and nobody ever interfered with me because they really didn't know anything about it. . . . We always used to have a joke, which I shared with him [André Deutsch], that until *Postman Pat* came along he would pass me on the street and not recognize me!'[27] Philippa Pearce, from whom she inherited the job of Children's Editor at Deutsch, summed up the position for Pam when she joined the company: 'André reminds me rather of my mother – if you don't go into the kitchen, you don't get asked to do a job! So just keep out of his sight and he'll leave you alone.'[28]

Freedom came at a cost, however; children's book editors were not well paid. According to Kaye Webb, 'People didn't think much of children's books; it was just a thing women could do. . . . I couldn't believe how humble all the [children's] editors were that I met . . . it never occurred to them that they were entitled to decent offices, or more money, or much attention.'[29]

Having their books largely ignored within their own companies and feeling themselves to be marginal brought children's editors from many companies together to share books, problems, information and ideas. It was clear that if they were to develop and succeed, they needed to learn from each other and make what they were doing more visible. Under the influence of Grace Hogarth, who hoped to bring to the British children's publishing world some of the best aspects of its counterpart in the United States, the Children's Book Circle (CBC) was formed in 1962. This was an informal organization where established editors and those with different kinds of knowledge, perhaps gained by working with publishers from other countries, came together in an alliance which was at once creative, co-operative and social.

The CBC was initially comprised of approximately twenty children's book editors; within four years it had grown to seventy-two members and had established (in 1965) the Eleanor Farjeon Award (see Chapter 3). All those involved in the early years of the CBC recall it as a vital forum in every way. Pam Royds sums up the general feeling:

> The chief thing was how really marvellously helpful people were. . . . I remember going to a meeting where Julia [MacRae] gave a terrific talk about how to cope with foreign rights and things; sharing all her skills and all that she had learned on various trips abroad. . . . The great bond we all had was that we were all second-class citizens.'[30]

The CBC established an annual cycle of evening meetings with both guest and 'in-house' speakers, covering topics ranging from illustration to publicity, occasional conferences, and what it called 'Grouch' meetings, where particularly irksome or thorny problems were aired. In 1989 the Patrick Hardy Lecture was inaugurated to commemorate the work of a visionary children's editor and publisher. Latterly the CBC has become a very different organization, less close-knit, open and instructive, though topics of general interest are still discussed at their regular meetings and many new to children's publishing (especially those involved in marketing children's books) find it a supportive source of general information and useful contacts.

Although editors worked closely through this forum and the social networks it established, during the years until the 1970s it was rare for them to share authors or illustrators. Each imprint had its own identity and its own style of book, and the idea of wooing someone else's writers or artists away was not just considered bad form, it was also regarded as having the potential to undermine the identity and character of a particular list. According to Judy Taylor, 'You didn't poach from each other. . . . this was so established that if you had an idea for a book and you very much wanted to do it with a particular person, you might approach the editor first – before you approached the author.'[31] This was one of the aspects of publishing which was to change dramatically during the 'Thatcher years' of the 1970s and 1980s.

Before moving on to consider how economic and technical changes in the final decades of the century have affected publishing for children, it is important to look more closely at the kind of audience for whom books were being made and the image of childhood they disseminated in the newly revitalized children's book industry.

We're not just here to make a profit

The majority of children's books produced in the years between 1945 and 1970 were chosen, edited and generally midwifed by a small group of white, middle-class women who felt passionately that 'only the best is good enough for children'.[32] Their idea of what was 'best' was largely based on their own tastes and experiences. Accordingly, they produced books which were aimed at and reflected the lives of white, middle-class, educationally successful children, and which generally assumed that boys were more likely to be at the centre of any action than were girls. (Looking back on her own work Philippa Pearce comments, 'I have noticed, in the first books I wrote the central character was a boy or boys, because I somehow thought that was

right. . . . it seemed more difficult to write a story with a girl in the centre.'³³)
Eleanor Graham was perhaps more up-front about the kind of child for whom
she was publishing than were her contemporaries. In a 1952 letter to Eunice
Frost, then an influential editor at Penguin, she set out her position:

> None of these three volumes (*Enjoying Painting, Going to a Concert, Going to the
> Ballet*) are [*sic*] likely to appeal to the general run of Secondary Modern children
> – who, I suppose, make up the greater part of the up to 15 age group. There has
> to be some consciousness: some extra upward yearning before they will bother with
> them, but this quality certainly lies in the make-up of the rather better educated –
> say Grammar School and High School level – from even 13 up.³⁴

For writer, critic and broadcaster Edward Blishen, this type of publishing was
epitomized in the books produced by Mabel George during her years at
Oxford University Press (see Chapter 4):

> She was not a popular publisher and had no intention of being one. Her notion of
> what was suitable for children was always a notion of quality. . . . There were
> actually people who were repelled at the idea of reading an Oxford book, and I'm
> sure there were as many school librarians who didn't buy them because they were
> Oxford books as school librarians who bought them because they were. . . . If
> children of other [than middle-class] backgrounds could be helped by being pre-
> sented with a less ambitious book, she wasn't interested. . . . Her interest was in
> the aristocratic reader: the best reader, in her view. She certainly had no wide social
> view about literature and its capacity to enlarge sensibilities or disadvantaged
> children, or anything like that.³⁵

Other editors were somewhat less dogmatic and overt in their approach to
publishing, but the effect was much the same, as Pam Royds recalls: 'To be
absolutely honest, when I started we probably were all publishing for a very,
very small percentage of the children of this country who went to libraries:
that really was a very small number of middle-class children.'³⁶

The post-war emphasis on good writing and positively nostalgic images of
childhood, backed with liberal resources and a burgeoning social optimism,
resulted in many fine works across the range of children's publishing (see
Chapters 3 and 4). In addition to their strongly middle-class bias, these were
circumscribed by a range of official and unofficial taboos and rules: no sex,
no 'language', no violence, and always a happy ending.

All of this began to change in the 1970s. By then, a noteworthy body of
work was established (a substantial proportion of which came out of Mabel
George's base at OUP). The work of writers and illustrators such as Joan
Aiken, Alan Garner, Charles Keeping, William Mayne, Mary Norton, Philippa
Pearce, Maurice Sendak, Rosemary Sutcliff, and Brian Wildsmith had begun
attracting serious critical attention. For instance, in 1961 Margery Fisher
published *Intent Upon Reading*, followed the next year by the first number
of her own children's book magazine, *Growing Point*; Brian Alderson was
appointed Children's Book Editor of *The Times* in 1967; Nancy and Aidan
Chambers founded *Signal* in 1970, and, in the same year, *Children's Literature
in Education* was launched and held a landmark conference where the new

breed of lecturers in Children's Literature exchanged ideas and information with critics, publishers, writers, illustrators, teachers and enthusiasts. It is another paradox of children's publishing that, precisely when it seemed to have 'come of age', two new pressures which were dramatically to affect its nature and future development came to the fore.

The first of these was financial. Government money for libraries and education was radically reduced, both in the UK and in the important US market. Over subsequent years the situation became so acute that in his 1992 Patrick Hardy lecture, writer and critic Michael Rosen declared,

> in spite of all the rhetoric concerning literacy levels [the Government] has declared war on the reading of books. Let's look at their weapons:
>
> * the closing of public libraries
> * the elimination of the library support services
> * the forced amateuring of school librarians – professionals can't be afforded
> * budget restrictions on school book buying as documented by the NAS and the Children's Book Foundation
> * the domination of fixed courses of study, set texts and testing that limit casual and pupil-led reading and browsing
> * the elimination of text books for home-reading and the consequent rise of the work-sheet.[37]

Publishers, then, could no longer depend on schools and libraries automatically purchasing hardback editions of every new book they produced (or even of specialist librarians making informed judgements about what to buy with their reduced resources). Additionally, throughout this period the costs of production – from materials to labour – increased dramatically. New selling techniques were imported from the United States, and though these largely pertained to adult books, they were generally applied to the children's division as independent publishing houses and/or their children's imprints were swallowed up in increasingly frequent corporate mergers (in 1970 there were forty-five independent publishers with recognizable expertise in publishing books for children; by 1995 only nine independent publishers were producing children's books[38]). 'Rationalization' meant that all of the imprints in any publishing house began to share design, production and marketing labour, which tended to homogenize appearance. Similarity in appearance was also encouraged by huge, centralised purchasers such as W.H. Smith, who generally refused to stock books which did not fit into their standardised display racks, and by publishers scrambling for 'market share' by imitating each others' best-selling titles. Financial constraints coupled with the second form of pressure – increasing awareness of newly topical issues – meant that publishers were simultaneously encouraged to look for new markets and to be alert to socially sensitive issues such as racism, sexism, and classism. This was the scene which the new breed of children's publishers inherited as the 1970s drew to a close.

The price of success? Publishing children's books in the 1980s and 1990s

In 1980, when Tony Lacey briefly assumed responsibility for the Puffin list, he did so with the conviction that it was time for change: 'It was middle-class, very girl/female oriented, and making certain demands of the reader that maybe not all of them could fulfil in terms of length and historical knowledge and so on.'[39] Trained under Patrick Hardy, Lacey had had drilled into him the importance of quality books and healthy balance sheets. Looking back at his years at Puffin, he is particularly conscious of the ways in which his age, class, and gender orientation influenced his management style and goals:

> Just because I am male, more things started to come in that were more obviously male, i.e., *You Can Do the Cube*! and the fantasy game books and . . . the football books for the eight to ten year olds by Martin Waddell. There was a certain kind of male influence; possibly more of a relationship with marketing. . . . We absolutely couldn't give up Puffin's constituency. . . . at the same time, I had this notion that you could work on the ways books were presented and also, just to get turnover, you could do books that might last but probably wouldn't. I very much encouraged speed of publishing during that time, too.[40]

Despite what Tony Lacey regards as the masculinization of children's publishing (and it is important to note that several prominent children's editors and publishers in the final decades of the century have been men – among them Paul Binding [OUP], David Fickling [Scholastic], Klaus Flugge [Andersen Press], Ron Heapy [OUP], Tom Maschler [Jonathan Cape] and, of course, the late Sebastian Walker, the first publisher to set up a specialist children's book list in this period), it continues to be dominated by women. Significantly, the positions many of them occupy are very different from those of their predecessors. One legacy from which many women in the field now benefit is the increasingly well-signed route to corporate power first marked out by women such as Julia MacRae, Judy Taylor and Kaye Webb. It is now no longer uncommon to find women working in children's books being appointed directors of companies. In this respect they differ significantly from other women in publishing, who argue that, as in many other professions, there exists a 'glass ceiling' which invisibly, covertly, impedes women's professional development: there is a point beyond which they cannot go. In January 1995 a report of the 'Women into Management Study': *A Case of Covert Discrimination*, showed that throughout publishing as a whole, 'men are more than twice as likely to become managers, and more than five times as likely to become a company board director' than are women.[41] Many of the women who do succeed in gaining entry to the 'top tiers' of publishing continue to do so through the children's route.

Interestingly, the study cites differences in culture and managerial style between men and women (for instance, men being more prepared to demonstrate high levels of commitment to the company through what is deemed a 'workaholic syndrome') which are to some extent contradicted in the history

of children's publishing in the period since the last war. A striking characteristic of the women editors of the 1950s to 1970s was their total involvement
with work. The majority of these women either had no children, or began
work when their children were grown; work for them took on the role of
surrogate family, as Judy Taylor observes:

> as not many of us were married, our work was our life. We didn't have to go home
> and cook or look after our husbands. It was my life, so if my authors or artists
> became my friends, then they would come to dinner and I would go to dinner with
> them, or we would go and spend the weekend together – it was an all-embracing
> thing.[42]

The situation is quite different for many women editors and publishers of
children's books in the 1990s. Most not only have children but have had their
children while continuing to work. This reflects social and legislative changes
which make it both more acceptable and easier for women with children to
continue to work, in whatever sphere.

The female presence in children's publishing may be a constant, and it
continues to be a reflection of the low status of children's literature in publishing companies;[43] everything else, however, has changed. No longer are
children's editors largely invisible and autonomous. Every book has to justify
its existence in purely financial terms and very rapidly, as Philippa Dickinson,
who was trained by Kaye Webb at Puffin, explains:

> That's the thing that's changed . . . in the old days I would not have worried about
> who a book was for; I would just have published it because I loved it. . . . now I
> have to put my personal selection in terms of money. . . . I don't suppose Kaye ever
> had to do that.[44]

As early as 1984, Marni Hodgkin was bemoaning the move to make the
marketing tail wag the publishing dog:

> What depresses me most [. . .] is that the way things are being stacked now, the
> best-sellers can't do anything to help the general cause. In times past, the selling
> titles helped to support those that didn't: the experimental books or those with
> minority appeal, or by unknown authors. But when books are marketed like soap,
> each one, we are told, must stand on its own feet. The result is that a title without
> mass appeal may easily go out of print within the year of its publication, before
> the hard-pressed librarians have had a chance to assess it or the children are able
> to have a go. Publishers are less ready to take risks, and new writers and innovative
> writing go to the wall.[45]

Kaye Webb concurred: 'The feeling of responsibility has gone, and it's been
replaced by making money and selling any kind of book.'[46]

Bound up with the newly aggressive economics of children's publishing is
the search for new markets and new readers, which has inevitably led to
changes in the image of the child contained in children's books as we approach
the end of the century. This process began in the 1970s as a quest for greater
recognition of the fact that Britain is not the monolithically white, middle-
class world represented in children's books before then. According to literary
agent Laura Cecil, who specialises in children's books, the first public attempt

to reconstruct the image of childhood in children's fiction took the form of a competition organized by the publishers, Collins, to find an 'ethnic-minority story'. The competition failed to identify an exciting new voice from any of Britain's ethnic minorities – it was won by a white, middle-class male. The experiment was not repeated.

It was not just ethnic minorities who had traditionally been excluded from the image of childhood in children's literature. Robert Leeson, who, both as critic and writer was instrumental in the transformation of children's literature, explains his motivation:

> People like me did not appear in children's books. People like me and my family were . . . underneath the Plimsoll line. I remember a phrase that was used quite frequently when I was a kid: 'the man in the street'. The man in the street always appeared in cartoons in pin-striped trousers and a black jacket. I never saw, when I was growing up, the man in the pin-striped trousers and jacket. The man in the street wore his overalls – or his Sunday best if you were going to the chapel. . . . I recognized as a kid the absence of people like me in these books, and when I came to review children's books, even though . . . post-war children's books opened up tremendously and children's books improved and began to be attractive to children compared with the stuff I used to get before the War which was uniformly brown: brown bound volumes. And yet, the new books, attractive as they were, were still very much socially orientated towards middle-class people.[47]

Robert Leeson's contribution to the changing face of and audience for children's books extended beyond the content to the nature of the book itself. Throughout the period 1945 to 1975 there was a clearly understood relationship between 'good' children's books and their appearance in hardback form.[48] This was in part an aesthetic judgement, but its economic implications when hardback sales were at three times their current levels were considerable. An author was likely to be paid a royalty in the region of 10 per cent of hardback and 7.5 per cent of any paperback sales (these percentages have remained more or less constant throughout). At 1996 figures, the price of an average hardback is £12; a paperback £4. Clearly more money is earned for everybody from hardback sales – as long as the sales exist. In the more competitive 1980s, not only did the bottom fall out of the hardback market, with even libraries often preferring to purchase paperbacks, but those, like Robert Leeson, involved in trying to bring children and books together became increasingly conscious that hardbacks were unaffordable for many of their potential readers. Moreover, with the pressure on publishers to turn over lists at ever increasing rates and the speed with which other media could deliver entertainment, many readers were not prepared to wait eighteen months or so for a book to come out in paperback. The result was a new breakthrough in children's publishing: books that were published as paperback originals.

One of the first of these was Leeson's *The Third Class Genie* (1975) which, at 30p a copy was specifically marketed as a 'pocket-money' book. However, for a paperback to earn as much as a hardback it needs to sell three times as many copies; for children's books to earn as much as adults the equation is approximately the same. Moreover, it doesn't cost less to originate a paperback, which means that it has much more to earn before it starts making a profit than is the case for paperbacks which are offset from hardcover editions. Thus, the problems previously outlined by Liz Attenborough are exacerbated by paperback originals. Nobody earns as much from them as from the traditional pattern of publishing. One response to this was to look for new ways of expanding the market for children's books through outlets such as mail-order book clubs and supermarkets.

If one way of reaching more children was by making paperback editions more affordable, another was by trying to move away from an image of childhood which was likely to be set in the writer's and/or illustrator's past to books which were more immediately responsive to young people's interests. Perhaps the best examples of this kind of book were the breed of Puffins brought out under Tony Lacey. Foremost among these were *You Can Do the Cube!*, a best-selling title written in a matter of days by a schoolboy during the brief craze for Rubik's cubes and which sold 700,000 copies in four months. This book coincided with a reappraisal of the Puffin list, which Lacey felt had to be modernised by up-dating covers, appealing to less literary readers, and, specifically, increasing speed of turnover with books like *You Can Do the Cube!* and the hugely successful 'Fighting Fantasy' series, which were less likely to become permanent fixtures on the Puffin backlist but which would make large profits immediately. Inevitably, best-sellers created internal demand for more of the same, and Puffin subsequently brought out books on other youth fads such as BMX bikes. The volume of sales generated by such books meant that the policy of looking for new kinds of readers had succeeded, but at what cost? One effect of high-profit high-turnover children's publishing was that many long-established writers of quality fiction suddenly found themselves labelled 'old-fashioned' and 'too literary'. At the same time, the loyalty which had existed between writers, artists, editors and publishing houses broke down.

Writing for children's publishers today

In the first Patrick Hardy lecture, given jointly by Jill Paton Walsh and John Rowe Townsend, the writer's perspective on the changes which have taken place in children's publishing since the 1970s was put succinctly by Townsend:

> When I was first involved in children's books, in the early 1960s, the leading editors, and their lists, were institutions. They seemed as solidly built as Stonehenge, or at any rate the Bank of England. . . . And the lists! The Oxford list, replete with Sutcliffs and Maynes, with Ardizzones and Wildsmiths and Keepings, all in print; all in hardback print, at that, in editions of ten thousand or more. There was security there, so far as there is ever security for artists and authors. Authors, as well as publishers, built up a backlist, and backlist books kept on selling. . . . how conditions have changed: the march of the big corporations, the rise in real prices coupled with a decline in the real budgets of schools and libraries, the cash flow problems, the dominance of the bottom line; above all, as a consequence of these

things, the emphasis on the short term. . . . Short-termism . . . has made such marriages [between author and editor] less frequent and more difficult. . . . Rather than marriages I sometimes think we now have one-night stands. . . . my observation suggests that many authors have transferred to their agent the trust and friendship they would once have shared with their editor; the editor becomes merely the buyer who may or may not stock your wares.[49]

Townsend is not the only writer to use a public platform to call attention to the plight of the writer now that so many of the practices which dictated children's publishing before the 1980s have largely disappeared. Michael Rosen, the keynote speaker at the 1994 UK Friends of IBBY (the International Board on Books for Young People) Conference, also took the opportunity to put the writer's point of view. His account of what it is to be a successful children's writer in the 1990s is a far cry from the days when publishers, editors and authors spent long hours crafting and polishing books, and thinking more about quality than marketability. Now, it seems, writers have constantly to produce more and more books at greater and greater speed; in some cases so little time is spent on editing and production that ludicrous mistakes can occur. For instance, Rosen himself had the experience of receiving page proofs for a book he had written many months earlier and subsequently revised at the editor's request. The page proofs, he discovered, were from the previously discarded version, but there was insufficient time to reinstate the corrections and improvements he had made. Problems are compounded by constant changes in personnel and the dictates of currently fashionable series publishing. No individual blame was ascribed, rather Rosen looked for the economic and ideological causes which have brought about this unsatisfactory state of affairs:

I think there are two processes going on here: in jargon terms: globalization and localization. Globalization is hot and strong, it's Disney, it's the international company, it's the we-must-sell twenty thou or forget it. It means return on investment must show within a year or clear the book off the warehouse shelf, it's taking up space and space costs money. It means more and more titles because any book stands a better chance of selling more in its first year than in any other year of its life, so ideally a publishing house should be a place that is selling hundreds of titles for one year. It is no strange artistic or economic mystery why seven thousand children's books a year are being produced in the UK. That's not something creative, critical people can alter by being pious and analytic about. It is the inexorable anarchy of capitalism that is insisting: more titles, more authors, quick quick, write write, no time to edit, no time to rewrite, get it out, sell it, drop it, pulp it. Publishing children's books is moving more and more towards the structure of publishing magazines. The impulse to localize is cool and weak. Very clever idealistic people are trying to set up outfits that are attempting commitment to a principle – bilingual books, for example, or multicultural books. They can't always pay authors and illustrators enough money to live off, they can't compete with the big geezers in distribution and publicity, so the buyers and readers find it difficult to get hold of the books or, to put it another way, they don't actually hear of them. . . .[50]

Conclusion

Townsend and Rosen speak from their positions as established and successful writers, but their anxiety about the changes which have affected children's book publishing in the final quarter of the twentieth century is echoed by many of those working at all levels and in every aspect of the industry. As the century – indeed, the millennium – draws to a close, children's book publishing faces challenges on almost every front. Many writers feel alienated from their editors, who in turn find their children's divisions run by managers and marketing departments who have little understanding of the special needs and patterns of their niche in the publishing business and for many of whom the old ethos, 'nothing but the best is good enough for children', no longer holds true.

The situation is not apocalyptic, however, and change is already in the air again. Like Michael Rosen, Piet Snyman, head of children's book publishing at Random House, looks at the emergence of small, independent publishers and forecasts that, as the century comes to a close, children's publishing will have increasingly to resist the out-dated and inappropriate structures of the huge, multi-national conglomerates which swallowed up so many imprints in the 1980s and 1990s.[51] Already companies such as Walker Books, Ragged Bears, Spindlewood, Frances Lincoln, and Mantra have become successful specialist children's publishers, but Snyman says the change will be more radical still:

> When the third golden age of children's publishing in Britain dawns (and it will) it will be on a publishing industry that has not only outgrown the current taxonomy of children's books, but that has been able to make books available to its readership through its ability to sell books where children, or adults buying books for them, want to buy them.[52]

Book sales are only one indicator of the health of the industry, however. If volume alone were at issue, children's publishing in the UK would seem to be thriving. The growth of new titles has been striking, increasing from 4,510 in 1986 to 7,080 in 1994. The industry has a turnover in the region of £215 million (excluding educational publishing).[53] Certainly more children's books have been published since 1980 than ever before; they represent a wider cross-section of the population than ever before, and, through new retailing initiatives such as selling books in supermarkets and through tying books to films and television programmes, many more young people have access to books. Children's books are currently experiencing a small revival in media coverage, and a healthy and wide-ranging number of prizes (see Chapter 3) help bring children's books to the attention of parents, children and teachers.

Despite these indisputable successes, there are also acute problems caused by the sheer volume and activity of children's publishing; the printed text and its creators are somewhat besieged by multimedia, hypertext and every other kind of alternative 'book'. Editors, writers and illustrators worry about the quality of many of the books published under present conditions, and there is an equally strong sense of uncertainty about the audience for their creations. In the face of competition from a range of leisure activities, will young people still make time for books?

Every generation this century (and many before them) has announced the death of reading. As she approaches the end of her career, Pam Royds puts present trends into perspective: 'I still think the standard is high, but I do think it's getting harder to maintain that standard.'[54] That is the battle for children's publishers in the twenty-first century.

References

1. J.S. Bratton (1981), *The Impact of Victorian Children's Fiction* (London: Croom Helm), pp.53–62.
2. Eleanor Graham has written about her time at Puffin in 'The Puffin Years', *Signal* no. 12, September 1973, pp.115–122.
3. L. Salway (1970), 'Pathetic Simplicity: Hesba Stretton and Her Books for Children', *Signal*, p.35.
4. P.W. Musgrave (1985), *From Brown to Bunter: The Life and Death of the School Story* (London and Boston: Routledge), p.243.
5. J.R. Townsend (1983), *Written for Children: An Outline of English-language Children's Literature*, second revised edition (Harmondsworth: Kestrel), p.209.
6. J. Tebbel (1981), *A History of Book Publishing in the United States, Vol. IV – The Great Change* (New York and London: R.R. Bowker Company), p.477. In the UK, few would dispute the claims of Grace Hogarth and Marni Hodgkin as joint holders of this title.
7. Ibid., pp.473–5.
8. R. Denniston (1993), 'A Children's Book Publisher of the Fifties', *Signal* no. 70, p.47.
9. Interview with Liz Attenborough, 8 February 1995; S. Gritten (1991) *The Story of Puffin Books* (Harmondsworth: Penguin), pp.25–7, notes the importance of the children's lists during the 1980s as well: 'The 1980s brought enormous pressure to Penguin Books. In the years from 1975 to 1980 volume sales fell from 42m to 39m. . . . By 1983 Tony Lacey was able to claim that 'one in every three Penguins sold is a Puffin'.
10. Interview with Pam Royds, 20 February 1995.
11. Interview with Kaye Webb, 7 February 1995.
12. For a discussion of variations in the pricing of nineteenth-century books, see Bratton, Chapter 2.
13. S. Unwin (1976), *The Truth About Publishing*, eighth edition (London: George Allen and Unwin), p.29. The decimal figures refer to 1976 prices.
14. Attenborough interview.
15. Interview with Judy Taylor, 21 February 1995.
16. For instance, Allen Lane read new Puffins with his children, Helen Hoke Watts (previously children's book editor at Holt, Messner, Reynal & Hitchock and McKay in the US) was actively involved in the children's lists developed by her husband's company, and Livia Gollancz assumed responsibility for the children's list begun by her father, Victor Gollancz.
17. Interviews with Royds and Taylor.
18. A. Durell (1982) 'If There is no Happy Ending: Children's Book Publishing –

Past, Present, and Future', *The Horn Book Magazine*, February, p.28; J.C. Giblin (1986), 'Children's Book Publishing in America: 1919 to Now', *Children's Literature in Education*, vol. 17, no. 3, Fall, p.155.

19. Taylor interview.
20. Attenborough interview.
21. Gritten, op. cit., p.14.
22. For a typical profile of publishing staff, see A. King and A.F. Stuart (1965), *The House of Warne: One Hundred Years of Publishing* (London: Frederick Warne and Co.,), p.63.
23. M. Clark, Introduction to Denniston, op. cit., p.46.
24. Philippa Pearce, who employed her, stresses that corporate procedures were followed and a formal interview conducted before the appointment was made.
25. M. Hodgkin (1984), 'A Personal Philosophy of Publishing for Children', the sixth Sidney Robbins Memorial Lecture, published in *Signal* no. 46, 1985, p.46.
26. Webb interview.
27. Royds interview.
28. Ibid.
29. Webb interview.
30. Royds interview.
31. Taylor interview.
32. Interestingly, this slogan was claimed as the company catch-phrase by many of the people interviewed for this chapter; Marni Hodgkin attributed the phrase to Grace Hogarth, which could explain its widespread use. However, in her article on 'Eleanor Graham', *Signal* no. 9, September 1972, Margaret Clark attributes the maxim to Graham, p.91.
33. Interview with Philippa Pearce, 31 May 1995.
34. S. Hare, ed. (1995), *Allen Lane and the Penguin Editors* (Harmondsworth: Penguin), p.142.
35. Interview with Edward Blishen, 20 June 1995. Laura Cecil, a literary agent specialising in children's books, offers a mild corrective to this view of Mabel George, pointing out that she embraced popular authors such as K.M. Peyton, and published 'working-class' illustrators such as Keeping and Wildsmith. Paul Binding, who took over from Mabel George at OUP agrees, adding that George was herself from an artisan background.
36. Royds interview.
37. Transcript of the 1992 Patrick Hardy Lecture, supplied by the Children's Book Circle.
38. Figures quoted in a talk given by Brian Alderson at the 25th anniversary conference of 'Children's Literature in Education', University of Exeter, 22–25 September 1995.
39. Interview with Tony Lacey, 16 August 1995. Lacey's strategy was an effective one for Puffin, which had been in an uncomfortable limbo during Kaye Webb's final years (she found it extremely difficult to hand over the management of Puffin, and continued to hold a post and wield influence after she had officially stepped down). Laura Cecil comments that Lacey pulled the list together and created a good working atmosphere during his time in charge of Puffin.
40. Ibid.
41. Quoted in S. Walsh and C. Cassell (1995), 'A Case of Covert Discrimination: Report of the Women into Management Study' (London: Bentinck Group and Women in Publishing Training Committee), p.7.
42. Taylor interview.
43. When interviewed for this chapter (7 March 1995), Philippa Dickinson underlined the correlation between the low status of children's book publishing in the industry and the small numbers of men who become involved in it.

44. Ibid.
45. Hodgkin (1984), op. cit., p.59.
46. Webb interview.
47. Interview with Robert Leeson, 26 June 1995.
48. Hostility to paperbacks was widely recorded, see, for instance, B. Alderson (1981), 'Prime Puffins', *The Horn Book Magazine*, p.20.
49. From the transcript of the first Patrick Hardy Lecture, supplied by Jill Paton Walsh and John Rowe Townsend, who jointly gave the address.
50. The full text of the IBBY address appeared in *Signal* no. 76, 1995. The extract included here is reproduced with the author's permission.
51. P. Snyman (1995), 'Towards a third golden age', the *Bookseller*, 25 August 1995, p.19.
52. Ibid.
53. Ibid, p.18. These figures include reprints and new editions/formats of existing books as well as new titles. According to the *Bookseller* report, *Book Publishing in Britain* (1995), in 1994 (the last year for which such figures are available), the children's market in Britain had a turnover of approximately £340 million pounds (table 4.6, p.94). The 1992 study, *Book Publishing*, by Key Note Publications, found that children's books (excluding school books) account for 28 per cent of the volume of all UK book sales and were the biggest growth area in the publishing sector (p.18).
54. Royds interview.

3   Prize-fighting

Keith Barker

The divided thinking which underlies so much of children's book publishing in the second half of the twentieth century is nowhere more clear than in the increasingly large and turbulent area of literary prizes. When adult novels receive awards it is always on the basis of literary merit, but in the world of children's publishing this is no longer seen as the sole criterion for judging a book. Accordingly, new prizes have accumulated in the post-war period, reflecting the differing social, aesthetic and financial forces circulating around juvenile publishing and reading.

The history of awards for children's books mirrors the general story of British children's literature in this period. In 1937, as Keith Barker points out, it was quite in order for the British Library Association to stipulate a tone 'in keeping with the generally accepted standards of good behaviour and right thinking' in all those children's books considered eligible for an award. Nearly sixty years later, awards were given to books that sometimes portrayed a very different world of parental discord, social misery and delinquent behaviour. Children's books were now no longer required to offer good examples pure and simple. They were instead increasingly expected to provide an honest picture of an occasionally flawed world within which some children in particular were receiving an exceptionally raw deal.

Who chooses books awards, and what criteria should they follow? Has increased commercialism devalued prizes, introducing both lower standards and too obvious links with book sales? Where do illustrated books fit in to the awards arena? These questions arise during all literary awards, but perhaps particularly where children's books are concerned. One judge's idea of what child readers need may be very different from that of another, sometimes reflecting an entirely different perception of what childhood itself is or should be all about. Different images of childhood have always been found in children's books; Keith Barker shows how they are present in any discussion about book awards as well.

In 1945 there was one children's book award; in 1995 there were over a dozen major awards as well as more localized ones and a significant international one. In 1945 the only award was presented by librarians and gained very little publicity; in 1995 a number of the awards are sponsored (two by food companies) and gain significant attention from the media. What happened in the intervening years to cause this shift?

To discover this, it is important to look at the children's book world immediately before the beginning of the Second World War. Many of the books published at that time promised much more than they delivered and the feeling which lay behind the foundation of the United Kingdom's oldest children's book award, the Carnegie Medal, reflects this. In the first editorial of *Library Association Record* for the year 1937, the British Library Association's trade journal, in announcing the medal, mentioned that one of its purposes was to encourage the improvement of standards. W.C. Berwick Sayers, one of the architects of the award, described the qualities which the winning books should possess:

> A book for a child somewhere between the ages of nine and twelve, but need not be absolutely within these age limits. Its appeal was to be universal, and therefore it was to be a book which appealed to both sexes equally, so far as any book could. It is possible that the greatest books for children do possess this equal appeal. In literary form it should be in the best English; its story should follow the line of the possible, if not the probable; its characters should be alive, its situations credible, and its tone in keeping with the generally accepted standards of good behaviour and right thinking.[1]

In its first year the selection committee pooled the results of its postal invitation for suggestions from chief librarians, and recommended to the Library Association executive committee that the first medal be awarded to Arthur Ransome for *Pigeon Post*. Second in the running was Howard Spring's *Sampson's Circus* and third Noel Streatfeild's *Ballet Shoes* (this practice of runners up was, in fact, dropped after the first year). Ransome duly received his medal at the Scarborough Conference of the Association in June 1937: it was presented to him by the president of that year, the Archbishop of York. Apparently Ransome thought it would have been better to have sent the 'blessed thing by post'.

Librarians were the main force behind this award, at a time when children's librarians were rare and librarians themselves were not perceived as a group likely to be at the forefront of literary innovation. It should not be assumed, however, that because the Carnegie medal was a low key affair, particularly in comparison with its modern, media-attracting counterparts, that it passed unnoticed. From the beginning, administrative decisions were questioned and the books chosen for honour were the source of some discussion. This was particularly true in only the second year of its existence, when the Carnegie Medal went to Eve Garnett's *The Family from One End Street* rather than to J.R.R. Tolkien's *The Hobbit*. Arguments at the time anticipated further heated discussions in the future over the respective merits of honouring innovative material, which at the time Garnett's book was, against trying to find a book which may (or more likely, may not) become a modern classic, as Tolkien's has.

One of the purposes of the medal was to encourage the improvement of standards, both in the writing and the production of books for young people at that time. As an editorial in *The Library Association Record* put it: 'Quite frankly, many of the books that are written for children are very poor; the field, however, is immense and so, too, should be its opportunities for good authors to distinguish themselves.'[2] This was also one of the original aims of the Newbery Medal, established in 1922 by the American publisher Frederic C. Melcher. It was an aim wholeheartedly supported by H.J.B. Woodfield who had begun *Junior Bookshelf* in 1936, a bi-monthly magazine devoted to articles and reviews about children's literature. As Woodfield wrote himself:

> There are, of course, varying opinions as to the value of such an award. We believe it will have a good deal of value. We believe that publishers will be interested, that they will feel there is some honour in publishing a book deemed to be the best children's book of the year. This again will lead to a competitive spirit of a type so very desirable – namely, competition for quality, and the ultimate result of a general raising of the average.[3]

However, despite this welcome, the Carnegie award made little impact: in fact, neither the 1937 nor the 1938 winner was even announced in *Library Association Record*. Nevertheless, one group which showed interest in the medal was the newly formed Association of Children's Librarians, which superseded the Circle of Library Workers with Children, and whose secretary was Eileen Colwell, children's librarian at Hendon. The group, which was not part of the Library Association, was particularly incensed that, at the meeting which chose Noel Streatfeild's *The Circus is Coming*, only two members of the committee were present. Eileen Colwell's frustration would appear to be mounting from a letter she wrote in 1944:

> For the final decision the committee meets for discussion, or rather, should meet. The Carnegie Medal has been awarded seven times to date but on only one occasion has there been a sufficiently representative committee to allow of useful discussion. On the other six occasions not more than a third of the members attended and remaining members voted by letter. What opportunity does this allow of reasoned discussion and a balanced judgement of the best book for the award? And when the award has been decided, how do librarians, booksellers and publishers advertise it? Scarcely at all. Surely if the award is worth anything, if it is to be a fitting memorial to the benefactor whose name it bears, it should arouse widespread public interest. It needs to be written and talked about, advertised in all libraries and book shops and awarded with some ceremony.[4]

No award was given for children's books in 1945, the second time during the war that the medal was withheld. In the years immediately after there were no dramatic changes. From the vantage point of the 1990s this seems like a fairly cosy and parochial period, both for children's publishing and for children's librarianship. One aspect of the awards procedure which was noticed, however, was the granting of the medal to established writers near the end of their writing careers. In 1947 Walter de la Mare received the medal for a collection of his short stories, none of which were new. The 1955 winner was Eleanor Farjeon. The selection committee 'regarded this as perhaps the last opportunity to recognise appropriately the work of one of the major writers for children of this century'.[5] The following year, a similar situation emerged when the medal was awarded to C.S. Lewis for *The Last Battle*, the final volume of the Narnia series. Alec Ellis has said, 'It has been suggested that in 1957, for example, C.S. Lewis won the medal because not only was *The Last Battle* considered outstanding but also he had already made a major contribution to children's literature in the other volumes of the Narnian Chronicle. Furthermore, it was suspected, correctly as it happened, that there would not, within the terms of the award, be another opportunity to honour this particular author.'[6] However, Peter Hollindale suggests, 'the award was obviously intended as much for the entire series as for the individual book, but it was nevertheless an unfortunate choice. *The Last Battle* is not a good novel, and is probably the weakest book in the entire seven-volume chronicle.'[7]

It was to be nearly twenty years after the introduction of the first children's book award before another was added to the list. In 1955, for the first time since 1937, a list of commended books for the Carnegie medal was also issued. In that year, Kathleen Lines's *Lavender's Blue* was specially commended: the committee had been suggesting for some time that an award similar to the Carnegie but for illustrated books be founded, and this was initiated the following year in the form of the Kate Greenaway Medal. This 'specially commended' was therefore felt to be a form of consolation prize for Kathleen Lines, a much respected critic and anthologist, and for the artist Harold Jones who, had events moved more quickly, would have been the first recipient of the Kate Greenaway Medal rather than Edward Ardizzone. The Kate Greenaway and other awards for illustration have created much less controversy than their counterparts concerned with fiction. Could this be because most observers are less confident about criticizing illustration?

The twenty-first anniversary of the first presentation of the Carnegie medal took place in 1957. To celebrate, the Library Association published a commemorative book, *Chosen for Children*. Its compiler Marcus Crouch, a well-known critic and librarian, while acknowledging that the quality of distinction is elusive, also entered an area of discussion which has dogged this and similar awards to the present day:

> Critics have sometimes faulted the assessors for awarding the medal to a writer whose appeal is to a rather limited audience. This is to apply the democratic principle blindly. The medal is not awarded as the result of a plebiscite; it is awarded by a small body of experts who bring to the assessment of the eligible books high standards of criticism and long experience of books and their readers. These judges are unlikely to be attracted by facile or meretricious qualities. This is not to say that the Carnegie medal books are unpopular with children. A book for children, however excellent in style, integrity and accuracy, is a failure if it lacks the elusive quality of personality which makes it acceptable to its audience. This is the quality shared by all the finest children's books; it is perhaps the one thing

common to all the medal-winners. It would however be as unlikely that such books, which make demands on the imagination and the concentration of their readers, should enjoy the widest popularity as that the novels of Virginia Woolf and E.M. Forster should be the most popular of adult books. A test of the good children's book, as of a book for adults, is that it receives the commendation of discriminating readers.[8]

The 1960s saw a great deal of change to the children's book world and consequently to children's book awards. It was a period when a flowering of talented writers, illustrators and editors came together to produce a new golden age in children's literature. Critics who focused entirely on children's books were beginning to be heard and published, such as Aidan Chambers, Margaret Meek and Brian Alderson. This attention was reflected in the founding in 1965 of the Eleanor Farjeon Award which is presented to a professional of extraordinary achievement involved in any aspect of children's books. Librarianship courses devoted specifically to the training of children's librarians were flourishing as more and more children's posts were being created. For the first time in thirty years, the winners of the Carnegie medal were selected solely by children's librarians, reflecting the increasing power of this group in the whole world of the children's book. However, it was also a time when the medals were examined more critically, both within and outside the library profession.

The early 1960s was a period when one publishing house, Oxford University Press, dominated the children's book world. This was reflected in the awarding of medals. At the 1964 presentation dinner, Frank Gardner said, 'it would be a curious year in which neither the Carnegie medal nor the Kate Greenaway medal went to an OUP book'.[9] In 1958, the Carnegie medal winner, *Tom's Midnight Garden*, and Rosemary Sutcliff's *Warrior Scarlet*, were both published by Oxford University Press. The firm even published a little paean of praise to itself in its house magazine:

> Why did we wander, Kate Greenaway, Greenaway,
> Over the meadow and down in the lane?
> See what they've done while we've been away, been away,
> Oxford have taken our medals again!'
> 'Mr Carnegie', said sober Miss Greenaway,
> 'Learn to face facts', (And he nodded assent).
> 'Oxford have done it before and got clean away,
> No use resisting a yearly event.'[10]

However, by the middle of the decade others were looking at the Oxford mafia with less affection. Aidan Chambers was unenthusiastic about Philip Turner's 1965 Carnegie medal winner, *The Grange at High Force*, describing it as:

> A book very typical of the O.U.P. productions which have figured often of late in the list . . . *The Grange at High Force* is typical of the kind of book, in story, writing and production, which, over the last ten years, has come to be considered,

it seems, by 'discriminating readers' *among adults*, the epitome of good-quality children's literature. It is intellectual, sophisticated, over-written, unremarkable for anything in the slightest 'questionable' in thought, word or deed. It reflects an adult's rather sentimental view of childhood. It is passionless, cautious in its opinion, conservative in its theme and treatment. It is one of 'the well-produced books of good quality' that gives a glow of satisfaction when dressed in their sparkling plastic covers, they line the library shelves, and the publishers offices. There in the main they stay.[11]

Other criticisms came in the late 1960s and often in arenas outside the library world. Criticism of the Carnegie medal was common, as is shown by correspondence in *The Times Literary Supplement*. The 6 June 1968 issue contained an article by Peggy Heeks, Chairman of the YLG (the Youth Libraries Group), the children's library section of the Library Association, which administered and selected the award. Writing about the selection of the 1967 winner, Alan Garner's *The Owl Service*, Mrs Heeks discussed the constitution of the selection committee and the lack of publicity generated. She described the selection procedure thus:

> Beginning by considering all the children's books published in the year, one reaches a plateau of finely written, beautifully designed books and from this rise the peaks, the books which it is appropriate to judge by the highest standards. We are not looking for the most popular book, the most promising book, the most socially useful book – although all these have been suggested in the past as desirable aims. Books of this kind may merit recognition, but what the Library Association has decided to recognise is quality, and quality full-grown, not in the bud.[12]

This provoked a letter from Brian Alderson, children's book editor of *The Times* and a frequent critic of the medal over the years. He criticised Peggy Heeks's apparent refusal to define precisely the qualifications of the selection committee and her failure to provide a full elucidation of medal winners' requirements. Given what he saw as the Library Association's 'primitive' approach to publicity, Alderson concludes, 'it would add greatly to our confidence in the Association if the announcement of the awards could be coupled with an intelligent critical account of the chief books considered, together with an elucidation of the reasons for selecting the winners'.[13]

This was the first occasion that criticism of the awards was made outside the library profession, albeit in a journal read mainly at that time by librarians, and the effect can be seen in two references made by Peggy Heeks in her short reply to Alderson's letter. She declared, not perhaps with total sincerity, 'It is heartening to find so much interest in the Library Association awards from someone who is not a member. Librarians are seemingly less energetic.' She also reminds him that, 'It was referred to by me in detail at the annual general meeting of Youth Libraries Group at the end of March, a meeting which Mr Alderson, although not a member, attended.'[14]

By this time another children's book award had been added to the list, the first from outside the library profession. The *Guardian* Award was established in 1966 as a direct reaction to the traditional winners of the Carnegie Medal. John Rowe Townsend, then the newspaper's children's books editor, has said,

'We had a feeling that an award which was made and administered by a particular body of people might tend to go to the same kind of book. In the three years before we decided to start our award, the Carnegie, as it happened, had been awarded to three successive sound, elegantly written, beautifully produced, Oxford novels, and we wondered, perhaps, if a different perspective might conceivably produce a different kind of winner.'[15] Just over ten years later, however, he was admitting, 'there has been rather more overlap between the *Guardian* and the Carnegie than I expected. Our winners and runners-up have frequently been winners or runners-up for the Carnegie as well.'[16] According to Townsend, the original purposes were 'to encourage writers in this field; to acknowledge merit; to stimulate the further emergence of good writers; and to play a part in the complicated process of getting the right books to the right children.'[17]

The general reaction at the time of the award's introduction was that it would rescue children's book awards from the staid, fusty image which the Carnegie apparently had. Several commentators made observations of this type. Janet Hill in her influential book, *Children are People*, wrote in 1973 that, 'It is mortifying that selectors of the children's annual fiction award instituted by the *Guardian* have almost consistently shown more acumen in choice of book, and certainly more sophistication in the analysis of the reasons for their choice, than YLG.'[18] There was also a general assumption that the *Guardian* award winners would find more favour with children: 'It is possible that the *Guardian*'s award may well go to a book less perfect than the Carnegie winner, but of wider significance to the reading of actual children.'[19]

However, the *Guardian* award has eventually proved to be as literary-bound as the Carnegie. As Townsend admits, 'No formal criteria for the *Guardian* Award have ever been put on paper. It is, however, a *literary* award. We have never required a book to have a social, psychological or educational purpose (which is not to say that a winning book would have to be without such values). We do not take account of popularity or likely popularity. We would rather find a good book and help to make it popular than find a popular book and proclaim it good.'[20] This has produced a list of winners just as eclectic as the Carnegie winners, some recognised as masterpieces, some forgotten, some totally eccentric choices.

There are also some international awards, the most famous of which is the Hans Christian Andersen Award, first awarded in 1956 by the International Board on Books for Young People (IBBY). In 1956 the award was given only to authors, but ten years later an illustrator category was added. After winning the very first award with Eleanor Farjeon's *The Little Bookroom*, the UK has not won this bi-annual award since, although some writers and illustrators have been runners up. Patricia Crampton, one of the British judges for a number of years, has spoken of the problems such an award causes, both practical and theoretical:

One of the biggest problems in serving on the international jury is Getting the

Books. We receive an average of ten books by each nominee and there are usually about thirty-two nominations – 320 books. The jury meets in April, so we hope to start receiving the books in the previous September – little enough time one would think. Inevitably the ideal is not achieved; 1978 provides a classic illustration. The Russian juror did not receive the works of Alan Garner and Charles Keeping, all despatched in good time, until long after the meeting had taken place. The work of the internationally popular Janusz Stanny reached scarcely any jurors and was reluctantly dropped from the list. The Spanish nominees decided on air freight as their method of despatch; jurors found themselves with invitations from Customs to come and pay for the release of the books at the airport. When claimed the books turned out to be only those of the author nominee, the illustrator's never arrived anywhere.[21]

As for the criteria for the selection of an international award by a jury of ten who are unlikely to be proficient in all languages represented, Crampton feels 'what is "fair"? Should we stick to excellence as the first criteria? (I think that in fairness, ultimately, to all children we should). Or should we to some extent at least cause the award to move around as a sort of congratulation for progress or to show our sympathy for effort (not the same thing!)? Should we broaden the scope of the awards?'[22]

One American judge, however, has praised the award for raising the profile of books which under normal circumstances would not be published in countries other than their origin. 'We have much to gain by reading and sharing the works of international authors and illustrators. Let's begin by learning who other cultures regard as their great writers, and then approaching them with the respect they deserve. The experience may be eye-opening.'[23]

As the 1960s began to explore the possibility of extending the boundaries of publishing for children, there began to be doubts that literary fiction alone was always the right way to reach most young readers. In 1969, writing about *Onion John*, a Newbery Medal winner which she had previously praised in a review, Rosemary Manning – herself a children's novelist – said:

> *Onion John* was one of the first of a growing number of novels that should, perhaps, never have been reviewed in a Children's Books Supplement. They should have been put firmly into the adult pages, and on to the adult shelves in the public libraries. There is a real problem here, for the teenager who might enjoy such books will probably have ceased to enter the Children's Department, while on the adult shelves a book is easily lost. Despite the praise that greeted *Earthfasts, The Owl Service, The Mark of the Horse Lord*, much the same might be said of them as of *Onion John*. Because they were by well-established authors they were, of course, guaranteed the notice of critics, which *Onion John* was not. What one could call the '*Onion John* syndrome' has produced a no-man's literature which may lead to certain first-class books reaching a very small readership of any age.[24]

The 1970s saw a larger concentration on aspects of children's literature than purely literary concerns. More books began to be published which reflected the changing structure of British society, a policy which was instigated by authors and publishers but often through the influence of teachers and librarians. The Other Award was introduced for non-biased books of literary merit in 1975. Its founder was Rosemary Stones, an influential feminist critic of traditional children's literature. She too had doubts about the direction the Carnegie Medal was taking. For her, 'Mollie Hunter, a fine children's writer, was awarded the Carnegie Medal for a book that was nowhere near her best; nor was it the best piece of writing published for children that year.'[25]

The Other Award was established to honour writing that reflected some of the new radical attitudes and ideas of the 1970s and 1980s. It selected a list of four or five titles, none promoted above the others; honoured writers like Farrukh Dhondy and Bernard Ashley; announced its decisions in an intelligent manner (unlike the bland praise at so many awards ceremonies); and was then terminated in 1988; 'not because all the "other" battles have been won but because it's time to think of new and imaginative ways of winning them'.[26] The basic criteria were the most specific of any children's book award in the United Kingdom:

1. Each book should have literary merit: an imaginative, interesting story line, rounded characterization, credible and recognizable situations, natural sequencing.
2. Each book should be free of the explicit or implicit values of competitive individualism, private property, hierarchical social organization, the inevitability of superior/inferior social divisions; alternatively, each book may combat these values in some way.
3. Each book should contain sympathetic and realistic depictions of all people, whatever their background or occupation.
4. Each book should contain, where relevant, a realistic and balanced depiction of sex roles.
5. Each book, where relevant, should be historically correct, and in particular provide a people's history of events, not just that of rulers and elites.
6. Each book should contain, where relevant, sympathetic depictions of blacks and other minorities both in the context of Western society and in the rest of the world.[27]

The 1970s saw a proliferation of new awards, although the majority of them were concerned with individual aspects of writing or illustrating. In 1972 *The Times Educational Supplement* introduced its information book awards; in 1976 the Welsh Book Council presented the first Tir Na n-Og Award, which was specifically concerned with books with a Welsh background; and in 1979 the highly regarded journal *Signal* introduced an award for poetry. Illustration was served by the establishment in 1979 of the Mother Goose Award for a new illustrator. Some awards were announced with a great flourish but rapidly disappeared: in 1979 the first Arts Council National Book Award had a children's category which was won by *The Animals of Farthing Wood* but in 1980 this category was dropped and in the following year the award itself disappeared. The *Observer* teenage fiction prize fared marginally better, lasting from 1981 to 1986.

In 1980 a new type of award was introduced, the Federation of Children's Book Groups' Children's Book of the Year Award. This type of award is very popular in America and is often known as a 'children's choice' award. The Federation was established in the 1960s and was designed for parents who wanted to know more about children's books. In all its branches it works closely with children and so it was inevitable that its award should use the views of children as a primary source. Pat Thomson, the original co-ordinator of the award, explains:

> It was inevitable, being the kind of organisation we are, that children should be involved in the judging. Parents have a very specific audience and if they get it wrong, they know at once! Any children's book award we gave would have to be approved by children. Consequently, the children's response is central to the judgement. As yet, there has been no fundamental clash. It must be partly because we are child-orientated to start with, but we have not been left sighing over literary gems while the kids choose unspeakable trash. We have, however, been made aware of how well a book works with children when our initial adult response has been only moderate.[28]

In recent years the policy of involving children in judging has been an integral part of a number of prizes. Since 1993 the overall winner of the Smarties prize has been selected by children from a list provided by adult judges. Recent years have also seen groups of children reading the Carnegie and Kate Greenaway shortlists, and sometimes providing an alternative winner or even the same winner beforehand. Such tactics help to dispel criticisms made of past winners of medals, for example:

> *The God Beneath the Sea*, the Carnegie medal winner, is an outstanding book; but it is not for children. This award reflects the attitude of too many children's librarians who are so concerned with the elevation of literary taste that they are blind to effective methods of raising it.[29]

> Not one child enjoyed *City of Gold*, and in fact we received criticism about the way the stories were re-told in the book ... Surely one of the most important characteristics of a book put forward as a contender for the Carnegie award is that it should be stimulating and enjoyable for children to read.[30]

Another correspondent, discussing the same book, claimed

> As regards the awards in general, why does the committee so often choose something that no 'ordinary' child will read? Every year there are books really offering something new and fertile which give children opportunities for growing; every year they are passed by.[31]

The 1980s saw two further major awards, one of which introduced a new element into the children's book award world, that of sponsorship. The Emil award, introduced in 1982, was in the more traditional mould. This is given to a book where text and illustration provide a harmonious whole, and was founded in honour of Kurt Maschler who introduced the very popular *Emil and the Detectives* to British children in translation in 1931. The Smarties prize was introduced in 1985 amid great controversy. It was the first children's award to be sponsored, in this case by Rowntree Mackintosh, the confectionery company, to the tune of £10,000. Neil Philip summarised the concerns:

At first sight this seems a spurious advertising venture, with publicity stressing that this is 'Britain's "biggest ever" children's book prize', and a panel of judges made up of television personalities. Purists used to the down-to-earth makeshift quality of the socially committed Other Award, or the sedate inoffensiveness of the Library Association's Carnegie Medal, may be forgiven for pursing their lips and looking worried.[32]

The Smarties has had a somewhat chequered existence. After the initial excitement of a wealthy children's book award, it soon changed its criteria and age categories. Originally there were three categories, one of which was for innovation. However, even within the first year there was some difficulty finding enough books for this category so that the categories were changed to books for the under 6s, 6–8s and 9–11s. However, this has also caused problems, with some judges trying to fit their favourites into these categories, so that, for example, Robert Westall's *Blitzcat* and Pauline Fisk's *Midnight Blue* both appeared in the 9–11s category, an age group for which both were unsuited.

Within two years Rowntree Mackintosh were reconsidering their decision to sponsor the award as it was felt that not enough publicity was being generated. Comparison was being made with the Booker prize, but children's books, unless written by a celebrity or member of the Royal family, rarely achieve the type of publicity which some adult books attract. Another blow was dealt to the Smarties when the late Janet Ahlberg and her husband, Allan, a highly regarded and prolific writing and illustrating team, let it be known that they did not wish any of their books to be considered for the award because of its association with sweets. In recent years the Smarties has attracted a good deal of publicity partly because final decisions are made by children from a shortlist compiled by adults. The announcement ceremony has featured regularly on the children's television programme *Blue Peter*.

In 1991 an even greater shock was revealed when it was announced that the UK's oldest children's book awards, the Library Association's Carnegie and Kate Greenaway medals, would be sponsored, albeit by the highly respectable library supplier Peters Library Service. The librarians on the YLG committee wished to distance themselves from the vulgarity of awarding a cash prize and instead each prizewinner is able to donate £1,000 worth of books to the organization of their choice. This sponsorship deal was successful in raising the profile of the award. Through it the services of a publicity officer has been secured who has been successful in gaining coverage in national newspapers (particularly when a controversial book has been chosen). Journalists regularly attend the selection meetings and a much more impressive venue is used for the announcements ceremony.

Another award to feel the change of sponsorship has been the children's book category of the Whitbread Award. This award, which consists of five categories including one for a children's book, has existed in various forms since 1972 and is sponsored by Whitbread, the brewing firm. In recent years the winning children's book has been named the Beefeater award (after the range of eating houses rather than anything connected with alcohol). Perhaps the Smarties' experience with Janet and Allan Ahlberg might have been a contributory factor to this careful separation. The Whitbread is a curious award. In 1978, six years after the award began, Samuel Whitbread, one of the directors of the firm, announced that 'their award was probably now the leading award in children's books'.[33] But it is difficult to justify this view from the list of winners or from the method of deciding an overall winner. The Whitbread is divided into five categories: novel, first novel, biography, poetry and children's book. Each category has its own set of judges, most of whom are experts in their field. When a winner has been decided by each set of judges, the five titles are examined by a different group of judges (many of whom are celebrities) who have to choose an overall winner. Children's books are the only category never to have won the overall title. One of the 1996 judges, Rachel Cusk, has criticized this process:

> Whitbread makes no claim to erudition; indeed, its only involvement is to do what it does best, namely administering large quantities of alcohol in comfortable surroundings. The business of comparing things which cannot be compared – a biography with a children's book or a volume of poetry, a mature novel with a first novel – is harder to dispatch. According to Hoggart [Richard Hoggart, chair of the judging panel], the chairman of Whitbread, Sir Michael Angus, cheerily likened the comparison to Crufts. That, perhaps, marks the point at which an innocence of literary politics becomes a troubling disregard for it.[34]

The most recently established UK children's book prize is also sponsored: the Marsh Christian Trust has pledged prize money of £750 for the best translation of a foreign book published in the UK by a British publisher. The Marsh Award is for translation and is given to the translator. Its purpose is to stimulate interest in the best books published in other countries for young readers. The first award was made in October 1996 to Anthea Bell for her translation of Christine Nostlinger's *A Dog's Life*.

A question that was frequently asked as the children's book world became more market-orientated was: do winning prizes help to sell books? Certainly in the United Kingdom the situation was very different from the United States where winning the Newbery or Caldecott medals definitely increased sales. However, perhaps things are changing in Britain, too. Elaine McQuade, at the time of writing Marketing Manager at Penguin Children's Books, estimates that sales of Carnegie winning titles have sold three or four times more copies than equivalent books by the same authors. She feels this is partly due to the far greater exposure these books receive than they did in the past (a development definitely helped by sponsorship). In the 1970s Penelope Lively attempted to examine the effects of children's book awards on sales of her own winning books:

> Trying to determine the effect of literary prizes on book sales is a baffling exercise. Two of my children's books have won awards: *The Ghost of Thomas Kempe* won the Carnegie Medal for 1973, *A Stitch in Time* the Whitbread prize for 1976. *Thomas Kempe* has done well ever since, *Stitch in Time* has not distinguished itself

particularly. But they are very different kinds of book, and I can't help feeling *Thomas Kempe* might have been more popular anyway, without the initial impetus of an award, though there's no doubt at all the Carnegie . . . does a great deal to help a book on its way. *Thomas Kempe* was doing quite well even before the announcement of the award – 4500 hardback in the first year – but this continued with another 5500 in the next, followed by a startling (to me at least) 63,000 paperback in 1976 . . . Now it has settled down to a steady 11,000–12,000 a year in paperback with over a thousand hardback and another 8,000 of a cheap hard-back educational version for sale to schools only . . . *A Stitch in Time* hit a point at which book sales seemed to be slumping all around – at least according to my publisher – and after an initial 5000 or so hardback in the first couple of years has settled to eight or nine hundred; no statements yet on the recently issued paperback. Sales figures are much the same as my other children's books, but *Thomas Kempe*'s are far superior.[35]

But as Liz Attenborough has said in another context: 'If an award goes to a bad book it won't help it sell, and it won't help it last.'[36]

One interesting aspect of modern awards is that, although in recent years close to seven thousand children's books are published in the United Kingdom annually (more even than in America), there does not seem a particularly wide choice among prizewinners. In the 1980s and 1990s, for example, six writers have won the Carnegie medal more than once. Does this point to the fact that there is less good material available among this wider variety or that award panels are sticking to the writers they know? Chris Powling, former editor of *Books for Keeps* as well as a children's writer himself, believes the latter:

For amongst the undeniable and deepening dross of the last couple of decades, it seems to me, there's actually been an increase in worthwhile writing for children. This leads to a double difficulty for today's award panellists. In the first place, it's harder to separate out the best titles . . . and in the second, it's harder to evaluate them against each other. Hence the likelihood of a loss of critical nerve and the near-irresistible temptation to play safe.[37]

However, the experiences of two recent judges of children's book awards do not bear this out. Simon Tait is one:

I had planned an uplifting and entertaining August judging my share of the entries for the 1995 Whitbread Book of the Year children's novel competition, but it was not to be. Assailed by ghosts, homeless and parentless children, and even the makings of sheer vice, I had to pick three or four novels. I made it – with difficulty. There was no great little book.[38]

Michael Morpurgo, himself an author and prizewinner, says of his involvement in the 1992 Smarties prize: 'I have to confess to being hugely disappointed: of the 300 I found less than 50 I liked. There was a mass of badly written stories, mediocre and imitative, poorly illustrated and unimaginatively designed.'[39]

The truth of the matter is probably that a different type of writing for children has emerged over the last decade which is less immediately attractive to adults, even professionals with children's interests at heart. Many modern children's books are certainly more racy in tone than in the past and more in key with other media forms vying for children's attention. Most panels no doubt long for such years as 1967 when the Carnegie Medal list consisted of *The Owl Service* as winner, Henry Treece's posthumous novel, *The Dream Time* (highly commended), and a commended list of Helen Cresswell's *The Piemakers*, Leon Garfield's *Smith* and K.M. Peyton's first book in the Flambards sequence.

The most frequently voiced criticism of children's book awards is that the various winners are often far too literary, thereby encouraging and endorsing an elitist approach to reading. Robert Westall has described how his writing was affected when he won an award for his first published work:

> And then *Machine-Gunners* won the Carnegie, and it felt like the whole world was watching; for a month I couldn't write at all. The burden of all their expectations was totally flattening. My target figure had grown from one to thousands; how could I please them all? To my shame, I tried. Crawlingly and contemptibly, though unconsciously, I tried. The amount of swearing in my books dropped; the intellectual content, the scholarship and research grew. I began writing books for the children of publishers, librarians and the literary gent of *The Times* . . . Now that I am at least conscious of what I was doing, I look around and see so many 'good' children's books written for the same bloody audience. Books that gain splendid reviews, win prizes, make reputations and are unreadable by the majority of children.[40]

From the beginning, the Carnegie medal was regarded chiefly as a literary award:

> It is hoped that any author who is awarded this medal will thereby receive a hallmark of excellence which . . . will encourage the production of better children's books. It is not to be assumed that we think that such writers as Walter de la Mare, Arthur Ransome, Kästner, Rose Fyleman, and several others who may be named, are not writers of the highest class for children; we need more such authors, and many more books.[41]

To the critic, this attitude is paramount but is not often practised by selectors of modern awards. Lance Salway has observed:

> Worthy historical novels like Mollie Hunter's *The Stronghold* and amiable fantasies like Penelope Lively's *The Ghost of Thomas Kempe* hardly reflect the present state of children's literature. Barbara Willard's Mantlemass books – surely the finest historical novels for the young in recent years – did not even feature on the Honours list for the Carnegie Medal. Such outstanding and challenging novels as Jane Gardam's *The Summer after the Funeral* and William Mayne's *The Jersey Shore* have been ignored too.[42]

However, is the rearranging of award-winning books just an interesting party game? After all, the books Salway cites as unjustly neglected have hardly become timeless classics. Perhaps John Rowe Townsend is right when he says,

> No sensible commentator would expect to find a list that fitted his own prescription exactly; everyone would agree that, with benefit of hindsight, it would be pleasant (though clearly impracticable) to reshape the list, remove the weaker titles, and bring in books that now seem to have been mistakenly passed over. No two people would agree on what should be discarded or introduced.[43]

Perhaps it was felt that newer, breezier awards would help to dispel the former elitist image. However, Julia Eccleshare, in her capacity as chair of the 1995 Smarties judges, began her announcement speech with expressions that would seem to agree with the originators of the Carnegie Medal:

> In the absence of reviews, prize winning books are the ones that command attention in shops and libraries: the books that will be the way into reading for successive generations of children. It became clear to us as Smarties Prize judges that, although we all read for slightly different reasons, we came up with a very high overlap of titles. In other words, the books that had a good plot, strong characters, the zap factor, the tingle factor or the ability to make a reader laugh – just some of the qualities that the judges were looking for – often had several of those characteristics at once. That is because good writing is a mixture of all these things, which in turn makes for good reading.[44]

There is still criticism of prizewinning books. In the mid-1980s one critic was referring to the sedate inoffensiveness of the Carnegie medal. In the 1990s the award has been criticized for that shibboleth of the right wing press, political correctness. The winner of the 1993 Carnegie medal, Robert Swindells's *Stone Cold*, is the story of a homeless teenager whose story runs parallel with and then eventually meets that of a serial killer. It provoked a furious outburst. In the *Daily Mail* Rosemary Anne Sisson asked:

> As we struggle to save our children from being subjected prematurely to horror and cruelty on the screen, do we really want to recommend to parents literature which invades their minds with the same dismaying message? Do we want everything that feeds their imagination to proclaim that life is nasty and brutish and that the world is a dangerous and cruel place? It is the publishers who are to blame and, even more, the 'children's librarians' [note the inverted commas – the writer obviously feels to give them their correct title would be wrong] whose choices are so influential for hundreds of parents who rely on their advice when looking for material for their children to read.[45]

Similar criticism came from Christina Hardyment: 'The whole tribe of children's writers and librarians are chronically over-anxious. Someone needs to bend their horrified gaze from the tabloid headlines, and give them a few statistics about the audiences that they are writing for and choosing books to please.'[46] Adding that she suspects the selection panel 'to be governed by a mixture of motives, all more to do with political correctness than literary quality' she gives the following advice to the selectors:

> Judges need to be able to compare like with like. It is time that the Library Association faced up to the new phenomenon of didactic teenage fiction (schools, for the use of) and treated it separately. Invent an award for such books by all means – the golden Doc Martin [sic], perhaps. But reserve the Carnegie Medal for its original purpose: 'The outstanding *children's* book of the year'.[47]

More fundamental criticisms of the medal were made by Chris Powling:

> For the truth of the matter is that Britain's premier prize for a children's book ceased long ago to be 'The Booker of the Playground' and traded upwards in the direction of the teen-scene. These days 'The Booker of Behind the Bicycle Shed' would be an apter description. As a result, the Medal now routinely passes over

the most important and perhaps the most difficult of all writing for children: the kind that creates readers in the first place.[48]

This provided the impetus for a re-examination of how the Carnegie medal could be altered to allow for the recognition of writers for the eight to twelve age group. However, after much discussion with its branches, YLG felt that the better solution was to encourage those suggesting titles for the shortlist to recommend more titles for the junior age range. It was felt that to introduce another medal specifically for teenagers would be to devalue those teenage books which had already won the Carnegie. Perhaps it is better not to be too restrictive about age grouping, as the Smarties prize has shown, particularly as there are variations in areas of the United Kingdom as to the suitability of books for different age groups.

The area of awards is almost a microcosm of the history of children's publishing since the Second World War. The 1930s and 1940s saw a searching for quality in order to combat much of the mediocrity of the period. This quality was discovered and nurtured throughout the 1950s and particularly the 1960s (remember that Carnegie shortlist of 1967 already referred to?) when imaginative and talented writers and illustrators were being nurtured by a growing band of children's book editors and their books were being bought and read by an increasing number of children's librarians. The 1970s saw a growing interest in books reflecting the true lives of the children who were reading them. In the 1980s and 1990s there was something of a dist-ancing from the ideals of the post-war period when it was felt that promotion of one book above another was a not particularly egalitarian method of selecting material.

So what do awards achieve? One thing is increased publicity about children's literature, which is no bad thing, at least as long as it is intelligent attention which is being aroused. Awards also provide a focus for organiza-tions wishing to sponsor children's books. Above all, awards create an arena for the discussion of children's books, including a starting point for contro-versy. Perhaps the ideals of the early pioneers of children's book awards are not that different from those of today's selectors and the winners of children's book awards will continue to enrage and captivate a new generation of children and the adults who select material for them.

References

1. W.C. Berwick Sayers (1937), 'The Library Association Carnegie Medal and Mr Arthur Ransome', *Library Association Record* no. 39 (5), May, p.218.
2. Editorial (1937), *Library Association Record* no. 39 (1), January, p.1.
3. 'Notes from the attic', *Library Association Record* (1937) no. 39(1), January p.21
4. Eileen Colwell (1944), 'The L.A. Carnegie Medal', *Library Association Record* no. 46 (1), January, p.14.

5. The Library Association minutes of the Carnegie Selection Committee, 6 March 1956.
6. Alec Ellis (1977), '40 years of the Carnegie medal: a hallmark of quality', *Library Association Record* no. 79 (2), February, p.77.
7. Peter Hollindale (1974), *Choosing Books for Children* (London: Elek), pp.64–5.
8. Marcus Crouch (1957), *Chosen for Children* (London: Library Association), p.2.
9. 'Prize-winning children's books', *The Bookseller*, no. 3048, 23 May 1964, p.1962.
10. *Library Association Record* no. 68(10), October 1966, p.378.
11. Aidan Chambers (1969), *The Reluctant Reader* (Oxford: Pergamon), p.67.
12. Peggy Heeks (1968), 'Looking for a winner', *Times Literary Supplement*, 6 June, p.578.
13. 'Carnegie awards 1968', *Times Literary Supplement*, 13 June, p.649.
14. Ibid.
15. John Rowe Townsend (1978), 'Ten years of the Guardian award', *Federation of Children's Book Groups Year Book* (Birmingham: Federation of Children's Book Groups), p.14.
16. *Library Association Record* (1988), p.184.
17. Ibid.
18. Janet Hill (1973), *Children are People* (London: Hamish Hamilton), p.142.
19. Carnegie medal 1966, *Library Association Record* no. 68 (10), October, p.378.
20. Townsend (1978), op.cit., p.15.
21. Patricia Crampton (1984), 'The Hans Christian Andersen award', *Books for Keeps* no. 25, p.16.
22. Ibid.
23. J. Garrett (1993), 'Far-away wisdom: three nominees for the 1992 Andersen prize', *The Reading Teacher* no. 46 (4), p.314.
24. Rosemary Manning (1969), 'Whatever happened to *Onion John?*', *Times Literary Supplement*, 4 December, p.1383.
25. Rosemary Stones (1988), '13 other years: the Other Award 1975–1987', *Books for Keeps* no. 53, p.22.
26. Andrew Mann (1975), 'The Other Award', *Signal* no. 18, September, p.145.
27. Personal correspondence, 13 September, 1983.
28. W.J. Murison (1971), 'When the best is not good enough', *Times Educational Supplement*, 4 December, p.162.
29. G. Bonfield and J. Hopkins (1981), 'Carnegie criteria', *Library Association Record* no. 83 (9), September, p.441.
30. Ibid.
31. Jennifer Taylor (1981), 'Extraordinary', *Library Association Record* no. 81 (11), November, p.540.
32. Neil Philip (1985), 'The Smarties prize for children's books', *British Book News Children's Books*, December, p.35.
33. 'Whitbread literary awards' (1978), *Bookseller*, 9 December, p.3453.
34. Rachel Cusk (1996), 'Books, beer and passion', *The Times*, 25 January, p.18.
35. Penelope Lively (1979), 'Winning reflections', *Author* no. 90(2), pp.70–71
36. Tony Bradman (1983), 'The awards business', *Books for Keeps* no. 20, p.4.
37. Chris Powling (1993), 'Contemplating Carnegie', *Books for Keeps* no. 82, p.3.
38. Simon Tait (1995), 'Children's literature', *Times Educational Supplement*, 24 November, p.12.
39. Michael Morpurgo (1992), 'When the best is not good enough', *Times Educational Supplement*, 27 November, p.10.
40. Ibid.
41. Editorial (1937), *Library Association Record* no. 39 (1), January p.1.
42. Lance Salway (1976), 'Kids' Oscars', *Times Literary Supplement*, 16 July, p.888.
43. John Rowe Townsend (1975), 'A decade of Newbery books in perspective' in

Kingman, Lee (ed.), *Newbery and Caldecott medal books 1966–1975* (Boston: The Horn Book), p.152.

44. Julia Eccleshare (1995), 'We've got the treasure, but where's the confidence?', *Bookseller*, 8 December, p.34.
45. Rosemary Anne Sisson (1994), 'What are we doing to our children?', *Daily Mail*, 15 July, p.9.
46. Christina Hardyment (1994), 'Slimy jeremiads of a serial killer', *The Independent*, 16 July, p.26.
47. Ibid.
48. Chris Powling (1993), 'Contemplating Carnegie', *Books for Keeps* no. 82, p.3.

4   Picture Books
Judith Graham

In fifty years of children's publishing, children's picture books in the UK have undergone great changes. Publishing aims and practices, printing procedures and possibilities, art styles, the balance between words and pictures and the content and assumptions about the child reader have all altered and combined to create a type of picture book today that was little in evidence before the early 1960s. The lull in production after the war, shortages of all kinds, problems in reproducing colour and an under-valuing of illustrators account for some of the characteristics of early picture books. More particularly, very few immediately post-war publishers, illustrators or authors fully exploited the unique power of the picture book to tell a story through two different, symbolic systems. Edward Ardizzone, Kathleen Hale, William Stobbs, Leslie Wood, Anthony Maitland, Harold Jones, V.H. Drummond and others all produced fine illustrated children's books in the post-war period but for the most part they did not seek to use illustrations to do some of the actual telling of the story. This close alliance of word and image was not unknown; Randolph Caldecott (1846–86) produced some superb picture books in his time, in which text and illustration worked intimately together. However, it took until the 1960s for the various threads of picture book storytelling to be woven together in Caldecott's way once again.

There are several illustrators and author/illustrators whose output spans three, four or, in the case of Shirley Hughes, nearly all five of the decades under review. Charles Keeping began providing covers and illustrating in black and white in the 1950s, and his picture-book career spanned just over twenty years until his death in 1988. Victor Ambrus, Quentin Blake, Raymond Briggs, John Burningham, Michael Foreman, Pat Hutchins, David McKee, Helen Oxenbury, Jan Pienkowski and Brian Wildsmith all began in earnest in the 1960s and are still at work now. Of those whose main work started in the 1970s, Nicola Bayley, Ruth Brown, Anthony Browne, Reg Cartwright, Helen Craig, Fiona French, Mairi Hedderwick, Colin McNaughton, Graham Oakley and Tony Ross are still prolific. Janet Ahlberg, whose first illustrations appeared in 1972, died in 1994.

The 1980s have seen many new illustrators, not least because of the energy and independence of such publishers as Julia MacRae, Klaus Flugge at Andersen Press and the advent of Walker Books, founded by Sebastian Walker in 1980. Those illustrators who made a significant mark include Angela Barrett, Patrick Benson, Louise Brierley, Catherine Brighton, Peter Collington, Philippe Dupasquier, Barbara Firth, Roy Gerrard, Satoshi Kitamura, P.J. Lynch, Jill Murphy, Jan Ormerod, Jane Ray, Posy Simmonds, Susan Varley, Charlotte Voake and Juan Wijngaard. Promising new author/illustrators since include Amanda Harvey and Claire Fletcher.

Publishing practices and the market

After the war, the publishing industry had been 'smashed to pieces', according to David Elliott, writing about the start of his publishing company, World's Work, in 1957[1]. Not only had authors and illustrators been away on war work (and some did not return) but paper stocks were still rationed, bombing had destroyed approximately twenty million books in warehouses, work space had been requisitioned for the production of arms (the publishers Blackie had given up 33 per cent of their factory space to the manufacture of shells) and printing plant was run down. Many picture books in the UK in the fifteen years after the war originated from abroad, particularly America. They were often printed using techniques which were not widely understood or available in this country. According to David Elliott, it was only by the mid-1960s that the UK finally possessed a viable picture book output, leading to a more balanced two-way traffic between the UK and the USA.

Frank Eyre's *British Children's Books in the Twentieth Century* reported that in 1952 there were 'fewer than a dozen publishers who maintained editorial departments specially for children's books and not more than five or six specialist children's publishers. But by 1970 there were some sixty publishers actively engaged in children's books.'[2] This growth continued. By 1980, Julia MacRae had left Hamish Hamilton to found her own imprint with its avowed emphasis on authors rather than balance sheets, and she has since nurtured some of the country's finest picture book creators. Sebastian Walker started Walker Books with an exclusive focus on children's books and particularly on picture-books. Walker Books is an extraordinary phenomenon as far as picture books are concerned, and would appear to owe a great deal of its success to an investment in illustrators unheard of in other publishing houses. It also has in Amelia Edwards a designer whose particular stamp of quality is on all Walker picture books. Though sometimes criticised for luring other illustrators from their former publishers, Walker Books has clearly raised the status and standard of picture books in the fifteen years it has been in business. There are still new children's publishers springing up, such as Orion, Orchard, Frances Lincoln and Studio Editions. According to Young Book Trust, in 1996 there were more than 100 children's book publishers in the UK. It remains to be seen whether this steady growth can continue. Certainly, publishers look with alarm at the cuts in the library service and in school requisitions, and express anxiety about the rise of video, CD Roms and other attractions that threaten the market for books.

Growth in publishers is matched by the increasing numbers of children's books published. Just after the war, there were fewer than 1,000 children's books published per year.[3] By 1960, the number of new children's books published had risen to approximately 2,000. Most of these titles were illustrated. By 1986, the figure was around 4,500 and by 1994 approximately 7,000, including new editions and reprints.[4] It is not easy to extract the number of picture books from these figures, but it can be assumed that their numbers increased steadily in line with fiction titles. The ratio of picture books to fiction titles between 1940–1960 was likely to be much smaller than in the latter part of the period under question. For reasons that this chapter explores, it was only after 1960 that picture books became easy, and more rewarding for publishers to produce. David Lloyd at Walker Books suggests that in the period 1945 to 1960 there would have been fewer than fifty picture books in any one year worth serious attention.[5]

As the number of titles on the market increased over the years so the print run for any one title tended to decrease, unless publishers found a best-seller on their hands. In this case, one or more reprints would be in order. Some of the contrasts here are spectacular. According to Ron Heapy, Managing Editor of Children's Books at Oxford University Press, a print run of 7,500 would be normal for a title in the late 1970s. By the mid-1980s, no more than 3,000 would be printed and by the end of the century, he suspects, a print run of a new title will be around 1,500.[6] An exception to this pattern was Charles Keeping's picture book based on Alfred Noyes's poem *The Highwayman*, which appeared in 1981. In anticipation of the high sales that did indeed follow, 23,000 copies were printed in paperback and 15,000 in hardback.

Klaus Flugge, Managing Director of Andersen Press, is proud of the sales of Ruth Brown's recent picture book, *Greyfriars Bobby* (1995) – 5,000 copies sold in the UK in two months – but remembers that it was not long ago when this figure was easily reached for every title.[7] Caroline Roberts, Managing Editor of Children's Books at Hutchinson, points out that the relatively respectable print run of 6,000 for *Snow White* (1991), retold by Josephine Poole with illustrations by Angela Barrett, would have been common for all titles in the early 1980s. It was only the prospect of occasional huge sales – for instance *The Whales' Song* (1990), text by Dyan Sheldon and pictures by Gary Blythe, which sold 50,000 hardback and 120,000 paperback in the UK – that made it possible for her company to take risks with newcomers and to support minority tastes.[8] This is also true of Walker Books, who can buttress less popular books with phenomenal sales (in the millions) of works like the 'Wally' books by Martin Handford or *Guess How Much I Love You?* (1994), by Sam McBratney and Anita Jeram. This last title sold 44,000 in the UK in three months, making it their fastest-selling book ever.

Another major change over the years is connected to shrinking print runs of all but best-selling titles. Publishers now need overseas sales to cover their costs. Only 1,500 copies of an average picture book may sell in this country but, with sales abroad, a print run of a commercially sensible size will still be possible. Indeed, many publishers do not offer a contract to an author or an illustrator until they have sold the rights either to the USA, Europe, Japan or South America.

British publishers are fortunate that English is widely spoken and that British books are often much sought after abroad. According to Ron Heapy, Brian Wildsmith sells around 25,000 copies of a new title in the USA and even more in Japan, where, at a recent exhibition of his artwork, queues formed round the block. Klaus Flugge mourns the insularity of our country in that we buy fewer and fewer books from overseas. Nevertheless he is grateful that he can sell his author/illustrator Max Velthuijs' books back to his native Holland in numbers of around 30,000, compared with sales here of 3,000. According to Caroline Roberts, at Hutchinson, a figure of 10,000 in a co-edition is required for any title to work financially. There is no children's book publisher for whom co-editions are not essential these days, which goes some way to explaining the frenetic atmosphere at the annual Bologna Children's Book Fair.

Picture books have always been published in both hardback and paperback. A number of publishers in the 1940s and 1950s produced their own paperbacks from their hardback titles. Faber & Faber produced paper-covered editions in which they re-packaged their own hardbacks, such as the Diana Ross/Leslie Wood titles and those from Gerald and Elizabeth Rose. They also bought paperback rights to well-known USA picture books by author/illustrators such as the Hobans, Virginia Lee Burton and Wanda Gag. Puffin Books brought out paperbacks of books originally published abroad and from a host of UK publishers, such as Methuen, Bodley Head, Longman and Hamish Hamilton, as well as from companies now taken over or no longer in existence, such as Worlds Work and Abelard-Schumann.

Puffin are still responsible for the majority of UK children's picture books in paperback, though Picture Lions (in existence for over twenty-five years), from HarperCollins, and Red Fox, a paperback imprint which was created at Random House in 1990, are also in the first rank. Other paperbacks are produced by Reed Group (Little Mammoths), now owned by Random House, Hodder Headline (Knights) and Macmillan (Picturemacs). Andersen Press paperback some of their own titles and sell rights to others elsewhere; Oxford has had its own trade paperbacks for decades, and Walker Books and some of the newer houses like Frances Lincoln also have their own paperback imprints.

Frequently with the change of format there is also a change in the size and shape of the book. Illustrations often suffer more than the written text here, as publishers tend to think that young readers need their print size left legibly large. It is the illustrations that are shorn, with detail and borders adversely affected. Colour may also not be as sharp as in the original. This is not always the case; sometimes a picture book first appears in a modest hardback format, does well, and is then reissued in paperback in a more generous production. On the whole the trend over the years has been towards more handsome and substantial paperbacks.

Not all titles re-appeared in paperback in the years following the war, any more than they do today. Even so, the number of paperback titles increased dramatically as picture books slowly went from strength to strength. In 1974, Valerie Alderson devoted an edition of *Children's Book Review* to paperbacks, claiming that 'For 1971, there was only a modest pile; for 1972, a large box; in 1973, there are two large and overflowing boxes (and these include only those received for review, nothing from Piccolo for example).'[9]

The traditional procedure for paperbacking was to publish a year or two after the hardback had been published. While this pattern is changing (see Chapter 2), it remains the case that reputations are built on hardbacks and certainly the reviewing process is still currently geared to the hardback. Ron Heapy predicts that hardback sales will eventually 'fall apart' and it is apparent that the 1990s growth of 'remainder' bookshops is built upon the publishers' need to shift slow-selling hardbacks from expensive warehouse space. It is not unusual to be able to find a hardback picture book at a third off the original price and to discover from the copyright page that it is still in its first year of publication.

Publishers do not, however, merely sit and bewail the situation. Libraries and schools may not be buying as many books as in the past, but marketing aimed at parents and children is ever more inventive. One can now buy picture books in a number of outlets, including supermarkets, and all sorts of re-formatting and re-packaging goes on. Anniversary editions; bumper books; books with tapes; books with torches, soft-toy characters, in-built mobiles, even with a knife, fork and spoon; books as fridges or as hamburgers; film and TV tie-ins; miniature editions, and much else are all common now. Big and small books packaged together have been tried, though book shops report that sometimes cellophane packages are opened and the little books have disappeared.

As an illustration of the diversity on offer, currently it is possible to buy six different formats of *Can't You Sleep, Little Bear?*,[10] a double award-winning picture book for the youngest child. This was described in a *Sunday Times* review as 'the most perfect children's book ever'.[11] As well as in its original format, it now appears as a paperback, in hardback, but over-printed in many different dual language versions, as a miniature book, in a Book and 3D Play Set (press-out characters and a panorama peep-show) and as one of the stories in a Walker Books' Bear anthology. The fact that there is as yet no enlarged book with a tape or one of the new Walker Book Charts does not mean that they will not eventually be available. One wonders what Sebastian Walker, the founder of Walker Books, would have made of all this. He regarded advertising, merchandising, even prize-awarding as a distraction from the central business of producing good books. 'All that counts is that a child says at the end of the book, "Tell it again, and tell it the same." Then its reputation will spread by word of mouth.'[12]

Special promotions are also frequent, such as vouchers in newspapers in exchange for books and, periodically, children's bookshops dress their sales staff up as favourite book characters. Some shops shelve their books according to characters known initially to their readers through TV and advertising (though advertising books on TV is usually out of the question, on grounds of cost). Many publishers supply to bookshops revolving stands, dump-bins, book-marks, stickers, competition entry forms, balloons, and much else, with the publisher's own trademark always clearly marked.

Booksellers and publishers of only twenty years ago, let alone those at work in the 1940s, 1950s and 1960s, would be amazed at this level of promotional activity. But in the current climate of competition from so many different areas, the book has to fight hard for attention. The collapse in 1995 of the Net-Book agreement has made the need for aggressive marketing even more urgent. At least the instant visual appeal of the cover and contents of picture books remains in their favour.

Printing matters and art styles

By far the most common visual aspect of picture books in the 1940s until well into the 1960s was the alternating of a monochrome page with one printed in often rather limited colour. Contrary to what my own children thought, that the monochrome pages had been generously left for them to colour in, this was then an economic necessity. It was not that coloured ink was particularly expensive; it was the process of separating the colours that proved so time-consuming. Had the war not intervened, it is likely that the process in use in the USA (to all intents and purposes today's system of photographic offset litho) would have been up and running in the UK also. As it was, laborious separation of colours was the order of the day.

Colour lithography was used in this country by William Nicholson, whose stories of *Clever Bill* (1926) and of *The Pirate Twins* (1929) were published by Heinemann and Faber & Faber respectively. It was also the method used for Jean de Brunhoff's Babar books, for Edward Ardizzone's early Little Tim books and Kathleen Hale's Orlando books before the war. In colour lithography, artists prepared individual plates (normally four) for each page of their artwork. Originally the plates were made of stone, later zinc, then plastic sheeting. Those parts that were to be tinted were drawn in black lithographic ink or chalk and artists identified which colour they required for each part of an image. After processing, based on the principle of grease and water not mixing, these plates were printed onto the same sheet of paper, one after another, in the colour order of cyan(blue), yellow, magenta (red) and black. The result was the convincing illusion of a full range of colours.

Whilst author/illustrators who did their own 'separations' complained about the time it took, assembling their written and illustrated text at the same time made it possible for them to conceive of the finished page as a designed whole. Prior to this, two separate processes were used for printing colour illustration and type. The former 'half-tone' method for reproducing colour also meant only the best glossy paper could be used. But the new process worked on matte papers, which were much cheaper. Comparing the exciting Babar books, reproduced lithographically, with the much plainer illustrated 'gift' books of the 1920s makes it possible to understand the enthusiasm for colour lithography shown by Kathleen Hale, among others. 'I designed the books the way I wanted to: the large Babar format, using seven colours – to hell with black and white! – and wrote the stories without length restriction.'[13]

Hale had completed two Orlando titles in the late 1930s. Noel Carrington, who wished to publish them, worked for the publishers Country Life and had become excited by autolithography during a trip to Russia. Initially, his printers, Cowells of Ipswich, had said that if Hale's seven colours were reduced to four and over-printing was used to achieve the subsidiary colours, they themselves would do the lithography before the printing of Hale's books.

The first title, *Orlando (The Marmalade Cat): A Camping Holiday*, was published in 1938 with the lithography done by Cowells from Hale's illustrations. But all the detail in the rabbits, snails, ferns, beetles and grasshoppers had pushed up the costs and Hale was told they would have to be cut. 'I refused to allow this, because I knew how much children loved details.'[14] So, from Cowells, she learned to do the lithography herself. In her autobiography, Hale writes with admiration and gratitude of the lithographers who taught her how to produce her own litho plates. She also describes the introduction of 'Plastocowell': grained plastic sheet material that was much less heavy to carry than zinc plates and which could be used on a light-box for easier registration. But one large-format book still took her four to five months, working seven hours a day, seven days a week producing the 128 plates needed for each thirty-two-page book.

Ultimately, the photo offset litho method was established here as in the USA and the burden was taken off the illustrator. A letter from Noel Carrington to the illustrator C.F. Tunnicliffe makes it clear that as early as 1948, Puffin Picture Books were switching to photolithography.

> The early Puffin Picture Books were nearly all printed from plates drawn directly by the artist, partly from economy, as the original books sold at 6d., and partly because of the difficulties during the war of getting photographic reproductions done. We are now reproducing most artists' work by photolithography, which would give you a complete range of colours, and also enable you to use pencil as much as you like on the black and white pages.[15]

It was only four years earlier that Carrington could be found explaining the older process of autolithography to another artist. Today the scanners used to produce colour-separated film for the individual colours to be printed are computer controlled.

Edward Ardizzone, admired as an illustrator for his full-colour books, was confined to alternating colour and monotone pages in those of his Little Tim books created after the war. His illustrative hallmarks – the small, rounded characters with tapering legs and expressive arms, the eloquent line that never gives too much away, the colour washes which give us huge, dramatic seascapes, grey and brown when disaster threatens, a brilliant blue when all is well, his balanced page design and his irresistible speech bubbles – are an essential part of his artistry. During his life, Ardizzone illustrated many of his own texts. His ability to capture mood, create a sense of place and convey a range of feeling in his small vignette line drawings also makes him a sensitive illustrator of others' texts, notably those of Walter de la Mare, Eleanor Farjeon, Philippa Pearce, James Reeves and Graham Greene.

Neither Hale nor Ardizzone was much affected by the more abstract styles of painting that had influenced other contemporary illustrators. American illustrators, often originally from Eastern Europe, were producing artwork influenced by cubism and the surrealists that questioned the whole notion of 'pretty' artwork for children. An illustrator such as Roger Duvoisin, whose *The Happy Lion* was imported into this country in the 1950s, claimed that 'literalness and realism are to the illustrator what the cage is to the bird' and 'freshness, force and interest can be lost when precision and detail are brought in'.[16] His work shows a use of flat colour and simple shapes and an absence of shading rare in children's illustration.

In this country, Leslie Wood's illustrations for *The Story of the Little Red Engine* by Diana Ross (1945) are clearly influenced by the modern style of Jan Lewitt and George Him. Originally illustrators from Poland, these two provided flat, two-dimensional shapes and blocks of colour for the first Ross book, *The Little Red Engine Gets a Name* (1942). Leslie Wood's colours, reproduced by lithography, are also very subtle; the illustrations continue over the double-page spread and are bled to the edge of the page. There are two memorable panoramic views of Taddlecome Station and of the open country-side accompanied by no written text at all. These features are quite common in modern picture books, but were both rare and unexpected in the 1940s. It was adventurous of Faber & Faber to publish them. Wood continued to illustrate the Diana Ross Red Engine titles up to 1971 but over the years some of his distinctive perspectives and free use of dramatic forms were lost.

V.H. Drummond used a very heavy line in her book *Mrs Easter and the Storks* (1957) and took a cavalier attitude to perspective and body shape. The bright red of the dust sheet and the primary colours within the book justly earn the accolade of the blurb writer: 'The book is most properly, energetically and colourfully illustrated by its author.' Whatever 'properly' might have meant, the Kate Greenaway judges must have agreed as the book won the award for that year (see Chapter 3).

Another illustrator in this country whose artwork had much in common with the more general art scene was Gerald Rose. His seemingly child-like drawing, visible brush strokes, disregard of perspective and bright solid colours combine with visual and verbal jokes to provide lively books for children. The brilliant double-page spread of seagulls and fish in *Old Winkle and the Seagulls* (1960) could easily be a 1950s curtain fabric.

Harold Jones provided something of a contrast during this period with his much more gentle line and wash illustrations for *Lavender's Blue* (1954), Kathleen Lines's collection of nursery rhymes. Jones's more traditional view of illustration is at odds with that of Roger Duvoisin, but the decade provided room for both approaches. For Jones, 'An illustrator should positively – even minutely – describe the text in every possible way but must go further than a prosaic description of facts.'[17]

The period from 1945 to the early 1960s is more notable for the black and white line drawing in fiction for older children than it is for picture books. The tradition of fine illustrative work found in artists like Edward Ardizzone, Mervyn Peake, E.H. Shepard, Faith Jaques, Robin Jacques, Diana Stanley, Joan Kiddel-Monroe, Lynton Lamb, Susan Einzig, William Stobbs, Pauline Baynes, C. Walter Hodges, Shirley Hughes and William Papas waned as the picture book developed.

Among those line illustrators were Brian Wildsmith and Charles Keeping. A notable landmark in the story of picture-book printing for children was Brian Wildsmith's *ABC*, published by Oxford University Press in 1962. Brian Wildsmith began his career with book jackets and line drawings for children's fiction. Eleanor Graham had been delighted with his illustrations for her *Life of Jesus* for the Puffin imprint in 1959. His work in Frederick Grice's *The Bonny Pit Laddie* (1960) was also full of understanding and feeling, no doubt connected with the fact that Wildsmith's father had been a coal miner. In 1961, Mabel George, editor of Children's Books at Oxford University Press, chose Wildsmith to illustrate *The Arabian Nights* in colour. The resulting, unusual book, was, in the words of Ron Heapy, 'taken to pieces' by an anonymous reviewer in the *The Times Literary Supplement* who wrote of 'aimless scribbles . . . splashed lavishly and untidily with bright smudges of paint'.[18]

Far from being discouraged, George was delighted that the artwork in a children's book was attracting attention and she proceeded to publish the *ABC*. As a printer's daughter who had also previously worked in the technical side of publishing, she already knew about the four-colour process. She was confident that photo offset litho techniques could preserve Wildsmith's vibrancy, visible brush strokes and depth. When her Austrian printer Bruder Rosenbaum used thicker-than-usual paper the end results were spectacular. The cover is of a red, pink and purple apple with the author's name cleverly interwoven in the title *ABC*. Grey endpapers (the letters A–M at the front, N–Z at the back) give no clue to the colours within. A clown holds up the lettering on the title page with his feet. The minimal text, consisting of the word chosen to illustrate each letter of the alphabet, in upper and lower case, is printed on to a range of flat colours in carefully designed lettering. The initial letters of the words are always in white but subsequent letters break out into colour. The facing paintings (also on flat-coloured backgrounds) admit very little white and are bled to the edge of the page. *ABC* was loved out of existence by my children who never had any problems with the paintings. They quite accepted that a mouse could be green or that a horse could appear without legs. This book won the Kate Greenaway Award for the year and, after thirty-four years in print is still available, though only in paperback with an altered cover, inferior quality paper and very different colour reproduction.

From this point, Wildsmith concentrated on illustrating in full colour. He produced a nursery rhyme collection, a counting book and the full-colour *Birds* (1967) and *Fishes* (1968), which also received great acclaim. He is still illustrating, frequently choosing folk tales and religious stories, and has tried his talents at a pop-up *Noah's Ark* (1994) and *Creation* (1995), which are not only typically colourful but also decorated with a great deal of gold. *Creation* was also produced in a CD-Rom version. Oxford University Press continue as Wildsmith's sole publisher, maintaining their tradition for bold, new initiatives in printing techniques. Wildsmith's declared intention in his picture books is 'to reconcile the beauties of the form and colour in pure painting with the problems of illustrating a given text. By attracting the child to the stories in picture form, consciously or unconsciously (it doesn't matter which), the shapes and colours seep into the child's artistic digestive system, and he is aroused and stimulated by them.'[19] Wildsmith's continuing popularity suggests he may be right.

After Wildsmith's *ABC*, picture books elsewhere began to blaze with colour. John Burningham started his picture book career with *Borka: The Goose with no Feathers* (1963) which filled classrooms with poignant fantasy stories and bold, stumpy creatures. Jonathan Cape, who had immediately responded to the naive style and particular use of colour in Burningham's book, has remained his publisher ever since, a relationship now into its fourth decade. Victor Ambrus meanwhile delighted readers with tales such as *The Three Poor Tailors* (1965), which used colour on colour, creating magnificent line drawing in paint and great movement across double-page spreads. William Stobbs illustrated fables such as *The Golden Goose* (1966), with dramatic end papers and a glorious yellow goose taking off across the title pages. In the same period, William Papas launched himself merrily into full-colour cartooning with *No Mules* (1964) and Shirley Hughes, Raymond Briggs and Quentin Blake were also actively exploring the medium. Michael Foreman, David McKee, Jan Pienkowski, Helen Oxenbury and Pat Hutchins were just starting their careers in those exuberant days. Of them all, it is Charles Keeping who produced some of the most startling artwork and unusual stories.

Initially Keeping had provided line drawings and covers for several publishers, including The Bodley Head and Oxford University Press. In 1966 he had his first two picture books published: *Black Dolly* by Brockhampton Press and *Shaun and the Cart Horse* by Oxford University Press. *Black Dolly* was printed using conventional autolithography, with Charles Keeping doing his own separated drawings on the same type of Plastocowell previously used by Kathleen Hale. Because he was both experienced and skilled, Keeping produced subtle effects with the overprinting of two or three colours. The flatness of the blocks of colour are relieved by fine line drawing, scraper-board and stippling effects.

The artwork in *Shaun and the Cart Horse*, on the other hand, looks as if the artist has suddenly been liberated from all considerations save that of creating a finished illustration. Brilliantly coloured inks and textured effects could now be reliably reproduced by Bruder Rosenbaum, the same Austrian printer used for Wildsmith's *ABC*. According to Douglas Martin, in an absorbing full-length study on Keeping published by Julia MacRae,

> The colour handling for *Shaun* – is quite different from that imposed by the Brockhampton Press, where Keeping had to make a separate line drawing for each colour printing. Colours are allowed instead to run into each other freely on the way to the paper and on the paper itself, and Keeping chose to work fast, using intensely brilliant Pelikan inks, broken and textured by wax resist as well as by sponge and by overprinting in body colour.[20]

Keeping continued to experiment with colour, notably in *Joseph's Yard* (1969) and *Through the Window* (1970), initially created as films for the BBC. He was then persuaded by Ron Heapy to give up colour work temporarily as his wordless books, *Inter-City* (1977) and *River* (1978), had acquired a 'fruit salad effect'. In his 'monochrome' work (actually two colours, brown and black) for *The Highwayman*, he returned to a less abstract style of illustration. The book won the Kate Greenaway Award, after which Keeping conceded that OUP 'knew what they were talking about'.[21] *Beowulf* (1982), *The Wedding Ghost* (1985) and *The Lady of Shallott* (1986) followed, all done in sepia. Modern methods of printing make reprints of these titles problematic as the camera under computer control 'doesn't know' whether to go for the line or the tone. Martin agrees that the printing quality of the early Keeping books published by Oxford University Press is unlikely to be matched by current printing methods.[22] Clearly all is not gain as time moves on.

Oxford University Press supported Keeping's experimentation with colour and sepia. It also accepted his exploration of some quite 'dark' themes, hitherto not the material of picture books for children, although Mervyn Peake had also created some occasionally disturbing picture books two decades before. Whether in his own texts or in those of others, Keeping's illustrations remain dramatic and emotional and always embody his declared intention to create an evocative mood. He never wanted simply to echo a text. Martin sees him as 'an immense influence in shaping attitudes to children's books over the past three decades and for the future'.[23] The emotional breadth and depth now visible in picture books owes much to Keeping's ground-breaking books, though few currently at work can hope to combine all his talents.

In the approach to the last decade of the century, diversity has been the hallmark. There is the wild and witty free line of Quentin Blake, the jewel-like perfectionism of Nicola Bayley, the big oil paintings of Gary Blythe, the mysterious coloured drawings of Angela Barrett and the painstaking cross-hatching and dramatic perspectives of Patrick Benson. There are also the primitive stick figures and robust sculptured shapes of Louise Brierley, the photo-realism of Caroline Binch, the surrealism of Anthony Browne, the classical page design of Catherine Brighton, the expressive, wavering line of the later John Burningham, the brilliant comic-strip work of Raymond Briggs and the atmospheric painting of Ruth Brown. These are just illustrators whose surnames start with B! There is, also a tradition of illustrating with wood-cuts and lino-cuts continuing in the work of such artists as John Lawrence, Derek Collard and Christopher and Mary Wormell. There is of course, development and change in all picture-book artists, but publishers know that an illustrator's personal and identifiable style helps establish the public identification and loyalty which is important for sales.

The balance between picture and written text

> Caldecott's work heralds the beginning of the modern picture book. He devised an ingenious juxtaposition of picture and word, a counterpoint that never happened before. Words are left out – but the picture says it. Pictures are left out – but the word says it. In short, it is the invention of the picture book.[24]

Over a century ago, Randolph Caldecott revealed his understanding of the pleasure to be gained when illustrations and text equally share the telling of the story in a picture book. In his *Sing a Song of Sixpence* (1898), for instance, the illustrations accompanying the familiar text tell a whole new story of how the poor farmer came by his pocketful of rye and how it was then used to lure the blackbirds for the pie. Maurice Sendak, the writer of the above lines about Caldecott, also left his 'wild rumpus' pages uncaptioned in *Where the Wild Things Are* (1963) and the last written line in the book, 'and it was still hot', appears without illustration.

One logical conclusion of this sharing of labour between written and illustrated text is that the written text can become more economical, and this striking change is evident in picture books through recent decades. David Lloyd of Walker Books says that if Kathleen Hale were to present her Orlando books to him now he would send her away to cut the text down to 300 words. For him, a written text which re-states what is shown in the illustrations is missing the point of the modern picture book. Hale argues in her autobiography that the delight for the child lies in listening to the words which can be checked against the detail in the picture. Her Orlando books did include extra details in the illustrations, but these were incidental and did not significantly add to the story. The pince-nez and the watch that the train is pictured wearing in *Orlando (The Marmalade Cat) Keeps a Dog* (1949) are amusing details but narratively inconsequential. But when children discover *unmen-*

tioned but significant details in illustrations they can take some pleasure in feeling more informed than the narrator or characters in the story appear to be at that moment.

There are instances in UK picture books between 1940 and 1960 of this Caldecott type of balance in picture books, but they are rare and on a modest scale. In *Tim All Alone* (1956), Ardizzone shows us little Tim raised to the right height at a restaurant table by sitting on a large pile of books; this is unmentioned in the written text and yet the story – our sense of Tim's smallness and the care he receives – is enriched by the detail. In *Old Winkle and the Seagulls* (1960), the rhythmic and sensuous language of Elizabeth Rose's text, 'their hands flicked and flew over the slippery fish', is duly illustrated by Gerald Rose, yet the illustration can never quite capture that 'flicked and flew'. Conversely, the written text does not comment on the one fish that we see slipping down the neck of the fisherman's guernsey. Accompanying the plain written text, 'and his cat grew very fat', we see a cat from whose smiling chops there droops a fish skeleton. This counterpointed shaping of a picture book was quite rare in its time.

When Pat Hutchins's *Rosie's Walk* was published in the UK by The Bodley Head in 1968, the 'Caldecott' exploitation of the medium began in earnest again. Pat Hutchins tells two stories: one of Rosie the hen, in the spare written text, and one of both Rosie and a predatory fox told in the pictures. It was Hutchins's New York publisher who made her pare down the written text so successfully.[25] She repeated this feat in her cumulative story *The Wind Blew* (1974), which can be fruitfully compared with a 1946 picture book on almost the same theme, *Whoo, Whoo the Wind Blew* (Diana Ross and Leslie Wood). If both written and pictured text are allowed to accumulate on each page, the book may become unwieldy. The Ross/Wood title suffers in this way, with the ever-lengthening text ultimately getting out of step with the illustrations. Hutchins shows the accumulating events in the illustration only, leaving her free to keep the written text succinct and to use it to focus on feeling and movement. In several of her subsequent titles, notably *You'll Soon Grow Into Them, Titch* (1983) and *The Doorbell Rang* (1986), this same disciplined sharing out of story between text and picture is evident.

Quentin Blake, an illustrator for over thirty years, has been particularly skilled at the illustrating of others' texts. His lively line and well judged selection of the key narrative moment is definitely a contributing factor to the popularity of stories written by John Yeoman, Joan Aiken, Roald Dahl and Michael Rosen. In his various picture books, including those where he is both author and illustrator, it is possible to trace a development towards a more understated, leaner written text and a more telling use of illustration. This development in one author/illustrator is indicative of the change in the picture book as it became more sophisticated over this period.

In early books, such as *Patrick* (1968) or *Jack and Nancy* (1969), everything is duplicated. We know that Blake thought of these books first in terms of pictures 'with bits written in underneath afterwards',[26] and indeed the Weston

Woods film of *Patrick* sets the book to music with no words at all. We see the objects on the market stall and the silver coin in Patrick's hand and the written text confirms what we have seen. If Jack and Nancy 'floated down between tall trees' and 'parrots were flying about among the branches' then Blake shows just that. Despite the glimpses of the witty detail that distinguishes all of his work, these early books seem flat today. In Yeoman's wonderful story *Mouse Trouble* (1972), engaging drawings of hundreds of mice create a great setting but, once again, when we are told that mice use the millstone as a roundabout and balance on the turning beams and slide down the grain chutes, this is exactly what we see them doing in Blake's illustrations.

In the Captain Najork books (Russell Hoban's texts, 1974 and 1975), there is more shared telling. Elaine Moss records Blake at this time saying: 'You leave a bit to the reader's imagination, the least you can do that enables them to see the joke better.'[27] By the time *The Wild Washerwomen* (Yeoman's text) appeared in 1979, Blake had hit upon a formula where he only repeats the written text visually when there is a dramatic requirement to do so. Thus every stage in the washing process is depicted – the sorting, the soaking, the soaping, the pounding, the rinsing, the wringing and the spreading out, one activity to each woman because these same processes are amusingly repeated when the woodcutters have to be cleansed of their disguises at the end of the story. But when the story moves on, we see the 'atrocities' involved in the women's rampage only in the illustrations; the text simply reports 'the people who tried to stop them didn't have a chance'. The final illustration of woodcutters and washerwomen having 'the time of their lives' reveals much amusing detail to the careful viewer, notably that there are no divisions of labour on gender grounds here. Blake pleases child readers both by allowing them to verify in the pictures what is said in rich, repetitive and rhythmic language while also saying to them: this bit I leave you to work out for yourself from a careful examination of the pictures.

In *Mrs Armitage on Wheels* (1987), Blake is prepared to let the climax of the story hang on an illustrated detail, the snagging of Mrs Armitage's bike's anchor on a passing branch. His *Cockatoos* (1993) plays a game with readers, asking them to spot the lost cockatoos hiding from the troubled Professor Dupont. The story must impress on the child reader the irritating regularity of the professor's behaviour; thus when 'he got dressed and tied his tie as he always did' and 'adjusted his spectacles as he always did' we see these actions pictured exactly. But Blake leaves it to his reader to spot the cockatoos in hiding in each room of the house, posing for instance as jug handles in the kitchen or as wine bottles in the cellar. The final drawing of the second exodus of the exasperated cockatoos is uncaptioned and all the more poignant (if your heart is with Professor Dupont) for that.

In *Simpkin* (1994), we come to the logical conclusion of this progression with a text that is only 100 words long – and a third of those are the word 'Simpkin'! Superficially this may appear to be a 'concept' book, involving pairs of opposites, yet each coupling contains an element of narrative as well ('Simpkin high' is balancing on a high but crumbling stone wall; 'Simpkin low' inevitably follows). A thread running through the whole also explores sibling competition, revenge and reconciliation.

The pattern I have described in Quentin Blake's work can also be traced in other illustrators who began in the early part of this period but who subsequently were able to benefit from printing and technological developments. They too show an increasing awareness of how to exploit the picture-book medium fully, appreciating the delight that children take in feeling they have done half the labour. Some of these author/illustrators also seem to have been influenced by certain post-modernist and metafictive developments in the world of adult literature, where readers are also more often invited to supply their own meanings to what they read. Publishers can also be influenced by such movements, sometimes welcoming picture books that are both popular with readers and experimental within themselves.

John Burningham is, like Quentin Blake, one of Jonathan Cape's mainstay author/illustrators. In the 1960s he created a quintet of texts based on five animal characters: Borka, Trubloff, Humbert, Simp and Harquin. The storytelling is classic realist, with the character, setting and situation conventionally described in words and pictures before the particular significant incident arrives. In the last of these five titles, *Harquin, The Fox Who Went Down to the Valley* (1967), we glimpse a growing willingness in Burningham to play with form. In five brilliant pages, the hunt flashes past, going from left to right over the gutters of the book, creating thrilling drama and tension to which the few written words carefully contribute. By the time of *Mr Gumpy's Outing* (1970), for which Burningham won his second Kate Greenaway Award (his first went to *Borka, The Goose with no Feathers*), bold blocks of colour and heavy outlining have now gone. In their place is a wavering line and gentle cross-hatching in colour. A different rhythm is set up with line drawings on the left-hand page and colour on the right. The animals look out, as if inviting readers to come along too; the book has a participant feel. The drama and splash of the capsized boat and the detail of the tea party are conveyed through illustration alone.

From this point onwards, Burningham's picture books develop through a shared telling between pictures and written text. Even in *The Snow* (1974), a book for babies, an important detail like a missing glove is evident from the picture before the text mentions it. In the 'Shirley' books, *Come Away from the Water, Shirley* (1977), and *Time to Get Out of the Bath, Shirley* (1978), the written text of the mother's monologue betrays no hint of the world of pirates or of the medieval world that Shirley is exploring.

By the time of *Granpa* (1984), the reader is required to supply the context and connections for the snatches of conversation (in two different typefaces) recorded in the written text, and also to 'read' the various sepia flashbacks and imaginings. One reviewer despaired of readers' grasping this book's meaning at all.[28] This is perhaps to ignore the time children seem willing to give to poring over pictures, and to discount the experience they bring from their television and video viewing. Burningham has continued to be wonderfully experimental in his picture books. He has occasionally returned to the dramatic use of colour characteristic of his early books – the dark industrial landscape towards the end of *Oi! Get Off Our Train* (1989) is clearly from the same brush as the London scenes in *Humbert* (1965) – but the principle of 'less is more' seems to guide both his written and his pictured text. The 'telling gap' is also brilliantly exploited.

Anthony Browne's picture books have also become progressively more skilled at letting the illustrations play an indispensable role in adding depth, irony and additional meanings to an apparently simple text. Julia MacRae, who has published all Browne's most significant titles, works with him on the written text and on its sound and rhythms. The pictured details in *Piggybook* (1986) contribute ironically to the theme of male-chauvinist piggery. The written text plays with metaphor (a great deal of snorting and snuffling goes on) but does not reveal the way that the male Piggotts have begun to throw swine-shaped shadows and develop snouts and large flappy ears in the illustrations. Prosaic details such as the grungey neck of the ketchup bottle and the stains on cloth and clothes (how eloquently Anthony Browne's stains speak in all his books) add depth to the story. The pink flying pig on the title page suggests a symbolic/ironic point about the likelihood of all this happening and the ending raises more questions than it answers.

Visually represented transformations are also something Anthony Browne does supremely well. In *Hansel and Gretel* (1981) visual clues link step-mother and witch, while in *Gorilla* (1983) father and gorilla share features. There are also breathtaking meltings of one character into another such as Nora into a toad (*Kirsty Knows Best*, text by Annalena MacAfee, 1987), the baby into a pig (*Alice's Adventures in Wonderland*, 1988), the boy into a stone statue (*The Tunnel*, 1989) and the kettle into a cat (*Changes*, 1990). In these picture books, not to read the pictures is to have no story at all.

Browne is also well known for his understated references to other literary and cultural texts. Kathleen Hale sometimes wittily employed detail to add interest, but Anthony Browne's detail, especially in his later works, is far less arbitrary and works below the surface of the text to expand rather than distract from it. He 'quotes' Walter Crane's *Red Riding Hood* several times in *The Tunnel*, since this fairy story permeates the life of the dreamy but ultimately powerful heroine of the story. A particularly generous reference comes in *The Night Shimmy* (text by Gwen Strauss, 1991), when the withdrawn Eric is reading in bed what the text tells us are 'the best stories'. Careful perusal reveals Maurice Sendak's *In the Night Kitchen* (1970), another study of inventive and transforming fantasy. Even in *I Like Books* (1989), created for younger children, there is subtle intertextuality and understated visual reference in Humpty Dumpty's uneasy glance at a fried egg book cover.

Allan and Janet Ahlberg have also been much applauded for their inventiveness in picture-book form. Their clever use of other texts to add resonance to their work is legendary. *Each Peach Pear Plum* (1978) weaves its story around nursery tales or rhymes, and each rhyming couplet's meaning can only be completed by close inspection of the illustrations (a game that many of the Ahlbergs' picture books invite us to play). The three 'Jolly Postman' books, of which *The Jolly Pocket Postman* is the last, are unique in the history of children's picture books. Noticing the interest that their small daughter took in the letters and junk mail that came through their door, the Ahlbergs hit upon the notion of a story where a postman delivered letters to various well-known nursery characters. The originality here lay in the book being created so that readers actually extract letters from pages folded into envelope shapes. Few concessions are made to children readers in the various formal, legal or commercial tones adopted by these letters. Contrary to expectations, neither the language nor the activity of extracting, unfolding and then refolding and returning the letters ever seemed to defeat children. The books have sold extremely well, despite the fact that, because of their physical composition, they could never appear in paperback. The Ahlbergs' editor at Heinemann, Judith Elliot, was amply rewarded for the risks and care she took in bringing these enjoyable multi-layered books into production in a manner which reflected so well the original conception of the author and illustrator.

Among the many delights in the last Jolly Postman book is the moment when the postman has a phone bill to deliver to the butcher, the baker and the candlestick-maker, all characters from the nursery rhyme Rub-a-dub-dub. Careful scanning of the picture reveals a small, empty boat, with Rub-a-dub printed round the prow. Are the crew drowned? All that remains propped up in the stern is a (mobile) phone. By the end of the book the postman is in hospital after a nasty bump: Puss in (football) Boots has come to visit; his boots were delivered by the postman before all his intertextual adventures started.

Ruth Brown, in *Our Cat Flossie* (1986), initiates the youngest reader into irony of another type. In her dead-pan cat's *curriculum vitae*, the line 'Her hobbies include bird watching and fishing' are accompanied by an illustration showing a cat intent on the budgie in the cage and attempting to scoop a goldfish from an ornamental pond. 'Flossie is a skilful climber' is accompanied by a portrait of Flossie, one ladder rung below her descending, unsuspecting owner. *One Stormy Night* (1992), was underrated in an *Observer* review as a pretty, ghostly tale, 'strong on atmosphere, short on narrative'.[29] It is more than that, and careful viewing enables the reader to follow the night-time visit of a long dead King Charles spaniel to the home where he used to live. A portrait of him with the children of the family in their lace collars still hangs above the fireplace; there is also a TV set and a newspaper dated 1992. The smile of one of those children, beneath the stone effigy of her parents in the nearby church, greets the spaniel's return at dawn to his position at the feet of his master. Ruth Brown is well known as a creator of multi-layered texts; it is worrying that a reviewer should miss such detail.

The fact that it is now possible to misread a children's picture book is a measure of the extent to which the genre has developed and taken on some of the characteristics of much modern fiction for adults: gap-filling, holding and revising data in the mind, hanging onto clues and bringing prior cultural and literary knowledge into play. But not all picture books have these ludic qualities; many others still offer more traditional fare. Young readers are fortunate to have access to such a range.

Themes and assumptions

The needs that teachers, librarians and parents exposed during the 1950s and 1960s was for books of wide social interest (see Chapter 1). It took some time for publishers and critics to recognise and accept this changing requirement. In 1971, Frank Eyre was uncertain about Charles Keeping's new and influential picture books. 'It is difficult to see how such an approach can be carried much further without taking picture books directly into the area of social commentary, and the age at which picture books are of value is still, I believe, too young for such conceptions.'[30] But though some critics express views of this type, picture books have continued to take on practically every issue while still appealing to a wide range of readers. Advocates like Elaine Moss have been particularly important here, urging eloquently that the qualities of the new picture books should be more widely recognised by teachers and librarians, especially those working with older children.[31]

Social/psychological issues such as anger, split families, sickness and death also came to be treated in picture books in both serious and humorous ways. Many of Anthony Browne's books reveal his belief in the role of the imagination in combating the difficulties of family and social life. Julia MacRae was quick to realise that children found Anthony Browne's particular way of exploring these themes fascinating and accessible. *Angry Arthur* (1982), by Hiawyn Oram and Satoshi Kitamura, tells of a small boy's anger filling and exploding a universe in wonderfully inventive, accumulative images but without the calm after the storm that completed Sendak's *Where the Wild Things Are*. In this respect, *Angry Arthur* is unusual for a children's story, disturbing some readers with its lack of resolution. It would not have found a publisher in the immediate post-war years, but Klaus Flugge of Andersen Press has frequently ventured into such territory on his list. He is also David McKee's publisher and has always encouraged his provocative and inventive work. Though the meanings are slippery in David McKee's complex and multi-layered picture book about adult strife, *I Hate My Teddy Bear* (1982), this indirect treatment seems preferable to those frankly 'bibliotherapeutic' picture books in which moral tracts masquerade as stories. Parental tension is also subtly indicated and resolved by Amanda Harvey in *Stormy Weather* (1991). Her very title draws parallels with storms that arrive but also pass.

There is no need to turn to formulaic constructions when many author/illustrators also produce sensitive and satisfying books touching on common problems or anxieties. Illness is at the heart of *The Ice Palace* (1994), where a sick child with waxen skin dreams of everything cool and cooling. This tender story by Angela McAllister gives magical opportunities to Angela Barrett's talent to make contrasts between the heat-filled room and the child's icy fantasies. Susan Varley's *Badger's Parting Gifts* (1984) was published in the same year as John Burningham's *Granpa*. No two picture books describe death as a completion of a full life more effectively. Animals and grandparents are the groups most often chosen for stories about death. It is still rare to find books in the UK willing to explore the death of siblings or of young adults in picture books as boldly as in the Australian picture book *Lucy's Bay* (1992) by Gary Crew and illustrated by Gregory Rogers. The same artist's *Way Home* (1994, text by Libby Gathorn) took on the subject of homelessness. This topic is also at the heart of Maurice Sendak's *We Are All in the Dumps with Jack and Guy* (1993) from America. There are still no equivalent British picture books on these issues.

War was an area largely avoided by publishers around 1945 and for some time after. Modern picture books have broken this taboo. Some of David McKee's and Michael Foreman's books comment on the folly of war in amusing ways, but Raymond Briggs's *When the Wind Blows* (1982) and *The Tin-Pot Foreign General and the Old Iron Woman* (1984) are still the most direct and affecting picture books on this theme, though not originally intended for children. The comic-strip format, broken at key points by larger pictures, seems to give increased resonance to Briggs's books. Picture books from other countries which touch on the holocaust also have no equivalent in the UK, although the poignant *Rose Blanche* (1985), a Christophe Gallaz story reworked by Ian McEwan and illustrated by the Italian Roberto Innocenti, was published initially by Jonathan Cape. Foreman has recently produced two personal and informative picture books about the First and Second World Wars: *War Boy* (1989) and *War Game* (1993), which could both make substantial and memorable contributions to school history teaching.

Ecological concerns are widely apparent in modern picture books. From his very early *Dinosaurs and All that Rubbish* (1972) to his more recent *One World* (1990) and *Peter's Place* (1995, text by Sally Grindley), Foreman has made visually arresting and accessible contributions in this area. Jan Pienkowski's pictures inspired Russell Hoban's text for *M.O.L.E.* (1993), a sobering but visionary view of the planet. Others who have contributed notably include Simon James, with his witty line, Helen Cowcher with her big paintings, Ruth Brown with her passionate defence of animals and the countryside and John Burningham in his perfect *Oi! Get Off Our Train* (1989), in which endangered species plead for protection. Charles Keeping's last book, *Adam and Paradise Island* (1989), showed his concern for a disappearing environment. This theme has long been present in children's stories, but it is new to find it so frequently now in picture books.

Some of these books are not intended for young children, and it is apparent over the years how picture books in their content and tone have become much more widely age-based. Helen Oxenbury, John Burningham and Jan Ormerod have created works for infants which have a subtlety and humour quite absent from more traditional 'baby' books. Other titles by Raymond Briggs, Michael Foreman and Fiona French build on Keeping's complexities and offer sophistication to ten year olds and above. In between, there are the enthralling domestic trials and tribulations successfully captured over the decades by Shirley Hughes in *Dogger* (1977) and *Alfie Gets in First* (1981). Tony Ross gives his own sense of subversive humour full rein in *Super Dooper Jezebel* (1988) and *Michael* (1990, text by Tony Bradman). Some of this wit is also apparent in other humourists such as Babette Cole, Claudio Munoz and Korky Paul. Mick Inkpen, Nick Butterworth and Colin McNaughton are also successful humourists, and Jill Murphy and Posy Simmonds appeal across the whole age range. Folk tales, legends, fairy stories and nursery rhymes continue to draw all illustrators. Illustrative work from Errol le Cain, Jane Ray, Charlotte Voake, Angela Barrett, Nicola Bayley, Juan Wijngaard, P.J. Lynch and Alan Marks offer sometimes startlingly different interpretations of this traditional material.

There are many picture books which, whilst explicitly conveying a belief or a message, can do much simpler things too, such as building an image of another country or indeed of a specific location in this country. Michael Foreman's early book *The Perfect Present* (1967) showed great attention to place. My children, as Londoners, loved his representations of buildings they could identify. In a later book, *Panda's Puzzle and his Voyage of Discovery* (1977), there are glimpses of China, Egypt, the USA, the Himalayas and the Far East. These convey a real and beautiful geography lesson, and many other Michael Foreman books reflect his worldwide travels. In *Panda and the Odd Lion* (1981), close-ups and aerial views disclose a detailed, blue-washed Venice. *Cat and Canary* (1984) provides a splendid bird's-eye view of the sky scrapers of New York as the cat of the title is kite-borne over the city. Foreman has also created many books set in Cornwall, and his war books bring alive the Suffolk locality with an immediacy that is melancholy and humorous in turn. Few early picture books are as specific about location, and some publishers do not welcome too much specificity because it may act as a barrier to overseas sales. Such caution is surely regrettable. A more positive welcome to such books could be found with teachers implementing the National Curriculum in different subject areas. A narrative text, illustrated with imagination and produced with care, can be most effective in conveying information memorably.

The Ahlbergs's *Peepo!* is also a social history lesson on the 1940s, complete with celluloid lampshades and a tin bath. Several of Philippe Dupasquier's books give a vivid flavour of the Wild West, Roman times or an eighteenth-century war ship. Catherine Brighton's splendid *Dearest Grandmama* (1991) builds up an authentic image of a sea voyage in the 1830s with all the paraphernalia of an explorer faithfully detailed. The overall context is the mystery surrounding the arrival of a silent boy, in fact a casualty of the

Marie Celeste disaster in 1830. Catherine Brighton's books are always carefully researched and have already provided a visually delightful education in locations as diverse as medieval England and Italy, turn-of-the-century Russia, Mozart's Salzburg, the Great Fire of London and the Brontës's life and times. *The Iron Needle* (1994), from Amanda Harvey, allows a close look at the inside of a foundry in a story which celebrates independence, the working class, mothers, girls and women generally.

That girls and women should have assumed more visible roles over the period is not surprising. Nor is the appearance of more black characters. One of the most successful picture books which puts a female child, who also happens to be black, centrally in the story is Mary Hoffman's and Caroline Binch's *Amazing Grace* (1991). In the sequel, *Grace and Family* (1995), the complex family relationships with which she grapples are faced. Eileen Browne's brilliantly coloured *Handa's Surprise* (1994), is set in Kenya and matches *Rosie's Walk* in its perfect balance of illustration and text. Jan Ormerod and Helen Oxenbury have also shown how black children in this country can appear unproblematically in picture books.

The brilliant paper engineering that often brings picture books close to toys is discussed in Chapter 5. In the right hands, the literary novelty book can now also be an aesthetic delight. In Lucy Cousins's delightful *Maisy Goes Swimming* (1990), readers can first disrobe Maisie in preparation for her swim and then dress her again for the book's next reader. This book was energetically promoted by Walker Books for young children.

Insufficient time has been devoted to the role of the comic strip, with or without words, which lends to the picture book something of the film with its differing perspectives and something of the comic with its witty use of frames (but see Chapter 6). The comic strip is less valued in the UK than in other countries, but a number of talented British illustrators following in the footsteps of the boundary-breaking Raymond Briggs have made the comic strip their own. Briggs's *Father Christmas* was published in 1973 and the wordless *The Snowman* for younger children in 1978. In Shirley Hughes's *Up and Up* (1979), another wordless fantasy involving flying, three features deserve our attention. Hughes's book has a girl as its protagonist at a time when adventures in picture books still more commonly happened to boys or to animals. The girl is totally and defiantly in charge of the drama of her magical flight over her town and the book is not in full colour but in black line on a creamy-pink background. Striking originality is also shown by Shirley Hughes in *Chips and Jessie*, (1985), a book which is not quite a picture book but more of a graphic novel. Inventive use of frames characterises Jan Ormerod's work. Peter Collington, Posy Simmonds, Philippe Dupasquier, John Prater and Colin McNaughton have also told witty and unusual stories through the clever use of frames in their picture books.

Advances in technology have resulted in a great many picture books being published. It is now easy to reproduce artwork; it is also possible to have an initially short print run and then reprint if the title takes off. This also has implications for quality which publishers have to face. It is not unthinkable that, through computers, readers will shortly be able to download any picture book from the screen, consequently spending less time in conventional book shops. The future may bring even more developments in visual terms, perhaps further blurring the distinction between books, toys, games and moving images.

But of the picture books that are currently available and of those that are now only accessible through libraries and collections, there are many that have been imaginatively conceived and executed, sensitively edited and carefully printed. When everything in the whole and complicated process of making a picture book comes together – the words, the pictures, the design and the printing – then there is a tangible, finished and very special object to put into children's hands, which can magically remain in their minds too.

References

1. David Elliott (1978), 'World's Work' in *School Book Shop News* no. 11, Autumn, p.14.
2. Frank Eyre (1952, second edition 1971) *British Children's Books in the Twentieth Century* (London: Longman), p.28.
3. Alec Ellis (1968), *A History of Children's Reading and Literature* (Oxford: Pergamon Press), p.192.
4. Figures supplied by The Publishers Association (1995), from *Whitaker's Cumulative Book List*.
5. David Lloyd (1995). Conversations with the writer.
6. Ron Heapy (1995). Conversations with the writer.
7. Klaus Flugge (1995). Conversations with the writer.
8. Caroline Roberts (1995). Conversations with the writer.
9. Valerie Alderson (1974) 'Paperback Review' in *Children's Book Review* vol. 4 no. 2 Summer 1974, p.51
10. Martin Waddell, illus. Barbara Firth (1988), *Can't You Sleep, Little Bear?* (London: Walker Books).
11. Molly Keane (1988), *The Sunday Times*, 27 November.
12. Mirabel Cecil (1995), *Sebastian Walker 1942–1991: A Kind of Prospero*. (London: Walker Books).
13. Kathleen Hale (1994), *A Slender Reputation* (London: Frederick Warne), p.205.
14. Ibid., p.211.
15. Steve Hare (1995), *Allen Lane and the Penguin Editors 1935–1970* (London: Penguin), p.138.
16. Roger Duvoisin (1974), *Children's Book Illustration: The Pleasures and Problems* (first pub. 1965), in Haviland, Virginia, *Children and Literature: Views and Reviews* (London: The Bodley Head), p.186.
17. Harold Jones (undated) in *The Box of Delights Children's Book Illustrations by Twenty one British Artists*, Newport Museum and Art Gallery, Gwent, p.42.
18. Anonymous (1961), *The Times Literary Supplement*, 1 December.
19. Brian Wildsmith (1965), 'Antic Disposition', *Library Journal*, 15 November, pp.5035–8.
20. Douglas Martin (1993), *Charles Keeping: An Illustrator's Life* (London: Julia MacRae), p.93.

21. Ron Heapy (1995). Conversations with the writer.
22. Martin, p.92.
23. Douglas Martin (1989), *The Telling Line: Essays on Fifteen Contemporary Book Illustrators* (London: Julia MacRae), p.49.
24. Maurice Sendak (1989), *Caldecott & Co.* (London: Reinhardt in assoc. with Viking), p.21.
25. Elaine Moss (1973), 'Pat Hutchins: A Natural', *Signal* no. 10, January, p.33.
26. Elaine Moss (1975), 'Quentin Blake', *Signal* no. 16, January p.35.
27. Ibid., p.37.
28. Julia Briggs (1984), *The Times Literary Supplement*, 30 November.
29. Kate Kellaway (1992), *Observer*, 29 November.
30. Eyre, p.51.
31. Elaine Moss (1981), *Picture Books 9–13* (Stroud: The Thimble Press).

Children's books

Ahlberg, Allan and Janet (1978), *Each Peach Pear Plum* (London: Kestrel/Viking).
Ahlberg, Allan and Janet (1981), *Peepo!* (London: Kestrel/Viking).
Ahlberg, Allan and Janet (1995), *The Jolly Pocket Postman* (London: Heinemann).
Ambrus, Victor (1965), *The Three Poor Tailors* (Oxford: Oxford University Press).
Ardizzone, Edward (1936), *Little Tim and the Brave Sea Captain* (Oxford: Oxford University Press).
Ardizzone, Edward (1956), *Tim All Alone* (Oxford: Oxford University Press).
Blake, Quentin (1968), *Patrick* (London: Jonathan Cape).
Blake, Quentin (1969), *Jack and Nancy* (London: Jonathan Cape).
Blake, Quentin (1987), *Mrs Armitage on Wheels* (London: Jonathan Cape).
Blake, Quentin (1993), *Cockatoos* (London: Jonathan Cape).
Blake, Quentin (1994), *Simpkin* (London: Jonathan Cape).
Bradman, Tony illus. Ross Tony (1990), *Michael* (London: Andersen Press).
Briggs, Raymond (1973), *Father Christmas* (London: Hamish Hamilton).
Briggs, Raymond (1978), *The Snowman* (London: Hamish Hamilton).
Briggs, Raymond (1982), *When the Wind Blows* (London: Hamish Hamilton).
Briggs, Raymond (1984), *The Tin Pot Foreign General and the Old Iron Woman* (London: Hamish Hamilton).
Brighton, Catherine (1991), *Dearest Grandmama* (London: Faber & Faber).
Brown, Ruth (1986), *Our Cat Flossie* (London: Andersen Press).
Brown, Ruth (1992), *One Stormy Night* (London: Andersen Press).
Brown, Ruth (1995), *Greyfriars Bobby* (London: Andersen Press).
Browne, Anthony (1981), *Hansel and Gretel* (London: Julia MacRrae).
Browne, Anthony (1983), *Gorilla* (London: Julia MacRae).
Browne, Anthony (1986), *Piggybook* (London: Julia MacRae).
Browne, Anthony (1989), *I Like Books* (London: Julia MacRae).
Browne, Anthony (1989), *The Tunnel* (London: Julia MacRae).
Browne, Anthony (1990), *Changes* (London: Julia MacRae).
Browne, Eileen (1994), *Handa's Surprise* (London: Walker Books).
Burningham, John (1963), *Borka: The Adventures of a Goose with no Feathers* (London: Jonathan Cape).
Burningham, John (1965), *Humbert, Mr Firkin and the Lord Mayor of London* (London: Jonathan Cape).
Burningham, John (1967), *Harquin: The Fox Who Went Down to the Valley* (London: Jonathan Cape).
Burningham, John (1970), *Mr Gumpy's Outing* (London: Jonathan Cape)

Burningham, John (1974), *The Snow* (London: Jonathan Cape).

Burningham, John (1977), *Come Away from the Water, Shirley* (London: Jonathan Cape).

Burningham, John (1978), *Time to Get Out of the Bath, Shirley* (London: Jonathan Cape).

Burningham, John (1984), *Granpa* (London: Jonathan Cape).

Burningham, John (1989), *Oi! Get Off Our Train* (London: Jonathan Cape).

Caldecott, Randolph (1978), *Sing a Song of Sixpence* (London: Routledge).

Carroll, Lewis, illus. Browne, Anthony (1988), *Alice's Adventures in Wonderland* (London: Julia MacRae).

Cousins, Lucy (1990), *Maisy Goes Swimming* (London: Walker Books).

Crew, Gary, illus. Rogers, Gregory (1992), *Lucy's Bay* (Queensland: Jam Roll Press).

Crossley-Holland, Kevin, illus. Keeping, Charles (1982), *Beowulf* (Oxford: Oxford University Press).

Drummond, V.H. (1957), *Mrs Easter and the Storks* (London: Faber & Faber).

Fatio, Louise, illus. Duvoisin, Roger (1955. USA 1954), *The Happy Lion* (London: The Bodley Head).

Foreman, Michael (1967), *The Perfect Present* (London: Hamish Hamilton).

Foreman, Michael (1972), *Dinosaurs and All That Rubbish* (London: Hamish Hamilton).

Foreman, Michael (1977), *Panda's Puzzle and his Voyage of Discovery* (London: Hamish Hamilton).

Foreman, Michael (1981), *Panda and the Odd Lion* (London: Andersen Press.)

Foreman, Michael (1984), *Cat and Canary* (London: Andersen Press).

Foreman, Michael (1989), *War Boy* (London: Pavilion).

Foreman, Michael (1993), *War Game* (London: Pavilion).

Foreman, Michael (1990), *One World* (London: Andersen Press).

Foreman, Michael (1996), *Seal Surfer* (London: Andersen Press).

Garfield, Leon, illus. Keeping, Charles (1985), *The Wedding Ghost* (Oxford: Oxford University Press).

Gathorn, Libby, illus. Gary Crew (1994) *Way Home* (London: Andersen Press).

Graham, Eleanor, illus. Wildsmith, Brian (1959), *Life of Jesus* (London: Puffin).

Grice, Frederick, illus. Wildsmith, Brian (1960), *The Bonny Pit Laddie* (Oxford: Oxford University Press).

Grindley, Sally, illus. Foreman, Michael (1995), *Peter's Place* (London: Andersen Press).

Hale, Kathleen (1938), *Orlando (The Marmalade Cat): A Camping Holiday* (London: Country Life).

Hale, Kathleen (1944), *Orlando (The Marmalade Cat) His Silver Wedding* (London: Country Life).

Hale, Kathleen (1948), *Orlando (The Marmalade Cat) Keeps a Dog* (London: Country Life).

Handford, Martin (1990), *Where's Wally?* (London: Walker Books).

Harvey, Amanda (1991), *Stormy Weather* (London: Macmillan).

Harvey, Amanda (1994), *The Iron Needle* (London: Macmillan).

Hathorn, Libby, illus. Rogers, Gregory (1994), *Way Home* (London: Andersen Press).

Hoban, Russell, illus. Blake, Quentin (1974), *How Tom Beat Captain Najork and his Hired Sportsmen* (London: Cape).

Hoban, Russell, illus. Blake, Quentin (1975), *Near Thing for Captain Najork* (London: Cape).

Hoban, Russell, illus. Pienkowski, Jan (1993), *M.O.L.E.* (London: Cape).

Hoffman, Mary, illus. Binch, Caroline (1991), *Amazing Grace* (London: Frances Lincoln).

Hoffman, Mary, illus. Binch, Caroline (1995), *Grace and Family* (London: Frances Lincoln).

Hutchins, Pat (1970), *Rosie's Walk* (London: The Bodley Head).

Hutchins, Pat (1974), *The Wind Blew* (London: The Bodley Head).

Hutchins, Pat (1983), *You'll Soon Grow Into Them, Titch* (London: The Bodley Head).

Hutchins, Pat (1986), *The Doorbell Rang* (London: The Bodley Head).

Hughes, Shirley (1977), *Dogger* (London: The Bodley Head).

Hughes, Shirley (1979), *Up and Up* (London: The Bodley Head).

Hughes, Shirley (1981), *Alfie Gets In First* (London: The Bodley Head).

Hughes, Shirley (1985), *Chips and Jessie* (London: The Bodley Head).

Keeping, Charles (1966), *Black Dolly* (London: Brockhampton Press).

Keeping, Charles (1966), *Shaun and the Cart Horse* (Oxford: Oxford University Press).

Keeping, Charles (1969), *Joseph's Yard* (Oxford: Oxford University Press).

Keeping, Charles (1970), *Through the Window* (Oxford: Oxford University Press).

Keeping, Charles (1977), *Inter-City* (Oxford: Oxford University Press).

Keeping, Charles (1978), *River* (Oxford: Oxford University Press).

Keeping, Charles (1989), *Adam and Paradise Island* (Oxford: Oxford University Press).

Lines, Kathleen, illus. Jones, Harold (1954), *Lavender's Blue* (Oxford: Oxford University Press).

McAfee, Annalena, illus. Browne, Anthony (1987), *Kirsty Knows Best* (London: Julia MacRae).

McAllister, Angela, illus. Barrett, Angela (1994), *The Ice Palace* (London: Hutchinson).

McBratney, Sam, illus. Jeram, Anita (1994), *Guess How Much I Love You* (London: Walker Books).

McEwan, Ian, illus. Innocenti, Roberto (1985), *Rose Blanche* (London: Jonathan Cape).

McKee, David (1982), *I Hate My Teddy Bear* (London: Andersen Press).

Nicholson, William (1926), *Clever Bill* (London: Heinemann).

Nicholson, William (1929), *The Pirate Twins* (London: Faber & Faber).

Noyes, Alfred, illus. Keeping, Charles (1981), *The Highwayman* (Oxford: Oxford University Press).

Oram, Hiawyn, illus. Kitamura, Satoshi (1982), *Angry Arthur* (London: Andersen Press).

Papas, William (1964), *No Mules* (Oxford: Oxford University Press).

Poole, Josephine, illus. Barrett, Angela (1991), *Snow White* (London: Hutchinson).

Rose, Gerald, illus. Rose, Elizabeth (1960), *Old Winkle and the Seagulls* (London: Faber & Faber).

Ross, Diana, illus. Wood, Leslie (1945), *The Story of the Little Red Engine* (London: Faber & Faber).

Ross, Diana, illus. Lewitt, Jan and Him, George (1942), *The Little Red Engine Gets a Name* (London: Faber & Faber).

Ross, Diana, illus. Wood, Leslie (1946), *Whoo, Whoo, the Wind Blew* (London: Faber & Faber).

Ross, Tony (1988), *Super Dooper Jezebel* (London: Andersen Press).

Sendak, Maurice (1967; USA 1963), *Where the Wild Things Are* (London: The Bodley Head).

Sendak, Maurice (1971; USA 1970), *In the Night Kitchen* (London: The Bodley Head).

Sendak, Maurice (1993), *We Are All in the Dumps with Jack and Guy* (London: HarperCollins).

Sheldon, Dyan, illus. Blythe, Gary (1990), *The Whales' Song* (London: Hutchinson).

Stobbs, William (1966), *The Golden Goose* (London: The Bodley Head).

Strauss, Gwen, illus. Browne, Anthony (1991), *The Night Shimmy* (London: Julia MacRae).

Tennyson, Alfred, illus. Keeping, Charles (1986), *The Lady of Shallott* (Oxford: Oxford University Press).

Varley, Susan (1984), *Badger's Parting Gifts* (London: Andersen Press).

Waddell, Martin, illus. Firth, Barbara (1988), *Can't You Sleep, Little Bear?* (London: Walker Books).

Wildsmith, Brian (illus). (1961), *The Arabian Nights* (Oxford: Oxford University Press).

Wildsmith, Brian (1962), *ABC* (Oxford: Oxford University Press).

Wildsmith, Brian (1967), *Birds* (Oxford: Oxford University Press).

Wildsmith, Brian (1968), *Fishes* (Oxford: Oxford University Press).

Wildsmith, Brian (1994), *Noah's Ark* (Oxford: Oxford University Press).

Wildsmith, Brian (1995), *The Creation* (Oxford: Oxford University Press).

Yeoman, John, illus. Blake, Quentin (1972), *Mouse Trouble* (London: Hamish Hamilton).

Yeoman, John, illus. Blake, Quentin (1979), *The Wild Washerwomen* (London: Hamish Hamilton).

Yeoman, John, illus. Blake, Quentin (1994), *The Do-it-Yourself House That Jack Built* (London: Hamish Hamilton).

Judith Graham wishes to thank the following for their help and interest:

Ron Heapy of Oxford University Press.

Caroline Roberts of Hutchinson (Random House).

Klaus Flugge of Andersen Press.

Anne McNeil of The Bodley Head (Random House).

David Lloyd of Walker Books.

Julia MacRae, who spoke to me at a very busy time when she was setting up her own consultancy.

Elaine Moss, who generously gave me time and space to study some of her older picture books.

5 Movable Books
Geoff Fox

Established children's books by well-known authors have enjoyed a good share of critical attention this century. Much less is known about the world of novelty books and other literature frequently regarded as ephemeral. Largely unreviewed by critics and unpurchased by schools or librarians, this type of literature often only had one constant source of support available to it: the interest and loyalty of generations of young readers themselves.

Most of us are familiar with at least one kind of movable book – the pop-up; but in this chapter Geoff Fox discusses a wide range of movable books whose effects may range from dissolving pictures to holograms. He looks too at differences in the quality of conception and paper engineering throughout the genre.

With the advent of electronic, multimedia texts the days of the movable book might seem to be numbered. Not so, argues Fox, who sees instead a resurgence in this area of book-making for young readers.

Perhaps the most contentious area Fox explores is the status of movable books – should they be dismissed as novelties which are primarily of interest for what they tell us about the times in which they are produced, or do they warrant more serious attention? Other questions raised in this chapter deal with the nature of the books themselves; for instance, how strong is the relationship between the movable parts and the text? Finally, this chapter looks at the future of the movable book in an age of multimedia, interactive publishing.

Introduction

A search along the 'Novelty Book' shelves of any large bookshop might well reveal anything from paper multi-decker burger buns filled with lettuce and squirming caterpillars to telephone books that ring, books that smell, books that play tunes, books that light up in the dark or a movable detective story ('Pull the tabs, lift the flaps and find the clues to discover who dunnit. Then turn the wheels, the clues will change and you can solve the mystery all over again . . . and again.') You might find a book which turns into a dolls' house 'Green Gables' with paper figures of Anne, Marilla, Gilbert and the rest, so that you can 'send your children on a spectacular journey inside the enchanting world of Anne's Prince Edward Island home' (clearly the anticipated purchaser is expected to be both adult and familiar with the original text). *A Walk in Monet's Garden* (1995) spreads out into the house and grounds at Giverny on a 75cm square base, with the great man himself at his easel beside the lily pond. The popular picture book, *Can't You Sleep, Little Bear?* (1988) by Martin Waddell and Barbara Firth is reincarnated as 'a full play kit'. A book-sized treasure chest about medieval knights (J. Howe, *Knights*, 1995) comes equipped with miniature weapons: 'Warning – the siege catapult should only be used with the missiles supplied. Serious injury can result from improper use of this machine. Never fire at point blank range.'

Some of the devices employed in these movable books have long histories. Alchemists and astrologers incorporated rotating discs as wheels of fortune in their manuscripts well before Caxton. Medical students in the nineteenth century used flap-books in their studies in anatomy. Lothar Meggendorfer's witty and ingenious *International Circus* (1887) is technically more complex than *A Walk in Monet's Garden*. At the turn of the century, the publishing house of Ernest Nister (German in origin but with thriving offices in London and New York) was very successfully creating books of 'dissolving' pictures activated by transforming discs; Brian Wildsmith uses a similar device to bring a flower bursting into bloom in *The Creation* (1995).

Enthusiasts for movable books suggest that the work of Nister and Meggendorfer, alongside that of the long-established British firm of Dean & Son throughout the latter part of the nineteenth century, created the first Golden Age of the movable book which came to an end only when the Great War severed the trading links between Germany and Britain. Those enthusiasts are also usually agreed that a second Golden Age began in the 1970s and continues to prosper in the 1990s. Movable books certainly entered new territories of artistic and technical ingenuity in that period; and a comparison of the numbers of titles produced in each decade since the war indicates the growth of the industry. An analysis based on the work of Ann Montanaro, the leading bibliographer in the field, produces the following approximate figures for the publication of movable books in the English language: 1940s – 90; 1950s – 80; 1960s – 110; 1970s – 310; 1980s – 800. These figures represent minimum totals; it is difficult to log the publication of movable books, since the bibliographer has only the title to work from: *Cinderella*, for example, may or may not have been transformed into a movable book. Many of the books recorded in the earlier post-war years were published in North America (and sometimes reprinted in Britain); while the later years show a marked increase of production by British publishers, at least to a state of parity. What these figures do not indicate is the size of the print runs in recent years: a publisher confident of success might well now order as many as 100,000 copies as the first run of a new movable book (compare this to the figures for standard picture books provided on page 62); and some titles might reprint as many copies again within a twelve-month period. These quantities, it has to be remembered, are for hardback books costing considerably more than any children's novel which, if published in board covers at all, might well be produced in a run of some 3000 copies.

Appropriately enough, the story of a product whose essence depends upon the unexpected is one of contrasts, where coincidence and chance often play decisive parts. The production process is complex: a pop-up book by a British author/illustrator for sale in a High Street bookshop could well have been originated in Britain, designed in California, assembled near a South American city better known as the headquarters of international drug cartels, and finally shipped in its pristine shrinkwrap to a British warehouse. The development of movable books over the last fifty years has been shaped by a relatively small number of artists, paper engineers and entrepreneurs of rare invention and daring business nerve. Several of them have had some connection with older traditions of paper-folding and cutting in former Eastern Bloc countries.

Considering the annual sales of movable books in Britain must now be measured in millions of pounds, there is surprisingly little information in print about their recent development; this chapter owes much to a few pioneering articles and the enthusiasm and generosity of their authors – notably Michael Dawson.[1] An account of all the varieties of movable books – books with lift-up flaps, peep-show books, panoramas, books with rotating wheels or tab-operated slats (circular, vertical and horizontal) – would require a volume to itself. This chapter is inevitably selective and concentrates for the most part on that most ubiquitous of movables, the pop-up book.

Louis Giraud, the Bookano series and the post-war period

> So here read, learn, and observe construction,
> And thank high Heaven that, freed from bombs' destruction,
> You may peacefully and, in your waking hours,
> Appreciate the blessings of democracy.

With these uneasy lines, 'The Wizard', depicted with pointed hat, flowing robes and black cat at his knee, welcomes readers to *Bookano Stories No. 12*, published in time for Christmas, 1945. The Wizard was S. Louis Giraud (1879–1950), originator, part author, paper engineer and publisher of the Bookano series which provides the first notable landmark in the publishing history of British movable books in the post-war period.

Giraud's genius did not lie in his feeling for verse. When The Wizard introduced what should have been *Bookano Stories No. 13* in 1946, he wrote:

> So let me try to ease the minds of those, the superstitious
> (Though, truth to tell, 'tis merely that I feel a bit capricious),

By leaving out the number and adopting 'pot-pourri'
As the 'mark' by which to recognise this latest book by me.

This 'pot-pourri' edition did, however, reflect his true strength, his resourcefulness as an entrepreneur, for Giraud included in it 'stockpiled' pop-up models which had been surplus to earlier issues – so that the four or five pop-ups found in one copy of the pot-pourri edition might be different from those in another. Giraud printed a list of eleven 'possibles' in the Contents, but even then added an 'etc.' to cover afterthoughts. The wartime spirit of 'make-do-and-mend' is evident in his strategy.

Giraud was descended from a refugee Huguenot minister. His branch of the family had settled in East Anglia, and by 1900 Louis Giraud was apprenticed to a general printer and compositor in his home town of Lowestoft. By the late 1920s, he was employed by Beaverbrook's *Daily Express*, with responsibility for producing books which were, in effect, spin-offs from the paper itself, such as the *Daily Express Song Book* and storybooks for younger readers.

Giraud's duties included the consideration of proposals offered to the paper by members of the public. In the late 1920s, a Mr Theodore Brown brought in a 'folded paper contraption'[2] whose potential excited Giraud so keenly that Brown's device was patented in both their names in February, 1929. The terms of the patent state, with nice precision: 'This invention relates to the use of a book . . . as a means for unfolding or expanding collapsible toys or models . . . that are fixed to the pages in such a manner that on opening out the said book . . . the said toys or models . . . are caused to be erected to an upstanding position.' One of the early uses of the invention was in the first five *Daily Express Annuals*, where the patent number is printed alongside the three-dimensional models. Rupert Bear (created by Mary Tourtel in 1920, and further popularised by Alfred Bestall from 1925 to 1965) features twice in the earliest issues in the series in 1929 and 1930. The need for the pop-up model to straddle the centre-fold generates a sharply creased smile more befitting the face of the tiger than the Nutwood bear, and several extra supports are needed to keep Rupert upright.[3] Nevertheless, young readers at the time must have been delighted to open the page – no doubt again and again – to find their hero rising magically to life before their eyes.

In their parents' childhood, the charming illustrations in Nister's books typically 'dissolved' into each other by means of tab-operated revolving discs set between pages, or appeared in layered tableaux lifted up by the reader. The characters in the books of the brilliantly inventive Lothar Meggendorfer (1847–1925) were portrayed in two dimensions, depending upon minute levers, coils and pivots for their startlingly lifelike movements. His elaborate and extensive three-dimensional tableaux, such as *The Doll's House* (1890) and *The International Circus*, have to be erected by the viewer, lifting and fixing flaps into place to provide support.

The most important features of Giraud's innovation, based upon Brown's

'contraption', are that the models in the early *Express* annuals and the subsequent Bookano series spring upwards, powered by the action of opening
the page; as the models stand at the centre of the double page and are painted
on both sides, they may be viewed 'in the round'. A dolls' tea-party, for
example, invites readers to rotate the book if they wish to see the faces – and
the backs – of all the guests seated round the table.

By 1934, Giraud had left the *Express* and established himself at 269
Ballards Lane, North Finchley, in order to publish pop-up books in his own
right as Strand Publications. Theodore Brown, his original collaborator, died
shortly after and appears to have played no part in the series of Bookano
books (the name echoes the trade name 'Meccano', the famous and much-
loved construction kits first produced in 1908). At first, stabling to the rear
at Ballards Lane accommodated Giraud's business, but before long it proved
necessary for the firm to take over the house while the family moved nearby.
Over the sixteen-year life of the series, the models became more sturdy and
sophisticated. The later Bookano books employed other writers and artists,
though Giraud, by all accounts a private, even secretive man, retained close
control of the paper engineering and the production lines. The individual
models were assembled to Giraud's designs by outworkers, and then collected
– in a small yellow van surmounted by a model of a Bookano book – and
returned to Ballards Lane for insertion into the books. There, when this stage
of production arrived, Giraud employed an assembly line of women to paste
the models down into the pages. Even when producing *The Daily Express
Annual*, Giraud had needed to bring in 50 women to put together the finished
volumes.

This glueing process required concentration and precision. Some of the
pop-ups are of the 'proscenium arch' variety, which provides a firm structure
for the model: a distant prospect of a castle seen through framing trees, for
example, with a cellophane lake in the foreground; or a splendid free-standing
dragon glowering down upon St George astride his charger, caparisoned in
brilliant red. Sometimes, there are small movements within a model as it
comes up off the pages: a Tyrolean cellist opens his mouth in lusty melody,
('He'll soon be moved to burst forth into song', declares an accompanying
verse); Giant Twoshoes' eyes roll as he sits up and gives a gap-toothed grin
to the nervous ranks of the mayor and corporation at his boots (both in the
Pot-Pourri edition). One hundred and fifty models were used over the years
in the series, and in one of the few which show how something actually
works, the roadway of Tower Bridge is raised and lowered. Physically, apart
from the pop-ups themselves, the books were unremarkable; Michael Dawson
notes the 'coarse, absorbent paper, crude photolitho printing and colour reproduction; cheap covers and bindings which (sadly) have rarely endured the
ravages of time unscathed',[4] though they are now much prized by collectors.

The intended readers of the Bookano series seem to have been between five
and ten years of age. The stories are often much concerned with fairies, elves,
goblins, princes and princesses, balanced by rather stronger informative pieces

on such matters as the ballet, the circus, the pantomime or the Tower of London, along with retellings of the plots of Gilbert and Sullivan operas and Shakespeare's plays. The style and subject matter are for the most part trapped in the middle-class conventions of the time, and lack energy. They contain not even a whiff of the rascality which marked comics and annuals of the time such as *The Beano* (first edition 1938) or *The Knockout* (1939–63). Here, we are closer to *Tiny Tots* (1927–59) or even Arthur Mee's *The Children's Newspaper* (1919–65). 'The Valley of Joy and Beauty', for example, begins:

> Cosily tucked up in their little beds in the night nursery, Angelina and Geoffrey were busily watching the reflections made by the flames of the fire and indulging in their favourite game of 'Magic Carpet'

and ends,

> What a lot they had to tell their parents that morning!

Here and there, however, are stories (perhaps by one of Giraud's hired contributors) which are charged with some humour, naive though it would seem to a child today. When the citizens of Puttemup Town are troubled by Gangster Mice, they are saved by Giant Twoshoes, 'a distant relation of Goody Twoshoes', who strides into town to meet the Mayor and Corporation:

> ... here the Giant had been trying to smother a sneeze (as he had a slight cold) and had to let it rip! Hats were blown in all directions, and I regret to say the Mayor's robe, and some other garments, were ripped off by the blast. In fact, when the sneeze abated, several of the assembled company were embarrassed to find themselves standing in their 'undies'.

Remarkably, the series kept going throughout the war and did not end until Giraud died in 1950. His daughter and other members of the firm attempted to continue publication, but their *Bookano Stories No. 17* (Christmas, 1950) failed to match the success of Giraud's issues and shortly afterwards the firm went bankrupt.

From such records as remain, Dawson infers that the books were produced in print runs of around ten to fifteen thousand. The books were promoted most vigorously in the London area, selling through multiple stores such as Selfridges and Harrods rather than through bookshops, which at this time might well not have had sections specifically for children; others were sold on market stalls around the city. Publishing details within the books include references to patents held in France, Germany, the United States and Canada, but this seems to have reflected Giraud's attempts to preclude imitation rather than his ambition to sell in these countries; in fact, the patent afforded him insufficient protection, for in the 1930s it seems probable that the American, Harold Lentz, closely imitated the Bookano technique in devising the pop-up models in his *Blue Ribbon* series, published in the 1930s in New York.

Bookano had few rivals in post-war Britain. Dean's, who claimed in the nineteenth century to be the 'originators of children's movable books', and Raphael Tuck, a firm of German origins in the 1880s but now based in Britain and North America, continued to publish a number of more modest movable books, with fairy tales and biblical scenes as perennial subjects. The glamour of all things American had a ready appeal for children who had grown up in wartime Britain. In 1951, Publicity Products Ltd, an imprint of Purnell & Sons, was reprinting books first published in New York with titles such as *Cowboys in Pop-Up Action Pictures* ('Here come the boys. Yipee – it's time for chuck! Chuck is cowboy lingo for food.'); and *How We Travel*, in which British children were offered pop-up models of streamlined trains, cars with huge tailfins and transcontinental buses which they would never see on their side of the Atlantic.

The influence of the American film industry was evident in Tuck's *Annie Get Your Gun. Seen through the eyes of a child* (1950), based on the MGM musical. Walt Disney was the inspiration for Dean's *The Cinderella Magic Wand Book* (c.1950); five of the illustrations, culled from the movie, require the use of 'magic' 3D spectacles, much like those issued at the time to excited cinemagoers. All eventualities are covered: 'Should you lose your spectacles, you can obtain another pair by sending 4d in stamps to Stephenson Bros., Ltd., Bradford.' An advertisement inside the rear cover extols the Stephenson range of furniture cream, perfumed wax polish and non-smear floor polish. Tuck's *Cinderella* (c.1953) was a 'scenic panorama book', with more than 40 slot-in stand-up characters: 'the second scene is a Grand Transformation Scene, which you will especially enjoy making up. As you will see, it has two sets of models, one for before the Transformation takes place, the other for after.'

Television, only just reaching out to the provinces in the early 1950s, shaped *Little Bo-Peep's Television Book of Nursery Rhymes* (c.1950). As the reader slowly turns a wheel, flickering forms of nursery rhyme figures are glimpsed through a cut-out black and white television screen on the front cover, in an effect reminiscent of silent movies. Brock's 1956 'Little Panorama Books' (15cm x 12cm) took the reader on a promenade through aspects of French rural life (*The Village, The Market, The Station, The Farm, The Seaside, The Mountains*). A pull-out opens, flap by flap, to 120 cm, showing a panorama of a French scene, accompanied by rather contrived stories by the novelist and playwright, Antonia Ridge. In *The Village*, a four-leafed clover allows everyone to have a wish granted that day: so, for example, Grandfather is able to sit fishing all day yet still have his vegetable plot dug and his cabbages magically planted – thus avoiding Grandmother's wrath when he gets home. We are urged to pick out details from the panorama: 'But quick: look at Madame Dubois and Madame Labise, kneeling on the river bank, doing their washing'; 'Hallo, what is happening over there, across the street?' The voice could have been borrowed from Norman Ellison's 1940s *Wandering with Nomad* on BBC Children's Hour ('Look at those birds over there, Nomad! They're black on top and white underneath.')

The only movable parts in Tuck's *Animated Little Red Riding Hood* (1949) are on the inside covers and depend upon a hand-moved tab, enabling Red Riding Hood to wave goodbye to her mother (one of the less excitingly visual moments of the narrative); whilst on the rear cover the wolf, in Granny's nightcap, opens and closes his jaws and eyes as Red Riding Hood nods her head with studied ambivalence. The book is one of a series of fairy tales which are noteworthy in that the publishing information records that they are engineered by the Duenewald Printing Corporation of New York, 'sole agents for Wehr Animations'. Tuck presumably bought the books from Duenewald who, in turn, had employed the paper engineer Julian Wehr, a European immigrant to America, to devise the moving parts of the book. In effect, this process was an uncomplicated precursor of what was to become a general and profitable practice from the 1970s onwards in the production of movable books: a 'packager' prepares the book before selling it on to a publisher, often in a different country, in fully-made format.

Collins's *Red Riding Hood* from the same period includes two discs enabling one picture to dissolve into another. There is little to excite the reader here beyond the interest of the device itself; the book lacks the wit which, eighty years earlier, Ernest Nister had shown in *Merry Surprises* (1897) where the reader turns the disc for diminutive figures to appear from nowhere and leap onto the backs of galloping horses. None of the work from the immediate post-war period shows a vestige of the comic energy which marked the work of Lothar Meggendorfer.

However, the spirit of Nister and Meggendorfer was about to be reawakened in Britain by an artist and an entrepreneur whose roots lay in Czechoslovakia. The artist was Vojtech Kubasta, whose influence is increasingly recognised in triggering the explosion of high-quality pop-up books in the 1970s. The entrepreneur was Leopold Schliesser, a Jewish banker from Prague, who had fled to London in 1938.

Vojtech Kubasta and Bancroft & Co

The introduction of Kubasta's work to the West was fortuitous in the extreme. He was 'discovered' by Schliesser, who had become the owner of Bancroft & Co., a London firm trading in fancy goods. In Prague in the 1950s, looking for cheap products for his firm, Schliesser had contacted Artia, the state-owned import/export business founded by the regime to trade with non-communist countries. Through Artia, Schliesser saw some card-backed versions of traditional tales designed by Kubasta, comprising pages with models which sprang off the page through a system of cut outs and folds. The pictures and words are printed parallel to the spine, so the book is read 'on its side'. As upper pages are lifted into a 90-degree position, they become backdrops to multi-layered pop-up scenes which have been pulled up into the vertical by the movement of the page. The models become both the scenery and the players standing in front of the backdrop, with the words set out just in front of the reader, 'downstage' – virtually as subtitles to the pictures. Schliesser arranged through Artia to translate and import Kubasta's work, to be published in the United Kingdom by Bancroft.

Kubasta's technique involved cutting shapes out of a single sheet and folding the paper against itself (in a kind of concertina fashion) to enable the models to stand as the book is opened; the technique is usually known as 'fan-folding'. Many of Kubasta's pop-ups incorporate a pull-tab whose manipulation may well induce a reader's smile. In the card-backed format of Kubasta's traditional tales, the same tab sometimes operates actions on both the cover and in the first opening. We make Jack jump up and down with excitement on the front cover as a tab is pulled, whilst the same operation causes the Giant's mouth and eyes to open and close on the reverse side (*Jack and the Beanstalk, c.* 1960). In the castle kitchens, a diversely talented cook picks out a tune on a lyre to prompt the hen to lay the golden eggs which, with the reader's help, she repeatedly does. The mirror, mirror on the wall (*Snow White, c.* 1960) switches from the step-mother's frown to Snow White's smile. In *Hop-o-my-Thumb* (*c.*1960), the woodcutter's three sons arrive at a castle. 'There, an old woman let them in, while her three daughters watched them from the windows.' As the tab is worked, one girl opens a window and looks out confidently enough, while two others peep out more quizzically – and the moon, which forms part of the pull-tab, comes out to see what's going on. The effect is conjured up partly by the bold caricatures of the girls, with their large noses and popping eyes, and partly by the slow movement of the windows revealing, little by little, their comically curious expressions. One tab is the end of the handle of a wooden shovel, a good 25 cm long, normally used for sliding the unbaked loaf into the oven; now we use it to propel the witch swiftly into the flames on Gretel's behalf (an operation likely to be of irresistible and frequent appeal to a young reader).

In such effects, the reader advances the story by the movement. In *Table, Lay Yourself* (1960), both hands are needed to make the free-floating club whack the wicked innkeeper of 'The Old Honest One' soundly on his bottom ('Out of the sack, Club!'). In *Tip and Top Go Camping* (*c.* 1961), one of a series about these two adventurous characters, 'Top was very excited: "I'm climbing this tree to get a better look," he said. And up he climbed.' And so he does, with whatever alacrity we choose.

Bancroft also published a series of a dozen tiny pop-up counting books for young children by Kubasta, and a set of single models (a Noah's Ark and a galleon, for example – subjects which have been copied as single models in the 1990s). These tableaux, and the fairy tales, are now particularly valued by collectors, although when Kubasta's books were first sold in the 1960s under the imprint of 'Bancroft and Co. (Publishers) Ltd/Westminster Books', they were very cheap, priced at 1/6d (about 7.5 pence), selling largely in penny bazaars and on market stalls. Michael Dawson found copies of the books in Collett's Bookshop in London's Charing Cross Road (one of the few booksellers to market Eastern European literature); in them, Kubasta's name is barely visible, merely a subdued signature somewhere within the cover illustration.

In the 1970s and 1980s, the tales were reissued in hard laminated covers first by Murrays Sales and Service Co. of London, and subsequently by Brown Watson (Leicester) Ltd, though the books were still printed in Czechoslovakia by Artia. Although the hard covers could no longer incorporate moving parts, some extra illustrations by Kubasta, along with two more pop-ups, have been included in several of the stories. The colours have been slightly altered in a number of illustrations – a palace courtyard is transformed from a purple wash to yellow paving stones. If anything, however, the colour is cruder and less intense in the later editions, and the line less precise than in the Bancroft versions. Some attempt has been made to appeal to a modern audience: the Brown Watson series is heralded as 'An All Action Treasure Hour Pop-Up Book'. By 1988, *Jack and the Beanstalk* has been given a new cover by Pamela Storey in which young Jack seems far more of a fashion victim from Disneyworld than he did in Kubasta's original rural weeds.

Kubasta himself worked on through to his death in 1992, by which time he had created some seventy pop-up titles. Unlike most subsequent illustrators of pop-up books, Kubasta was responsible for the book's origination, illustration and paper engineering. Some of his work published in the 1980s suggests an increasing inventiveness. *The Magic of the Circus* (illustrations copyrighted by Kubasta in 1976, and by Artia in 1982) contains a series of sleights-of-hand; a kitten conjuror makes flowers jump out of a basket, butterflies dance about a pig's face, a troupe of frogs nervously performs a balancing act. Finally, Kubasta invites his readers to join in the fun with a spot of legerdemain themselves: 'Push the butterfly on "10" down and you will be able to see 10 young hares, push it up again quickly and then there will be only nine.' Other books reveal working steam trains and drumming drummers. Sometimes the models include elements floating free of the page on paper supports: two dwarves sit swinging on a set of scales in the baskets they've been using to collect apples, and animals take a ride in a fairground swing-boat.

Artia eventually produced thirty million copies of Kubasta's pop-ups, translated into seventy or more foreign languages, including Chinese and Japanese. It is difficult to estimate an individual print run of a Kubasta book – the plates were simply kept and the stock renewed as required. The pages could be stamped and die cut, then strung at the spine relatively simply; there was very little use of glue, so they did not require the intensive labour forces used for the Bookano books and, on a much larger scale, for the movable books of the 1970s and after. In the 1960s, it was rare for an author working behind the Iron Curtain to be published in Western Europe; the fortunate visit by Schliesser in the 1950s, looking for something else, enabled Kubasta's work to be available (if not critically recognized), not only in Western Europe, but also in the United States.

Kubasta's work moved pop-up books available in Britain forward in terms of engineering (though Kubasta was not the only one to use cut-and-contrafold in this way). In addition, in contrast to the largely static images of the Bookano books, the pictures in Kubasta's tales require more active mental and physical engagement of the reader. The movement of the pop-ups serves to advance the narrative, to draw readers into that process – and often to make them smile at the ingenuity and wit involved.

Kubasta's achievements are all the more remarkable given the limited nature of the resources available in an Eastern Bloc country, though Czechoslovakia provided a cultural context rich in its use of animated figures and cartoon, as films of the period demonstrate. The sense that Kubasta was working within a tradition is confirmed, in other pop-up works by artists of Czech origin published by Bancroft in the 1960s, such as the nine books of the *Animalia* series (produced in the 1960s), with illustrations by Rudolf Lukes. The words are by George Theiner, a Czech émigré living in Cheltenham. His familiarity with the English language is evident – to an extent – in *A Visit to Animalia* (1963):

> As we are about to leave, a lovely Toucan flies up to the King, asking whether he might not be allowed to come with us.
> 'Toucan, one can't,' decided King Leo the First. 'You must find another bird to go with you.'
> And so we can go home accompanied by Kenny the Kangaroo, the Toucan, and a Hornbill, who will prove most useful, as he can sound his horn to clear the way for us.

There is a definite, if ironic, link with Kubasta's books of the 1960s and the next major landmark in the development of movable books in Britain. Like Giraud and Schliesser in their times, an individual entrepreneur provided an extraordinary impetus to what was about to become a highly profitable sector of publishing for children.

Wally Hunt and Intervisual Communications

Waldo ('Wally') Hunt was a Los Angeles advertising man based in New York. On a visit to London in the 1960s he saw Kubasta's books and was at once enthusiastic about the possibility of selling them in the States. He contacted Bancroft and inquired about the feasibility of obtaining a quarter of a million copies of each of four titles. Not surprisingly, Bancroft sent their editorial and productions director, Michael Thomas, to Prague in person. The story goes – and it may have grown in the telling – that Artia, the agents, were responsive, but they pointed out that such a massive rise in production would require the agreement of those who ran the printing works. Out of the question. The factory turned Thomas down flat. An order of that size could not be met, the managers insisted, since it had not been written-in to the firm's Five Year Development Plan.

Hunt's disappointment seems to have been matched by his determination; his subsequent perseverance was a major factor in the growth in quality and numbers of movable books in the West. Hunt decided that rather than publishing the books – for which he was not equipped – he would co-ordinate authors, illustrators, designers, paper engineers, printers and those who physically assembled the books. This 'package' he would then sell to a publisher (or to make the operation viable, to several publishers in different countries simultaneously). Since the number of copies to be sold would be agreed before production, all the financial risks and the hazards of marketing would rest with the publisher. The scheme shrewdly took out of publishers' hands the problems which deterred them from entering the specialist movable book market – the lack of expertise needed to design and manufacture a book from start to finish. The involvement of a 'packager' has become almost standard practice in the production of movable books.

Hunt began in the mid-sixties by working with Random House. Among the initial batch of six titles produced by his newly founded Graphics International was *Bennett Cerf's Pop-Up Riddles* (1965), which was successful enough to provide the operation with a secure platform. Much like Bancroft and Raphael Tuck, he also marketed three-dimensional greetings cards and table decorations, physically producing these, and the books, in Japan. In the next few years, the company did well with such classics as *20,000 Leagues Under the Sea* (1969) and *The Wizard of Oz* (1968), a title which has appeared in at least eleven different pop-up versions. From the outset, Hunt was able to sell his packages to several publishers in different countries. In Britain, Hunt's early titles were sold by R.H.S. Publications, owned by Roger Schlesinger, who had formerly worked for Bancroft. As yet, the mainstream general book publishers remained largely uninterested in the movable books market.

Hunt's developing team at Graphics International was, after some years, merged with Hallmark Cards (yet again, producers of fancy goods). In 1975, Hunt's contract with Hallmark finished, and he returned to his native California to form Intervisual Communications. This firm has now become Intervisual Books Incorporated, and though the field is large enough to allow other packaging firms to have prospered, Hunt's business remains very much the market leader, perhaps half of the output of pop-up books worldwide passing through their hands. Their success is due no doubt not only to Hunt's business acumen; he is a passionate enthusiast and collector in the field himself. It is not surprising that in 1979 Intervisual produced facsimiles of some of Ernest Nister's books for Collins and a collection of Lothar Meggendorfer's illustrations, prefaced by a brief essay by Hunt which pays homage to the artist, alongside an appreciation by Maurice Sendak.

The number of full-time staff members at Intervisual is not large, and most are employed in administrative or marketing roles. The artistically creative side of the work, including the paper engineering, is usually carried out on a contract basis. Paper engineering is an art form in itself, and the names of these craftspeople now always appear in the publishing information within a book, if not on the front cover itself. Some of the paper engineers who have worked for Intervisual are British, such as Ron van der Meer and Keith Moseley, who also regularly work with British based packagers such as Sadie Fields, which has its own publishing outlet, Tango Books.

Among the paper engineers frequently employed by Hunt is Tor Lokvig, who worked on one of the books commonly cited as the text which persuaded major British publishers they could not afford to stay out of the pop-up trade, Jan Pienkowski's *Haunted House* (1979), winner of the Kate Greenaway Medal, the most prestigious award for illustrated books in the United Kingdom (see Chapter 3). Pienkowski's publisher, Judith Elliott, then at Heinemann, had been quick to note the brilliant success of Robert Crowther's *The Most Amazing Hide and Seek Alphabet Book* (Kestrel, 1977). It could well be argued that *this* was the breakthrough movable book in the British market, in terms of both its originality and the daring scale of its production. The book at first glance seems simply to offer an alphabet, printed in black, two or three letters to each landscape page (31cm × 23cm). But as tabs are pulled and flaps are lifted, animals peep out, waving a trunk or wiggling a tail or stretching a neck.

Crowther sent the proposal for the book, unsolicited, to Patrick Hardy, the distinguished children's book editor at Kestrel. In a humorously anguished saga relating the book's production, Hardy reveals that, having decided to do the book, his first impulse was to print 15,000, but the expense involved made that size of run impractical.[5] Eventually, Hardy found the courage and confidence to go for an initial print run of 40,000 for Kestrel and 30,000 for its American sister company, Viking. Kestrel had discovered, through contact with Hunt and Intervisual, that assembly lines in Colombia could be used to produce the book economically. In these early days of the packaging process, communications with Columbia were intermittent. Copies arrived unannounced in unscheduled batches and at times no one knew whether shipments were in Hamburg, Paris, on the high seas or still in South America. In the event, 40,000 proved to be far too few, and within two years Kestrel had (in two reprints) sold a further 145,000 copies and the book was rarely off the children's best seller list, which it had topped soon after publication. Crowther's book remains, with its several successors such as *The Most Amazing Night Book* (1995) and *Robert Crowther's Pop-Up Olympics* (1996), in demand to the present day.

Pienkowski had little knowledge of pop-up books, but when invited by Judith Elliott to devise one, he thought, 'well, I did do a bit of paper cutting when I was a child – it's a very strong Polish tradition, so why not?'[6] With his assistant, Jane Walmsley, he bought half-a-dozen mechanical books and took them to bits to see how they worked.

Pienkowski and Elliott noted that most of these books had been processed by Hunt's Intervisual Communications Incorporated and so they turned to Hunt to prepare their new book. By 1995, the Pienkowski–Hunt combination had produced more than a dozen movable books and generated sales of some seven million copies, one million of them being for *Haunted House* alone.[7] No doubt such sales yield a very satisfactory return, but an artist's royalties may not correspond to the 7 to 10 per cent which a novelist normally earns. The originator of the book – the artist – must decide whether she or he wants a contract with the packager or the publisher. Suppose the contract is with the packager: according to the American Robert Sabuda, who is both an illustrator and a paper engineer,

> If you are the author/illustrator (or maybe a paper engineer) for a pop up book that retails for $20.00, you do not get $2.00 (the customary 10% paid to an author). A $20.00 book has been marked up by the publisher 75%–80% from the base price which in this case makes the base price about $4.50. If the royalty is 10% you get 45 cents for each book.[8]

However, where the hardback print run of a novel might be 3000 or so, the print run for a quality pop-up, as opposed to a 'pot-boiling' fairy tale or counting book, could be as high as 100000 copies (probably in several languages with several publishers). Since the publisher buys the whole of a print run from a packager, the author–illustrator contracted to a packager has a guaranteed, and speedy, return.

The packager oversees a number of processes: the editor, the art director, the paper engineer, and the production co-ordinator all work on the book before it is sent to the factory where the book is assembled; at this stage a minimal number of further physical changes might still need to be made. If artists wish to retain a greater involvement in the book as it goes through different production stages, they might prefer to make their contracts with a publisher, although even then control can hardly be closely exercised. In such cases, an author–illustrator's royalty is presumably calculated on the receipts of sales in the normal way.

The assembly of the book may be an aspect of production to trouble the consciences of purchasers in the affluent countries where the majority of pop-up books are sold. Jan Pienkowski's *Haunted House* and *Robot* (1981), for example, were put together by women working in the village of Papayan, near Cali, in Colombia. By the late 1970s, the majority of the finest pop-up books were assembled there; other centres have now been developed in Singapore, Hong Kong, Thailand, Ecuador, Mexico, China and Tunisia. South America may seem a long way from North Finchley and Giraud's assembly line at 269 Ballards Lane, but we do not know what Giraud paid his workers during the depression and the war years. These complex books require cheap intensive labour if they are to be produced at a cost which makes them acceptable to the current market.

In the late 1970s and early 1980s, Pienkowski twice visited the factory where his books were made:

> I was very impressed. All the work is done by girls, and conditions are no worse than they'd be in an English printing works. In some ways they're even better. They don't get paid very much, which is why we can afford to do these books at all, but on the other hand it's very warm, there's a constant pleasant temperature and

daylight, food is plentiful and not expensive, it's a very attractive place and the girls seem to enjoy their work.

When I went to Papayan for *Haunted House*, there were about 200 or more girls working there. This year when I went back for *Robot* there were nearly 500. They have had an absolute explosion. These books have brought wealth and prestige to Papayan – it's the only industry there. That's very pleasing.

The production line was supervised by Inés Calvache whose skills deeply impressed Pienkowski:

She's Miss Fixit on the production line and she translates my work and the engineer's work into reality. She's extremely experienced, and trained as a jeweller – so she's got the skill in her hands (all the girls seem to have very delicate hands and fingers which is why I think they're so good at doing these books) and Inés figures out ways of putting these things together, of getting the bugs out.[9]

The Chinese Mainland women employed by Hong Kong packagers reportedly have banished men from their assembly lines as being too clumsy. The fact is that in this sector of children's book publishing, a majority of the artists, entrepreneurs and paper engineers have been men (with notable exceptions, such as the illustrator and paper engineer Claire Littlejohn); apart from editorial roles, women have performed the more menial tasks on the assembly lines.

From 1980 to the mid-1990s

In the 1970s, Dean's – the longest established publisher in the movables field, had concentrated on a very young audience with perennial themes such as circuses and fairy tales, or titles such as *My Baby Jesus Book* (1972) and *A Little One's Prayers Pop-up Book*. Five different titles drew on Mabel Lucie Attwell's illustrations and they twice visited The Magic Roundabout (the popular French television programme which was first broadcast in England in the 1960s), with an ABC and a storybook. These books usually involved four straightforward models alternating with pages of text and evidently were sufficiently successful for many of them to be reprinted in the 1980s, sometimes in larger 'De Luxe Editions'.

In the early 1980s, Dean's were bought by the Paul Hamlyn group, which continued to use the name as an imprint. It may well be that they hoped to re-establish themselves with titles such as their 1984 feature on the Royals, *The Royal Family Pop-Up Book*: 'Call it a souvenir or a memento, here is a fascinating record of one of the most exciting periods in the lives of the Royal Family' declares the back cover. Dean's recruited a former editor of Debrett's Peerage to write the words, as they had in 1953 for their pop-up celebration of the Coronation. A 'distinguished portrait artist' was also enlisted, but to little avail. A pop-up Mark Phillips woodenly thrusts a drink towards Princess Anne watched (with a grimace) by Her Majesty, sausage and tongs in hand, presiding over a Balmoral barbecue with Prince Philip. At the pull of a tab, on the balcony of the Palace on their wedding day, Di and Charles delicately kiss – and part. A kangaroo erupts out of a bush in front of a popping-up Ayers Rock as the honeymooning pair speed smilingly by in their four-wheel-drive. Even the technical skills of one of the leading paper engineers, Vic Duppa-Whyte, could do little to redeem a text of this feebleness.

For the most part, however, in the 1980s and 1990s, the range of pop-up and movable books expanded rapidly, though not always with much originality. Series of fairy tales remain popular, but have not yet been treated with the subtlety and power of retelling provided, for example, by Anthony Browne, Susan Jeffers or Errol le Cain in flat book format. A 1991 *Little Red Riding Hood*, packaged by Intervisual and published in the United Kingdom by Child's Play International, is so stunning in its ineptitude that one suspects the book may chiefly be marketed either to provoke adult merriment or in the commercial conviction that all pop-ups have a guaranteeable sale. The movable elements are simply two talking pop-up heads on each page; the reader is expected to pull the tab and mouth the script. This 'Chatter Book' series assures its readers that,

> You can change the words. These characters know just what you want them to say. By the way, the real name of one of them is the same as yours. And the others can have the names of other actors or people you know.

Even if six-year-olds can make sense of that, they may still balk a little at the closing exchange between Red Riding Hood and her pipe-puffing rescuer:

> WOODSMAN: It was lucky I was passing. Otherwise, the wolf would have just got his dessert, instead of his just deserts.
> RED: I have learned once and for all not to talk to strangers. Thank you for saving Grandma and me.
> WOODSMAN: Think nothing of it, my dear. Perhaps I could come and share your delicious health food lunch.
> RED: I am sorry, Sir, but you are a stranger, too. And you should give up smoking. It is bad for you.
> THE   END

Most of the favourites of young children, old and new, have been transformed into pop-up formats: Alice, Peter Rabbit, Peter Pan, Pooh, Bambi, Orlando the Marmalade Cat, Thomas the Tank Engine and Paddington Bear. Not all are well-served by the form. Alice cannot readily shrink into the confines of the few pages of a pop-up book. Even Babette Cole's lively illustrations to *The Wind in the Willows* (1983) do not clarify what must be a confusing experience for a young reader unfamiliar with the full text. All that can be offered are brief unconnected episodes from the original – edited highlights, as it were – mostly involving exploits such as Toad shinning down knotted bedsheets (with the help of the reader) to escape from Toad Hall and his exasperated friends. There is a particularly effective model where one steam engine, carrying the pursuing policemen, enters a wood just as the desperate Toad (in another engine) comes out the other side. In fact, the paper engineering in this book is particularly good – Intervisual employed the designer

Dick Dudley and the well-known paper engineers James Roger Diaz and Keith Moseley; but within the constraints of its length, the book cannot be much more than a coffee table curiosity.

Other recent movable versions of classic texts include titles such as Belloc's *The Bad Child's Pop-Up Book of Beasts* (1987) and Stevenson's *A Child's Garden of Verses* (1987) in which, somewhat unusually, the illustrator Claire Littlejohn is also the paper engineer of the four pop-ups. Some American comic book heroes lend themselves well to the form. Peter Parker opens a door, nips through and comes out the other side as Spiderman in time to save Mary Jane from The Green Goblin. In *Stan Lee Presents the Incredible Hulk Pop-Up Book* (1980), 'As a building blazes, the mighty Man-Monster bounds high into the air to save a frightened, falling woman' – and at the tug of a tab the bulging green form soars upwards to catch a shapely brunette in mid-air.

Father Christmas is, not surprisingly, another popular figure. Clement Moore's 1823 classic poem, 'The Night before Christmas' was produced in ten different versions in the 1980s alone. Descendants of Pienkowski's *Haunted House* are also numerous, including Stephen Wylie's *Ghost Train* (1992) – 'With Six Spooky Holograms' – where the reader tilts the book this way and that to 'come haunting with the gruesome ghostly trio as they appear out of nowhere to scare you!'

Among much rather repetitious and banal work, however, there have been several areas of exciting innovation. Other artists whose work is highly praised in flat books have been attracted to the field. Raymond Briggs's *The Snowman Pop-Up Book* (1986), which included a musical device playing the theme tune from the filmed version, 'Walking in the Air', is not simply a reworking of the original story. Much of the book is taken up by the boy travelling and partying with the Snowman and his friends. The Snowman, with the boy clinging to the pillion, hurtles through the night on a motorbike, startling owls, pheasants, foxes and rabbits as he goes – one rabbit is caught forever suspended in the headlight beam. Briggs's *Fungus the Bogeyman Plop-Up Book* (1982) – 'This book really stinks' – also extends the original text. 'NOW! For the first time in Human History is revealed to YOU, personally, in breathtaking STEREO-BOGIC THREE DIMENSIONS the true-life interior of a Bogey Bedchamber'; or 'Fungus inspects his trousers which have been marinading overnight', as he pulls them, dripping green slime, out of the domestic water tank.

Michael Foreman, Arnold Lobel, Taomi de Paola and Edward Gorey have also created pop-up books; Gorey's *The Dwindling Party* (1982) fuses form and content as an Edwardian family visits the grounds of a stately home, Hickyacket Hall, and are plucked, one by one, into the undergrowth (unnoticed by the survivors) by monsters who emerge as we pull the tab.

Two of the most striking movable books of the 1990s, *Noah's Ark* (1994) and *The Creation* (1995), have been originated by Brian Wildsmith – for more than thirty-five years, one of the leading British illustrators for children. The models recall the pioneering work of Giraud's Bookano stories, for they too are to be viewed 'in the round' as they rise up from the centre of the page – though to consider these works of Wildsmith and Giraud side by side is to recognize the huge advances in technical skills, in artwork and in the quality of the paper used. In *The Creation*, a great multi-coloured fish skims above an ocean in which a whale surfaces and spouts and dives again. God – who is at once male, female, black, white, coloured and oriental – soars in cruciform above the universe, holding Planet Earth aloft. There are tabs and dissolving discs, while hidden beneath flaps lies a text which echoes 'Genesis' itself.

Wildsmith 'interrogated himself' about the process of working on *The Creation* for *Books for Keeps*:

> Once an image is firmly in my mind I make a rough model. This is then sent to Intervisual Books in Santa Monica, California. They have wonderful talented paper engineers there who work out how to make the image fold. Each shape is dissected into its separate pieces and then sent to me to paint. . . . There are 175 glue points in the final assembly, with over 100 different cut-outs to be glued into place.[10]

He describes how his wishes have sometimes to be tempered by what the paper engineers decide can be managed; in the Garden of Eden a tree had to be moved from the centre of a double page spread to the right hand page; or, 'I'd have liked the woodpecker to be able to tap the tree trunk, but for the mechanics to do this would have involved more cost'.

The work of Pienkowski, Wildsmith and Briggs has so far largely consisted of fine set-piece tableaux. There are, however, other authors and illustrators interested in developing narratives. *Dinner with Fox*, first published in 1990, provides an example, with text by Stephen Wyllie, pictures by Korky Paul, and paper engineering by Claire Littlejohn. This is very much a British publication, since the packager is Sadie Fields of London and the 1995 edition is published under Fields' own Tango imprint.

Much of Paul's work in the 1980s treated such traditional pop-up subjects as nursery rhymes and counting books, but here an original narrative is developed in which the movement of the models plays an integral part. The illustrations have the razor edge of a Steadman or a Scarfe in this chronicle of the devious tricks of Thin Red Fox who cunningly invites White Hen, Brown Hare and Pink Pig, in sequence, to join him for dinner – as his main course. All goes well until, now Plump Red Fox, he ends up in his own oven, outwitted by Huge Grey Wolf. There are doors to open, other people's tiny letters to fish out of mail-boxes to read, cupboards and cooking pots to peer into. Both Hans de Beer's *Ahoy There, Little Polar Bear* (1995) and Mick Inkpen's *Where, Oh Where, is Kipper's Bear?* (1994) require the assistance of their young readers to drive the stories along. De Beer's Lars, the diminutive polar bear, slides off an ice floe and is caught up in a trawl net: 'the net was emptied and Lars fell down into a pile of fish, landing so hard he fainted.' With the help of a highly ingenious mechanism involving a winding thread, Lars spins downwards head over heels to land among the fish. (Children will probably enjoy his return ascent even more, since Lars spins over and over at even greater speed as the mechanism is rewound.) In Inkpen's book, the reader must repeatedly help the doleful canine Kipper in his search for his lost teddy bear by pulling tabs, lifting flaps and so on before the search is resolved. In these three books, the pictures sometimes confirm the narrative and sometimes extend it, much like the flat-picture books most admired by critics of children's literature in the 1990s.

A further development has been the increasing quality of the instructional use of pop-up material in information books. Perhaps the first notable, even disconcerting, use of the form was *The Human Body* (1983: text by Jonathan Miller, designed by David Pelham). A skinless head leaps out at the reader on the first opening, surrounded by cross-referenced sections of text explaining the model on the flat surfaces of the pages (the larynx, the nose, and so on). Many of the pop-ups are worked by tabs, others employ layered flap sections which take you ever inwards beneath the skin by way of the chest, the ribcage, the lungs and the kidneys. Miller and Pelham also produced *The Facts of Life* (1984) in which the sexes' genitalia are open for inspection in three dimensions. Their books are a brilliant use of the form – intriguing, instructive and accurate; marred only by the excess of dense small print.

The *National Geographic* magazine produces two books per annum for young readers with such titles as *Whales* (1990), *Explore a Tropical Forest* (1989), or *Creepy Crawly Creatures* (1995). Some of the most praised information flat books of recent years have been Stephen Biesty's minutely detailed cross-sectional drawings. Three of them (a fire engine, a space shuttle, and a rescue helicopter) have been transformed into *Stephen Biesty's Incredible Pop-Up Cross Sections* (1995).

There is a miraculous series of movables created by Gallimard in France and published by Larousse in the United Kingdom as 'Kingfisher Kaleidoscopes'. A book such as *Ce que voient les Peintres/What the Painter Sees* (1994) fascinates both adult and adolescent readers: a transparent overlay illustrates how perspective works in Hobbema's 'The Avenue, Middelharnis' or a Guardi view of Venice; a tubular mirror – a silvered sheet stored in a pocket inside the back cover is placed by the reader upon a distorted image in the text; in the mirror, the image becomes clear – the transformation known as anamorphosis. Other pages open out into a 'Guernica' some 50cms long. It is a physical delight to handle this series.

In Jay Young's *The Most Amazing Pop-up Science Book* (1994) the reader rotates a record slowly to listen to Edison's 'Mary had a little lamb' phonograph message; and uses the book, in turn, as a dangling pointer to fix magnetic north, a microscope, a camera obscura, a kaleidoscope, a sundial and a periscope. In a characteristically speculative lecture in 1969, the illustrator Charles Keeping (1924–88), asked his wary audience of teachers and librarians, 'What about a book that stretches or squeaks or does anything? What about a round book? What about one that is a circular tube with lots fitting inside it?'[11] Jay Young's book would have pleased him.

The absent critics

Little critical attention has so far been given to movable books. They are increasingly reviewed, but the children's literature academy has either ignored or dismissed them, preferring a limited range of flat-picture books – especially those often described as 'metafictive' – where more familiar literary analysis can be applied.

Brian Wildsmith points to an area where more information would be useful as a preliminary to critical discussion. 'When you think of it,' he says, 'for the amount of intensive manual labour involved, pop-ups are amazingly cheap to buy and they can soon become collectors' items.'[12] *Haunted House* sells at £11.99, while the average price of most high-quality pop-up books is between £13.00 and £15.00; for the most part they cannot reappear in cheaper paperback versions. Few children will independently spend this sort of money on books. Moreover, the vulnerability of movables requires that the complex pop-up will frequently be offered shrinkwrapped on the bookshop shelf, precluding examination by inquisitive hands. Large bookshops might well be willing to sacrifice a sample copy for a potential purchaser, but smaller booksellers cannot afford that luxury and report that they are therefore reluctant to stock movable books at all. For similar reasons, children are unlikely to find them on the shelves of their school or public library. So, the adult mediates the purchase of movable books even more powerfully than conventional books. As Wildsmith suggests, it may well be that many of the books most admired by adults are seen as 'collectible'; and that publishers are aware of this possibility. As a result, we know little about how, or why, children come into contact with pop-up books, or, for that matter, what kind of children experience them. It is quite probable that movable books are even more the preserve of the middle class than flat books.

It is also not at all clear what child readers do with many of the movable books published for them today. Some movable books (*Haunted House* would be a case in point) are so strong in their 'plots' that they implicitly teach children how they must be read. What does a child do, however, when confronted with the arbours and pathways of *A Walk in Monet's Garden*? And even a book such as *The Creation* might leave a child nonplussed. Is this a book or an attractive toy which is rather too fragile to be played with? You need to spend reflective time with Wildsmith's illustrations – much as a reader of poetry must spend time walking around 'inside the poem', allowing its images to resonate with each other. This is a learned skill. Some pop-up books work more richly if the reader allows memories of other narratives to play around the texts – an area which is complicated for readers with relatively little literary experience. As yet beliefs about how children 'read' movable books have been subjected neither to empirical study nor to the hypotheses of criticism. It may be that children marvel briefly at the technical ingenuity involved, but then move on. The only evidence seems to be anecdotal, and generally parental.

Critics might also usefully consider the strengths and limits of the form, starting with what may seem self-evident. Movable books clearly have potential as information books; they are interactional, offering models to be pored over, sometimes to be manipulated, if their secrets are to be shared. In a radio interview, Ron van der Meer (who has created several fascinating information packs) claimed that research conducted at Amsterdam University demonstrated a far higher retention rate among learners who used 'packs' of 'hands-on' movable materials than those who worked with print or illustrated books.[13]

In more literary areas, the form depends to a degree upon a relishing of the unexpected or the ingenious. Movables are an excellent medium for surprise (*Haunted House*) or for spectacle (*The Creation*); and for conjuring up the enchanting or the magical in fairy tales, notably in Kubasta's versions. They work less well when the narrative needs to hurry on, when the reader is at all impatient to know what happens next; a pop-up model, especially if it incorporates tabs to pull or flaps to lift, insists far more strongly that the reader gives it time to make its effects; the model shouts for attention for its own sake. There are exceptions, where concealment and discovery are at the heart of the story itself. Young readers no doubt love lifting the flaps to explore the mousehole of Anne Merrick's *The Very Visible Mouse* (1995) or to follow the maze in *The Amazing Anthony Ant* (1993) by Lorna and Graham Philpot.

Ultimately, the format of the movable book seems more rigid than that of the flat book for narrative purposes. As we have learned more about how to read a Sendak or an Anthony Browne, we know that a first reading will probably be rapid ('to find out what happens') but that a savouring of the pictures, and how they chime together with the words, will require far more leisurely re-readings. Children often learn this quickly, as their requests for the same book again and again indicate. Once the moments of surprise with the pop-up book have passed, what function does the model continue to serve as a reader re-visits the book?

The future development of the movable book is, appropriately, unpredictable. It might be thought, for example, that CD Roms would render movable information books obsolete – and even story books, for Little Red Riding Hood and some of her companions have already made their debuts in this format. But all ways forward may not lie along electronic highways. Perhaps the most loved movables of the last decade have been 'The Jolly Postman' books from Janet and Allan Ahlberg (1986; 1991; 1995), which depend upon their creators' sure understanding of how most children 'work' as readers, including their delight in handling the variety of correspondence the books contain. Movable books have already withstood the challenge of other forms of technology, much as live theatre and even the very art of reading have retained their particular appeals alongside the satisfactions of film and television. What they will surely continue to depend upon will be the fusion of the inventiveness of a Meggendorfer, a Kubasta, a Crowther or a Pienkowski, the innovations of modern paper engineers and the vision of entrepreneurial publishers. To date, there is no sense that the limits of the form have been reached.

References

1. The research of Michael Dawson was a shaping influence in the preparation of this chapter (See notes 2 and 4 below). He is at once historian, collector and bookseller (through Ampersand Books, Ludford Mill, Ludlow, Shrops. SY8 1PR). With absolute generosity, he shared his enthusiasm and his extensive knowledge of the field, both in lengthy conversation and in correspondence. He was kind enough to read this chapter in manuscript. I am most grateful to him.
2. See M. Dawson, 'S. Louis Giraud: The Wizard of Bookano' in *Antiquarian Book Monthly Review* no. 18, 1 June 1991, pp.250–6.
3. I was able to examine *The Daily Express Annual* and very many more of the books mentioned in this chapter through the kindness of Tessa Rose Chester, curator of the Renier Collection at the National Museum of Childhood at Bethnal Green. She and her colleagues were always welcoming and helpful, especially in providing access to the Renier and Saekel-Jelkmann Collections which are housed at the Museum.
4. In Dawson, 'S. Louis Giraud and the Development of Pop-Up Books' in *Antiquarian Book Monthly Review* no. 18, 1 May 1991, pp.218–22.
5. See P. Hardy, 'Top of the Pop-Ups', in *Bookseller 29* September 1979, pp.1546–7.
6. This comment, and the subsequent descriptions of Jan Pienkowski's visits to Colombia, are taken from an interview the illustrator gave to Tony Bradman. The photocopied article (which does not ascribe its source) is in the resources of the National Museum of Childhood at Bethnal Green.
7. Reported in J. Elliott, 'The Perennial Pop-Up' in *Books for Keeps*, no. 95, November, 1995.
8. In R. Sabuda, 'Movable Stationery' in *Movables*, vol. 3, no. 4, June, 1995.
9. See Note 6 above.
10. In B. Wildsmith, 'Creating The Creation' in *Books for Keeps*, no. 95, November.
11. Keeping was speaking at a Children's Literature conference at St Luke's College, Exeter, in the summer of 1969. His talk is printed in *Children's Literature in Education*, vol. 1, no. 1, March 1970.
12. Wildsmith, op. cit.
13. Ron van der Meer was interviewed by Libby Purves in 'Midweek' on BBC Radio 4, 20 March 1996

Movable Books

(In this list, 'pe.' indicates 'paper engineering')
Ahlberg, Allan and Janet (1986), *The Jolly Postman* (London: Heinemann).
Anon. (1897), *Merry Surprises*, (London: Ernest Nister).
Anon. (1949), *Little Red Riding Hood Animated* (London: Tuck).
Anon. (*c.*1952), *Annie Get Your Gun. Seen through the eyes of a child* (London: Tuck).
Anon. (*c.*1953), *Cinderella. Scenic Panorama Book*, illus. Molly Benatar (London: Tuck).

Anon. (*c.*1950s), *Little Bo-Peep's Television Book of Nursery Rhymes* (London: PM Productions).

Anon. (1953), *Little Red Riding Hood* (London: Collins).

Baum, L. Frank (1968), *The Wizard of Oz* (retold by A.G. Miller), illus. Dave Chambers and John Spencer (New York: Random House).

Belloc, Hilaire (1987), *The Bad Child's Pop-Up Book of Beasts*, illus. Wallace Tripp, pe. John Strejan (London: Methuen).

Biesty, Stephen (1995), *Stephen Biesty's Incredible Pop-Up Cross Sections* (London: Dorling Kindersley).

Briggs, Raymond (1982), *Fungus the Bogeyman Plop-Up Book*, pe. Ron van der Meer (London: Hamish Hamilton).

Briggs, Raymond (1986), *The Snowman: A Pop-Up Book with Music*, pe. Ron van der Meer (London: Hamish Hamilton).

Cerf, Bennett (1965), *Bennett Cerf's Pop-Up Riddles*, illus. Art Leonard (New York: Random House, and London: RLS Publications).

Crespi, Francesca (1995), *A Walk in Monet's Garden* (London: Frances Lincoln).

Crowther, Robert (1977), *The Most Amazing Hide and Seek Alphabet Book*, pe. James R. Diaz (London: Kestrel).

Crowther, Robert (1995), *The Most Amazing Night Book* (London: Kestrel).

Crowther, Robert (1996), *Robert Crowther's Pop-Up Olympics* (London: Walker Books).

de Beer, Hans (1995), *Ahoy There, Little Polar Bear*, pe. Vicki Teague-Walker (London: North-South Books).

Dreany, Joseph. E. (1951), *Cowboys in Pop-Up Action Pictures* (London: Publicity Products).

Giraud, S. Louis, (1929; 1930), *The Daily Express Annual* (London: Lane Publications, Daily Express Books Department).

Giraud, S. Louis, (1945; 1946; 1949) *Bookano Stories Series* (North Finchley: Strand Publications).

Gorey, Edward (1982), *The Dwindling Party*, pe. Ib Penick (London: Heinemann).

Grahame, Kenneth (1983), *Kenneth Grahame's The Wind in the Willows*, illus. Babette Cole, pe. James Roger Diaz and Keith Moseley (London: Methuen).

Inkpen, Mick (1994), *Where, oh where, is Kipper's Bear?* pe. Ariel Apte (London: Hodder & Stoughton).

Kubasta, Vojtech (*c.*1960), *Hop o' my Thumb* (London: Bancroft).

Kubasta, Vojtech (*c.*1960), *Jack and the Beanstalk* (London: Bancroft).

Kubasta, Vojtech (1960), *Table, Lay Yourself!* (London: Bancroft).

Kubasta, Vojtech (*c.*1961), *Tip and Top Go Camping* (London: Bancroft).

Kubasta, Vojtech (1984), *The Magic of the Circus* (Leicester: Brown Watson).

Kubasta, Vojtech (1988), *Jack and the Beanstalk* cover by Pamela Storey (Leicester: Brown Watson).

Levin, Ted and Linny (1995), *Creepy Crawly Creatures*, illus. Warren Cutler, pe. Rick Morrison (Washington: National Geographic Society).

Marchand, Pierre (1996), *What the Painter Sees* (London: Larousse); originally published (1994) as *Ce que voient les peintres* (Paris: Gallimard).

Meggendorfer, Lothar (1978) (facsimile), *The Doll's House* (London: Kestrel).

Meggendorfer, Lothar (1979) (facsimile), *International Circus* (London: Kestrel).

Merrick, Anne (1995), *The Very Visible Mouse*, illus. Tessa Richardson Jones (London: Bloomsbury).

Miller, Jonathan and Pelham, David (1983), *The Human Body*, illus. Harry Wilcock, pe. Vic Duppa-Whyte and David Rosendale (London: Jonathan Cape).

Miller Jonathan and Pelham, David (1984), *The Facts of Life*, illus. Harry Wilcock, pe. John Strejan, James R. Diaz, David Rosendale and David Pelham (London: Jonathan Cape).

Montague Smith, Patrick (1984), *The Royal Family Pop-Up Book*, illus. Roger Payne, pe. Vic Duppa-Whyte (London: Dean's International Publishing).

Montanaro, Ann (1993), *Pop-up and Movable Books: a Bibliography* (Metuchen, New Jersey and London: The Scarecrow Press).

Philpot, Lorna and Graham (1993), *Amazing Anthony Ant* (London: Orion).

Pienkowski, Jan (1979), *Haunted House*, assist. illus. Jane Walmsley, pe. Tor Lokwig (London: Heinemann).

Pienkowski, Jan (1981), *Robot*, assist. illus. Jane Walmsley, pe. James Roger Diaz, Tor Lokwig, Marcin Stajewski (London: Heinemann).

Ridge, Antonia (1956), *The Village* (et al.) (Leicester: Brockhampton).

Rinard, Judith E. (1990), *Whales: Mighty giants of the sea*, illus. Ned and Rosalie Seidler, pe. James Roger Diaz and Rick Morrison (Washington: National Geographic Society).

Row, Richard (1994), *The Anne of Green Gables Pop-Up Dollhouse*, pe. Rick Morrison (Toronto: Key Porter Books).

Stevenson, R.L. (1987), *A Child's Garden of Verses*, illus. and pe. Claire Littlejohn (London: Sadie Fields Productions).

Strejan, John and Murphy, Chuck (1980), *Stan Lee Presents the Amazing Spider Man Pop-Up Book*, pe. Tor Lokwig (New York: Marvel Comics Group).

Theiner, George (1963), *A Visit to Animalia*, illus. Rudolf Lukes (London: Bancroft).

Vartanian, Raymond (1951), *How We Travel* (London: Publicity Products Ltd).

Verne, Jules (1969), *20,000 Leagues Under the Sea*, adapted by A.G. Miller (New York: Random House).

Waddell, Martin and Firth, Barbara (1995), *Can't You Sleep, Little Bear?* (London: Walker Books).

Winston, Peggy (1989), *Explore a Tropical Forest*, illus. Barbara Gibson pe. John Strejan (Washington: National Geographic Society).

Wylie, Stephen (1990), *Dinner with Fox*, illus. Korky Paul, pe. Claire Littlejohn (London: Sadie Fields Productions).

Wyllie, Stephen (1992), *Ghost Train*, illus. Brian Lee (London: Sadie Fields Productions).

Wildsmith, Brian (1994), *Noah's Ark*, pe. Dennis K. Meyer and Ariel Apte (Oxford: Oxford University Press).

Wildsmith, Brian (1995), *The Creation*, pe. Bruce Reifel and José R. Seminario (Oxford: Oxford University Press).

6 Picture Stories and Graphic Novels

Philip Pullman

Literature purchased directly by children often provides a strong contrast in both treatment and theme with those children's books that many teachers and librarians have tended to prefer. This is particularly true in the case of comic-strip publications. In this chapter, Philip Pullman looks at favourite post-war comic strips, concentrating on the semi-anarchic world of the Beano *and* Dandy, *the more gentle heroism of* Rupert, *and the visual pyrotechnics offered by the adventures of Dan Dare in the* Eagle. *Their influence was such that over time established authors such as Raymond Briggs and Shirley Hughes also began to experiment successfully with comic-strip techniques.*

Printed texts which rely on pictures as part of the narrative process are still widely assumed to be directed at young, inexperienced and unsophisticated readers. Analysis of the semiotics of the picture book has in fact revealed that visual narratives are often involved in radical experimentation and invention. By contrast, the graphic novel, because it is told using styles and techniques first developed in the comic strip (largely reviled by adult institutions), has so far received little recognition either as literature or art. Yet, as Pullman explains, it is precisely these elements which give graphic texts their ability to exhibit and challenge orthodoxy. From early examples of powerful intellectual female characters, such as the Eagle's *Professor Peabody, to explorations of the relationship between art and auotobiography (*Maus*), the combined storytelling efforts of writers and illustrators (or writer–illustrators) have raised questions which are as probing as any encounter in 'proper' literature.*

There are other reasons for the popularity of comic-strip publications with children beyond the occasional breaking or stretching of literary conventions. Progress from one picture to another involves a type of visual energy highly pleasing to the young. The various special visual effects used by comic-strip artists to suggest anything from excess speed to deep embarrassment have been much appreciated by readers of comics over the years. Picture reading

110

*is an older technique than print; it is not surprising that children are often
drawn to it at a time when their reading skills may not be highly developed.
And, because this type of literature is broadly shunned by British adults, the
comic-strip world has become something of a private space for child readers.*

*The following study celebrates the achievements of those who have con-
ceived and developed the picture story to make texts of undeniable literary
and artistic merit. Not the least of these achievements must be the genre's
ability to appeal to disaffected readers; especially adolescent boys. Yet the
dark side of these stories should not be forgotten, and readers need to recall
that for every Professor Peabody there have been many hundreds of female
characters simultaneously objectified and denigrated in comic-strip stories.
Philip Pullman is particularly well qualified to write about this form of story-
telling since he is not only a collector, enthusiast and historian of picture
stories and graphic texts, but also a writer who has explored how graphic
elements can be incorporated into his own writing for young readers.*

Definitions

According to the Oxford University Press lexicographers, the first printed
usage of the term 'graphic novel' occurred in 1978, in the title of Will Eisner's
A Contract with God: A Graphic Novel.[1] Whether or not Eisner (who had
been thinking and writing about the form for many years) actually invented
the term, it was clearly needed. Ten years after the first publication of *A
Contract with God*, it was well established. By the mid to late 1980s, you
might not have been able to buy more than one or two graphic novels in an
average, well-stocked bookshop, but no bookshop assistant would have been
in any doubt about what you meant if you asked for one.

What the graphic novel actually consists of is a lengthy comic: a single
story in the comic-strip format printed in one volume. Thus an episode of
The Bash Street Kids isn't a graphic novel, because it's only one of a number
of short stories in a weekly comic; and a Rupert story isn't either, because,
although it's long and between hard covers, it isn't in the comic-strip format.
However, a Tintin story is, although the term hadn't been coined when the
first full-length Tintin stories were published.

In this chapter I intend to look at a wider range of phenomena than
those limited by current definitions of the graphic novel. Rupert needs to be
considered, because of his vast popularity, and so does the work of Leo
Baxendale in the *Beano*, for his continuing influence. I have given a good deal
of space to an examination of the first six months or so of the *Eagle*, which
seems to me not only to encapsulate some of the best comics-form work this
country has ever produced, but also to evoke very powerfully the atmosphere
of a particularly attractive time in our history. I continue with the work of
Raymond Briggs, who is original and powerful enough to shape the language
of comics and make it say what he wants, and that of Art Spiegelman, who

has produced what to my mind is the greatest work yet in the form; and I conclude with a (necessarily) brief survey of the present state of the graphic novel.

First, though, a definition of the form itself. Essentially graphic novels consist of a story told in successive pictures, with the addition of words set into the pictures: words of particular kinds, each kind indicated by its own smaller frame. These are speech balloons, think bubbles, captions, and sound effects (which usually don't have their own frames, but share the space with the pictures). This graphic vocabulary is so natural-seeming, intuitive, reader-friendly, that it seems to have come to the understanding of most of us very early in our reading. A curious question is why, given this naturalness (and the fact that, unlike photogravure, for instance, it needs no special technical development before it can be printed: there was no *technical* reason preventing Caxton or Gutenberg from printing comics in the fifteenth century), it took so long to arrive. Claims have been made that the Bayeux Tapestry, Egyptian hieroglyphics and Mayan temple inscriptions are all ancestors of the comic strip, and so they may be, but any ancestry that remote is usually more boasted about than proved. Then there are the various ways in which speech has been represented in pictures, from the elaborate scrolls emerging from the mouths of barbecued Protestants in *Foxe's Book of Martyrs* (1563) to the (apparently only partly inflated) balloons sagging with their weight of text across the gross form of the Prince Regent in Gillray's popular caricatures. More plausibly the work of Rodolphe Töpffer in the middle of the nineteenth century has also been claimed as ancestral. His narrative technique used successive panels of drawing with a commentary underneath, thus bringing words into play as well; but his work had few direct imitators, and there can be little doubt that the first recognisably comic-strip comics were those that came into being within ten years of the birth of the cinema, as did comics' first masterpiece: the *Little Nemo in Slumberland* (1905), strip drawn and written by Winsor McCay for the *New York Herald*.

The first strips were short – a page in length at most. Writers and artists soon needed more space to contain the growing complexity and depth of the works they wanted to create; but before the graphic novel proper was born, another words-and-pictures work had already begun to spread itself on a larger scale. This was Rupert Bear.

Rupert

It seems slightly perverse to begin this survey of the graphic novel with a consideration of the adventures of Rupert Bear, because they are nothing of the sort. However, in any survey of British stories told in pictures and words, it would be even more perverse to leave Rupert out, if only because of the immense popularity of the stories over seventy-five years – much of that time (1935–65) in the hands of Alfred Bestall.

As I have pointed out elsewhere,[2] the design of a Rupert page works so well because it works with the grain of the nature of pictures. The largest elements on the page are the four central picture panels, and the two verbal narratives – the couplet under each picture and the prose at the foot of the page – are both in the present tense, which acknowledges the present-tense-ness of the pictures. There are actually two other elements that also tell the story: the headline at the top of each page, and the two little figures on either side of it. One of these is always Rupert, and his picture is always on the outside, so that the reader can use it as a flicker-book, producing a little 'movie' of Rupert in action. (The prose at the foot of the page was ignored by most readers, if anecdotal evidence is anything to go by; though one eminent academic of my acquaintance, who always read it, claims to have selected her friends according to whether or not they did.)

Rupert was introduced in the *Daily Express* in 1920 in order to compete with the successful *Teddy Tail* strip which was running in the *Daily Mail*. The creator of the strip was Mary Tourtel. Paul Vaughan, in the memoir *Something in Linoleum* (1993), shows how Tourtel's Rupert struck one child of the 1930s:

> I loved Rupert, with a deep and unquestioning love, and I don't believe Mary Tourtel, his inventor, has received her due . . . [The Rupert stories] were quintessentially of the 1930s, and must have occupied a commanding place in the reading life, and quite possibly shaped the moral universe of an entire generation of middle class children . . . Mrs Tourtel's imaginative world was eventually too much for the *Express* management: the paper was committed to a policy of comfortable, thumbs-up optimism, which applied to absolutely everything – and the Rupert saga was casting a dark shadow across the heart of the paper. When Mary Tourtel was forced to retire through failing eyesight, Beaverbrook gave orders that her successor, Alfred Bestall, should cut the witches, dwarves, ogres and wolves: henceforth the stories would be brighter, cheerier, cosier – and incomparably more dull.[3]

Bestall was already well-known as a *Punch* cartoonist – at a time when *Punch*, under A.A. Milne, was at its most mimsy, specialising in cartoons depicting sweetly adorable children asking adorably embarrassing questions of their indulgently adoring parents. The one thing that redeems the toe-curling pages of a 1920s volume of *Punch* is the artwork, by such artists as E.H. Shepard, much of which is superb. Bestall's cartoons were not as emetic as some, and his pen-and-ink artwork was well up to the standard of the rest, but he would hardly be remembered today if it were not for Rupert.

The *Rupert Annual* was first issued in 1936 (dated 1937), and by the outbreak of the Second World War it had become so popular that Daily Express Publications continued to issue it despite wartime restrictions. To quote the publicity for the facsimile reprint of the 1940 *Annual*:

> In the darkest period of the Second World War, Lord Beaverbrook, owner of the Daily Express and Minister of Supply in the War Cabinet, decided that it was important for morale to continue to publish the annual which had become a Christmas treat for so many children. Paper was strictly rationed however, and for that reason it was probably the *only* annual published that year.[4]

No doubt Beaverbrook was entirely motivated by patriotism, and in his capacity as Minister of Supply would have decided in favour of the *Daily Mail's* Teddy Tail had he been as popular as Rupert. The 1940 Annual was the first to be printed in colour throughout, and in form (once allowance has been made for advances in printing techniques) a Rupert page from this one is exactly the same as every page that Bestall drew from then on. It is in these Annuals that the Rupert form reaches its perfect state. It reached it early, and never fell away, and despite the reservations expressed by Vaughan and others, Bestall's work does have a rich flavour of its own; to most people who are adults today, Bestall's Rupert *is* Rupert.

Bestall drew the strip for thirty years, and continued to work on the annuals after 1965. He has two particular strengths. One is his delicate and charming artwork, which reaches the peak of its achievement in the endpapers in the later Annuals: landscapes from a fairy-tale England, or an imaginary China, with Rupert and his friends doing what they did most of the time: having innocent fun. Bestall's other strength is his fantasy. When I think of the Rupert stories I enjoyed as a child it is the fantastic elements that come back to me: Rupert flying an improbable little aeroplane up to the kingdom of the birds, or tumbling down through the roots of a tree to an underground world where gnomes operate complex machinery. Bestall drew it all with great grace, and with a certainty of imagination that created a solid and lovable world.

Rupert continues in other hands, notably those of John Harrold, whose style is inevitably different from Bestall's, but who has maintained the form impeccably. There seems no reason why Rupert should not live to be a hundred.

D.C. Thomson, *Beano*, and Leo Baxendale

For all its power and popularity, Rupert isn't a comic. Comics proper in Britain began with Ally Sloper (this character first appeared in *Judy* 1867, his adventures were gathered together to form the first comic book in 1873, and in 1884, with the publication of *Ally Sloper's Half-Holiday*, set the mould for the layout of British comics[5]) and *Comic Cuts* in the 1890s, but they really took off in the decade before the Second World War under the imprint of D.C. Thomson & Co. of Dundee.

This firm had been in the publishing business since 1905, and had issued 'boys'' papers since the 1920s. *Adventure* (1921), *Rover* and *Wizard* (both 1922) were the first, and lasted until well into the 1960s. They began as story-papers, with prose narratives about such figures as Wilson, the athlete who was over 100 years old and who broke every record known. As these papers grew older, the proportion of pictures to text increased, until finally some of them gave in altogether and became vehicles for the comic-strip.

D.C. Thomson's most successful titles were not adventure papers, however, but *Dandy*, first published in 1937, and *Beano*, from a year later. The latter has always been slightly more popular, no doubt because of the vitality of the favourite characters, such as Dennis the Menace. The Dennis strip began in 1951, the work of David Law, and was one of the early inspirations for the most famous and influential of all *Beano* artists, Leo Baxendale.

Baxendale's first contribution to *Beano* was Little Plum your Redskin Chum, whose vendetta against the greedy bears ran for many years. Baxendale says[6] that he intended Litttle Plum as a Red Indian Dennis the Menace, but Baxendale's world was always richer in surrealistic detail. When Little Plum has a driving lesson, for instance, a vulture follows the car carrying a knife and fork. A detail like that in a Dennis strip would have distracted, because the imaginative focus of a Dennis story is the straightforward mischief of Dennis himself. The imaginative focus of a Baxendale strip is the entire picture area, and the appearance of everything matters. For example, Baxendale thought carefully about the effects of the printing process:

> When the reader opened *The Beano*, the right hand held five sheets together, so they were opaque, but the left hand held a single sheet, and this, taken with the apparently finer quality paper used for the cover, allowed light to filter through from the front (full colour) cover, thus giving a luminosity to the inside cover feature.
>
> This luminosity helped give an atmosphere to the set; it softened and enhanced the solid reds and the pink and grey lines produced by the Process Department's 'Ben Day Tints' dots and stipples.
>
> Even the solid blacks which I used liberally (to give weight to the sets) received softness and depth from this luminosity.[7]

The same care is evident in his remarks about the Bash Street Kids. Commenting on the reason for giving Teacher a mortar board, he says:

> Black mortar board and gown had two purposes: on a page printed by letterpress,

those patches of solid black gave weight to the page and drew the reader's eye to Teacher (the solid black trousers and skirts of the Bash Street Kids were to the same purpose) . . . Fatty's purpose in Bash Street derived from his shape: in a clump of characters of even, stocky size, his larger, circular shape was a visual contrast (and Plug was created tall and gangly, and Wilfrid dwarfish, for similar need of visual variety).[8]

But it was not only the appearance of his work that Baxendale considered carefully. Teacher's mortar board and gown had two purposes, as he points out above, and the second purpose was a connotative one: it 'made the status of Bash Street School ambiguous', in order, 'to seize the widest readership'. However, this blurring of identity, 'caused me unease whenever I did it, since I believed that art, and in particular comedy, should be specific'.[9] Baxendale's unease over this point is indicative of his scrupulous attention to the meanings as well as the origins of his work. He is frank about his sources: the Bash Street Kids, for example, was inspired by a Giles cartoon of a mob of children running out of an urban primary school. Each of his creations has a quite distinct moral atmosphere. Of Minnie the Minx he says:

> I intended Minnie to burst the bounds, to make, not a 'bad girl' but a little girl of boundless ambition, desirous of every high post on earth (including that of world heavyweight champion) and an Amazonian warrior to boot . . . The titanic struggle of will between Minnie and her Dad is both a literal physical struggle, and one of psychological attrition.[10]

One of his editors sums up the differing implications of the most famous Beano strips in a passage that again reveals Baxendale's own brooding over meanings:

> Twisting round in his chair with a grin, Ken declared: 'Dennis is a bad lad, the Bash Street Kids mean well but things come to pieces in their hands; *but Minnie is a psychopath.*'
>
> I thought he was hard on Minnie, but that was by the bye. I considered his summing up of the Bash Street Kids: they 'mean well but things come to pieces in their hands'.
>
> But there lay the *ambiguity*, that had entered the work with the removal of the frowns and leers of intent: *did those beams and smirks betoken gormlessness or guile?*[11]

Whether an artist's work is ultimately improved by being the subject of its own creator's intellectual analysis is doubtful; Baxendale was good not because he intellectualised but because he was funny. His work in recent, post-*Beano* years has been less certain: his *I Love You Baby Basil* strip, for instance, which ran in the *Guardian* in the late 1980s, veered between the facetious, the tender, and the lewd, and never seemed quite sure what it was saying. However, Kevin Carpenter's judgement that Baxendale is, 'the most inventive, most prolific, and most influential of modern British comic artists' remains true.[12] And the *Beano* remains popular. Now in full colour throughout, it still features Baxendale's best creations, Minnie and the Bash Street Kids. Teacher has given up his gown, but his mortar board is still in place; so important is it that he has to tie it on with string during a high wind in a recent issue. Like all the best situations, Baxendale's are capable of endless variation.

Eagle

Popularised by the *Beano* and its stablemates, the comics form spread quickly, and was almost as quickly demonised. The story of the great horror-comic scare of the 1950s has been well told in Martin Barker's *A Haunt of Fears* (1984) and does not need retelling here; it suffices to say that the power of the comics form was recognised by concerned adults as something worth harnessing. One of the most notable of these was the Revd Marcus Morris, the Lancashire clergyman who persuaded Hulton Press Ltd to publish *Eagle*.

The first issue of *Eagle* appeared on 14 April 1950. It looked spectacular, with a large format and with a lot of full-colour printing. The cover story,

Dan Dare, was an immediate and continuing success, which was largely due to the artwork by Frank Hampson. Panels were drawn from the most dramatic, or cinematic, angles, and edited brilliantly: a close-up of Dan Dare's face, with the famous inverted tick at the end of his eyebrows, would be followed by a picture of the rocket base from above, complete with modernist architecture (the Festival of Britain was less than a year away), which would cut to a shot (how easily the cinema terminology lends itself to the discussion of comics) of the rocket ship streaking through the blackness of space. The lighting was especially dramatic: Hampson specialised in a lit-from-both-sides technique in which Dan Dare's face had a line of shadow following the contours of brow, nose, lips and chin with tremendous vividness.

But the artwork was not the only reason for Dan Dare's success. The stories are intriguing, too. The very first one involves a plan to grow food on Venus, compress it, and ship it back to Earth, 'vast areas' of which 'have been exhausted by bad farming in the past'. This plan meets with some opposition from the Venusian Treens, who are both green and mean, and their leader, the Mekon. The Mekon doesn't actually appear until the thirtieth issue, but, like Orson Welles's Harry Lime in *The Third Man*, he's worth the build-up. The Mekon is unforgettable. His tiny spindly body and his vast domed green head give him the aura of some interplanetary Professor Moriarty, intent on monstrous (and highly intelligent) evil; but most impressive of all is the little saucer he sits on, which floats above the much taller but equally lean Treens and from which, skinny elbows on twig-like knees, he dominates any frame in which he appears.

Any story is the better for a good villain, but villains are easy. It's much harder to create a hero who's both attractive and interesting. Dan Dare himself is undoubtedly the first, but not always the second. However, he is by no means the only protagonist in the history of literature, or of comics, of which that is true (the great Tintin is a case in point), and the Dan Dare writers allowed for it by surrounding him with characters whose quirks could make up for the hero's own lack of them. The most important of these is Digby, his batman: a stout Lancastrian with a double chin, a quiff of white hair, a fondness for fish and chips with lashings of salt and vinegar, and a propensity for ludicrous mishaps. Digby has an Aunt Anastasia, who arrives when the story needs some comic tension (Digby himself supplying the comic relief); there is also a Mrs Digby and five children. Mrs Digby is pictured in issue no. 25, beside a coal fire in front of which washing is drying on a line. The year, we are told, is 1995, but they couldn't be expected to get everything right.

Other important characters are Sir Hubert Guest (OM, DFC, etc.), Dan Dare's boss, an upright and old-fashioned gentleman who looks like Charlton Heston playing Sir Anthony Eden; and, not least, Professor Peabody. The Professor is, 'a first-class geologist, botanist, agriculturalist' and, 'a qualified space pilot as well'. However, those qualifications pale beside the astonishing fact that Professor Peabody is a woman, and a glamorous one, too. Dan Dare himself is fairly cool about this, but Sir Hubert is disgusted ('Women! Pah!'), and this allows for some comic by-play later on. In issue no. 6, Professor Peabody refuses to relinquish the controls of the rocket ship to Sir Hubert, telling him he's not as young as he was; and in issue no. 19, when the two of them are about to be engulfed by 'a great vitreous silicon mass' on Venus, Sir Hubert accidentally compliments her on her courage, at which she blushes (the colour printing showing this process clearly) and he finds himself disconcerted by his own gallantry: 'Never expected . . . hrrmph . . . female to behave so well . . . um . . . very cool . . . er, good show . . .'

In fact, the Dan Dare stories were confident enough to be witty. The cover of issue no. 25 was a mock newspaper front page (*The Daily World Post*) which, in the context of the ongoing story of the food shortages on Earth, includes a paragraph under the headline SUCCESS IN EAST AFRICA – PEANUT ARRIVES IN LONDON:

> There was a touching ceremony at the Strachey Memorial in London yesterday when a whole unblemished peanut was handed to the Minister of Food by a delegation representing equally the native tribes in the groundnut area and the survivors of the Strachey scheme.

This reference to the Minister of Food's abortive Tanganyika groundnut scheme is one of the points at which a present-day reader, seduced by the skill and authority of the presentation, is suddenly brought up short by the realisation that this story comes from the last exhausted days of the post-war Labour Government. Our vision of that world is of a drab, grey place, derived as it is from murky monochrome photographs and black-and-white films, as if colour itself had been rationed along with food. The first children who saw the blazing colours of *Eagle* must have found it satisfying a hunger they didn't know they had.

Dan Dare was the star, but the comic was full of good things. There were several other comic-strip serials: one about 'the famous radio policeman', PC 49; a cowboy story called 'Seth and Shorty'; a black-and-white strip about Rob Conway, an ATC Cadet who gets involved in a yarn about smuggling and gangsters, and on the back cover a full-colour strip called 'The Great Adventure'. This was the story of St Paul; it was the only overtly Christian part of the comic, but it was not in the least like the sort of thing you might have learned in Sunday School. The story is full of fights and hairsbreadth escapes, with vivid colour in the artwork and a particularly dramatic use of strong intense blacks.

As well as the comic-strip serials, there were prose stories (including a 'gripping new serial' by Chad Varah called 'Plot against the World'); there was a feature in comic-strip format called 'Professor Brittain Explains', showing a genial boffin telling a boy and a girl all about radar; there was a Captain Pugwash strip, by John Ryan; there was a half-page strip of Cricket Coaching tips, featuring Learie Constantine ('This week, The Late Cut'); there was a dauntingly technical model-engineering spot, showing you how to make a model racing car; there was a full-colour cutaway drawing showing, 'The New Gas Turbine-Electric Locomotive'; there was a strip called 'Real Life Mysteries' – and so on.

A long-established tradition in periodicals for the young was the editor's page, on which the readers were addressed directly. A good example of this is Hamilton Edwards's *A Chat With the Chief*, from the first issue of *Cheer Boys Cheer* ('The Paper Every Boy Can Show His Parents'), May 1912:

> Of late years the boys' reading market has been flooded with a lot of sensational trash. The sensible, intelligent lad can find no interest in this sort of reading. He wants exciting reading, but he wants good reading, and, most of all, he wants common sense . . .
>
> In this chat I want to play the part of an elder brother, and if [my readers] are in trouble, to give them good, sound advice which they can follow for their own benefit . . . In short, I want to establish between my readers and myself a bond of brotherhood and confidence. I want them to realise that in me they will find a real friend . . .

For all the modernistic splendour of *Dan Dare*, the Editor's Page in *Eagle* comes directly from this older tradition. In the first issue, we are told about the importance of being a MUG:

> There are really only two kinds of people in the world. One kind are the MUGS. The opposite of the MUGS are the Spivs – also called wide boys, smart guys, hooligans, louts or racketeers.

The MUGS are the people who are some use in the world; the people who do something worth-while for others, instead of just grabbing for themselves all the time.

Of course the Spivs snigger at that. *They* use the word Mug as an insult. 'Aren't they mugs?' they say about people who believe in living for something bigger than themselves.

That is why someone who gets called a MUG is likely to be a pretty good chap . . .

That is the authentic tone of a certain kind of Church of England parson. I remember it very well from my own grandfather, who was one himself, and I can see it today in the editorials of his parish magazines from the 1950s, which I still have. At all events, it touched some sort of chord. *Eagle* instituted a Mug of the Month Club, and soon a small photograph of a boy or girl would be regularly featured over a paragraph explaining why s/he was a Mug. Looking after the home during the illness of a parent certainly qualified you; so did saving people from drowning, an activity that seemed to take place with suspicious frequency.

The Editor's Page also explained why the number of pages varied from issue to issue. Issue no. 3 said:

> You will see that this is another 20-page issue of EAGLE – like the first one. For the time being, we are planning to make it 20 pages one week and 16 the next. This is because of the difficulty of getting enough paper which is still very scarce. So many copies of EAGLE have to be printed to satisfy the demand that we can't manage enough paper for 20 pages every time just at present.

In fact, demand was so high (according to E.S. Turner, the initial sale was almost a million[13]) that by issue no. 7 they had to reduce the number of pages to sixteen every week. In the very first week, sixty thousand readers wrote in, and by issue no. 17, the *Eagle* Club had a hundred thousand members. The *Eagle* Club had been inaugurated with the first issue, and was clearly a big attraction. 'There will be, from time to time, special expeditions for selected members . . . for example, a trip to the T.T. Races in the Isle of Man, to the Edinburgh Festival, to the Monte Carlo Rally, to the 1951 Festival of Britain, and to interesting places abroad.'

We can learn something about the readership from the reports of these expeditions, the first of which took place in May 1950. There were three girls among the twenty-five members taken to the Silverstone Grand Prix Races, and that proportion remained roughly constant among *Eagle* Club members taken on trips or commended for saving people from drowning in later months. *Eagle* never called itself a boys' paper, but its sister paper, which joined it within a couple of years, had no qualms about specifying who it thought would read it, and called itself *Girl*. *Girl* had the same high production values as *Eagle*, but there was no doubt about which title was the bigger and more inclusive. I remember attending the crowded *Eagle* Exhibition at Olympia in 1956 or so, and queuing to get the autographs of the artists and writers of the most popular strips ('Best wishes from Storm Nelson and the crew'); and I remember quite clearly that it was labelled *Eagle* Boys' and Girls' Exhibition. Professor Peabody would have fitted in at once.

As well as pleasing the boys and girls, *Eagle* met with instant approval from the grown-ups. The *Times Literary Supplement* Children's Books supplement of 16 June 1950 greeted it warmly:

> Ten numbers of *Eagle*, a strip cartoon weekly addressed to children (Hulton Press, 3d) have now appeared, and already it is possible to hail this new venture as an established success ... It has worked out an excellent formula for combining amusement and interest ... *Eagle* is already turning into a source of furtive pleasure for parents ... It seems likely that *Eagle*, which overtly sets itself a standard as high as can be consonant with a national circulation among children from every type of home, will perform a most valuable service by offering plenty of unpretentious entertainment without tumbling into reckless sensationalism at one extreme or vapidity at the other.

Amusement and interest good, reckless sensationalism bad: it was a formula Hamilton Edwards would have echoed. *Eagle*, too, was definitely 'The Paper Every Boy Can Show His Parents', and was proud to be.

Eagle lasted roughly as long as the post-war consensus, which in many ways it exemplified. But bright and cheerful modernism combined with fundamental decency were perhaps too mild (or to use Michael Frayn's term, 'herbivorous') a mixture to satisfy the savage palate of the late twentieth century. By 1970 it was gone (the last number was dated 26 April 1969), having been swallowed first by the International Publishing Corporation and then by the *Lion*. Attempts were made later to revive it, but without success.

Dan Dare up to date

The first *Eagle* story of all, about food shortages on Earth and the prospect of relief from supplies grown on Venus, had an ingenious and brutal reworking in a true graphic novel published by Xpresso Books in 1991. Called simply *Dare*, it was written by Grant Morrison and drawn by Rian Hughes in a skilful updating of the visual style that keeps the essential Dare features – the lantern jaw, the famous eyebrows – but the story evokes a different world.

It begins with the funeral of Professor Peabody, who has committed suicide. Then it gets bleaker. This is a Britain in which the Unity Party, led by a dominant, charismatic woman, seeks its fourth election victory in a row. The space fleet has been privatised, buildings are crumbling, city streets are full of rubbish, and the atmosphere is the one we know so well, perhaps the endemic atmosphere of the twentieth century itself: corruption, violence, and incipient fascism. Dan Dare himself, now retired and walking with a stick, discovers a video in which Professor Peabody passes on the awful truth:

> Our **government**, the Unity Party, led by **Gloria Monday**, has been collaborating secretly with the **Treen** dictatorship on Venus.
> In return for an answer to Earth's food shortages, the Unity Party is offering human **lives** to the Treens.
> The people who've come to threshold on the training scheme aren't being given work.
> They're being **murdered** and their bodies are being broken down into **biomass**.
> Hundreds, thousands of them . . . **teenagers**, mostly . . . dumped into the **vats**, screaming for their mothers, screaming for someone to help them.

Digby's response is immediate: 'Bloody hell,' he says. That seems to sum it up.

Dare is a vigorous and respectful tribute from the art of today to the inspiration of the past. Few things could better encapsulate the change in mood from the Festival of Britain–National Health Service–welfare state–Butler Education Act–BBC Third Programme–New Elizabethan world of optimism and civic decency to the bleak and savage expectations of the end of the century. Still, *Dare* isn't for children so much as for those who were children when to be a MUG was still to be a pretty good chap. And the elderly, limping, compromised Dan Dare comes up trumps in the end:

> I'm almost glad you taught me that England only ever existed in my head. It means it can never really be destroyed. Unlike the sick, cruel, heartless thing you erected in its place . . .

And he blows everyone up.

Raymond Briggs

Raymond Briggs is the creator of several of the most notable books in comic-strip form to have emerged in this country in the past twenty years. His first, *Father Christmas*, was and remains such a success, both artistically and commercially, that it comes as a slight surprise to learn that he did not intend it to have that form at all.

It became a comic strip almost by accident, he says, when he realised that he had far more material written than would fit on to thirty-two conventional picture-book pages. His method is to write the dialogue first and then draw the pictures, and when he saw that he needed eight or nine pictures per page, he knew he had to do something new. 'That's how it came about, just trying to get the material in with this maddening limitation.'[14]

His method often relies on this kind of serendipity. When *Father Christmas* was reduced for paperback publication he saw that the pictures were just as legible at postage-stamp size, and realised he could get many more pictures on a page. That in turn allowed the contrast in *When the Wind Blows* (1982) between the little pictures and the big double-page spreads.

His meticulousness shows on every page, but it takes endless time and patience. The initial writing is fun, he says, because that's straightforward, but,

> The worst thing is allotting the space to it. That's the part I dislike most – it's the bugger of planning the space – you've got that line [of dialogue] and then the curtains are in the way, simple things like that. The worst thing is the endless repetition, drawing the same bloody thing over and over again. I keep thinking I ought to do something more simple, but it creeps into this realistic style, and you end up drawing boring things like boxes of tissues and bloody phones and his blasted radio, drawing all the little buttons on the radio, that sort of thing, calculators and radios . . . Oh, God . . .'[15]

There's a certain *Father Christmas*-like tone to these remarks, which will be familiar to anyone who knows that marvellous book. But just as Father Christmas delivers the presents despite grumbling every inch of the way, so his creator unfailingly delivers the pictures. The comments above refer to his book *The Man* (1992), an extraordinary mixture of earthiness, delicacy, anger and love. Formally, it is like nothing else, and like *Father Christmas*, it came about as the solution to a technical problem – that of finding enough space for the dialogue. There is a great deal of it: enough to fill over 100 pages, he says, if he had drawn it as a conventional comic strip. When he realised how long it was going to take to do, he came up with a new answer.

The bulk of the dialogue is set out as prose, the Boy's speech being differentiated from the Man's and from his Parents' by the use of different typefaces

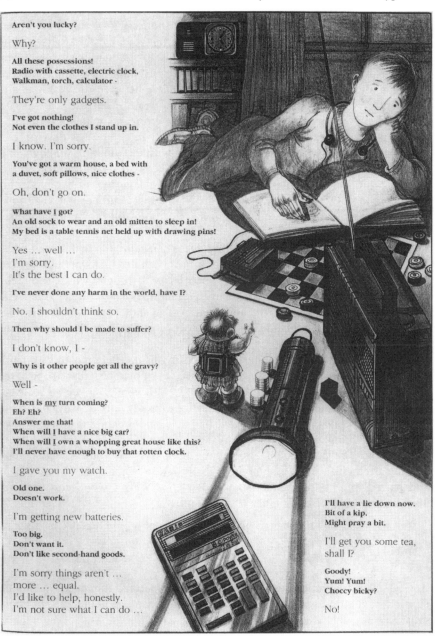

(big, slender, and lower case for the Boy, big and upper case for the Parents, small and bold for the Man: just like them). There are pictures on every page, some of them with speech balloons and some without, so it is a mixture of comic-strip and more conventional illustration.

Shirley Hughes, in the *Chips and Jessie* (1985–86) books, also put comic-strip techniques to a hybrid use, combining them with a conventional prose narrative. Her use of it is delightful and her pioneering of this method has been very influential, but there seems to me an unavoidable clash between the past tense of the narrative and the present tense of the comic-strip pictures. Briggs avoids that in *The Man* by the simple expedient of doing without narrative altogether. It works brilliantly; we move between the dialogue and the pictures with no sense of discontinuity or strain, as if the white space around the words were inhabited by the undrawn figures who speak them.

The pictures themselves are some of Briggs's best. He has developed a technique in the use of watercolour overlaid with crayon which allows him to express gradations of tone and form as well as all those buttons on the blasted radio, and which is an unfailing delight. His depiction of hair, for instance: the Boy's wispy and trailing, the Man's spiky and upright, his round skull showing through where it's thinning, and both full of subtle richnesses of red.

Briggs has not stopped experimenting. He is constantly searching for a good paper to work on, for instance, because he uses both pen and watercolour, and they need different surfaces; and his method with roughs varies too. Like Charles Keeping, he doesn't like them in general, because, 'quite often you put your heart and soul into it and then you've shot your bolt and it goes dead on you'.[16] His latest idea is to photocopy a rough on to watercolour paper and work on that.

This experimentation is all in the cause of realism. There has to be a truth in it, a danger. In *Bear* (1994), for instance, the polar bear has to be large and cuddly, but it has to be a bear none the less: 'I wanted to keep it realistic, so that he could put his paws round her in a cuddly sort of way, but there are still those claws, and you know if he has a bad dream and just goes like *that*, her face comes off.'[17]

Similarly, *The Man* could easily have been a sentimental tale of a boy looking after a little man, and no more than that. In fact it is full of resentment and hatred and clumsy tenderness, and it ends with a wonderful spelling-mistake-pun in the Man's letter:

You wer moR kind to me thaN aNNy won els in the hole of my life.
YOU AR A GOD BLOKE
Yor old MATE
Man.

If God is indeed uncertain, nervous, and immature, inexplicably finding Himself having to look after a querulous, sentimental, demanding, but easily satisfied humanity, it would explain a lot.

Penguin, the graphic novel, and *Maus*

In the mid-1980s, when media interest in the graphic-novel form was growing, some mainstream publishers decided to enter the field. The most important of these, if only because they brought Art Spiegelman's *Maus* to British readers, was Penguin. No doubt any publishing venture is risky, but there did seem to be, if not a new market, at least sympathetic interest in the established one.

However, in the mid-1990s, things look slightly different. According to Ravi Mirchandani, the editor who was responsible for the development of Penguin's graphic novels list, the attempt now looks like, 'an honourable failure'. If there was a bubble, it has burst. 'What we did wrong', he says, 'was to be too arty.'[18]

Typical of the arty end of Penguin's list were the three volumes of *Raw*. This compendium of 'High Culture for Lowbrows', or 'Open Wounds from the Cutting Edge of Commix', or 'Required Reading for the Post-Literate' (to quote its own covers) was edited by Art Spiegelman and Françoise Mouly, and the three volumes that appeared (1989–91) contain a mixture of the bad, the weird, and the wonderful. They were handsomely produced by Penguin in a smaller than usual format (the size of a wide paperback book) and printed on a mixture of papers: Issue no. 2, for instance, contained one story printed in colour on newsprint, and a chapter of Spiegelman's own *Maus* printed in black and white on paper with the faintest of grey tints. It also included an episode from the unpublished 19 000 page epic created by the eccentric Chicago janitor Henry Darger (1892–1972) and called *The Adventures of the Vivian Girls in What is Known as the Realms of the Unreal or the Glandelinian War Storm or the Glandico-Abiennian Wars, as caused by the Child Slave Rebellion*. The Penguin *Raw* lavishly reproduced in colour (on fold-out pages, too) the author's own spidery writing and his obsessively detailed paintings depicting hundreds if not thousands of doe-eyed children undergoing strenuous ordeals in bizarre landscapes. Darger was clearly a naive genius on the same scale as the postman Cheval, who built a dream-palace out of concrete and junk, and he clearly had not a hope of ordinary publication, let alone mass-market success; so it is to Penguin's great credit that we can look at this minute fragment at all.

The three issues of *Raw*, like most of Penguin's list, did not sell especially well. Bookshops, which had also become excited about the graphic novel, found their initial enthusiasm waning as the titles were well browsed but less often bought. There are two exceptions in the Penguin list, however. One is *Tank Girl* (1990), by Jamie Hewlett and Alan Martin, cheerful nonsense about a shaven-headed foul-mouthed gun-toting beer-drinking tank-driving girl and her kangaroo lover, which according to Ravi Mirchandani currently sells over fifty thousand copies annually at the non-arty end of the spectrum; and the other is Art Spiegelman's *Maus*, which has been reprinted ten times since the first volume was published in 1987.

Maus might or might not be a 'classic'; it is a hundred years too soon to tell. But it is interesting to look at it in the light of Harold Bloom's remark: 'One mark of an originality that can win canonical status for a literary work is a strangeness that we either never altogether assimilate, or that becomes such a given that we are blinded to its idiosyncrasies.'[19] In one way *Maus* stands squarely in the comics tradition, observing many of the conventions of the form: a story about anthropomorphically depicted animals, told sequentially in six square panels per page, containing speech balloons with lettering in capitals and emphasis in bold, with sound effects to represent the noise of rifle fire, and so on. It also refers to older traditions. The stark black and white drawings, the lines so thick in places as almost to seem like woodcuts, hark back to the wordless novels of Frans Masereel (1889–1972) such as *Passionate Journey*, with their expressionist woodcut prints; and those in turn take their place in an even older northern European tradition of printmaking that goes back to Holbein and Dürer. Spiegelman, in telling a story about Germany, uses a very German technique to do so.

Yet in other ways *Maus* does have a profound and unfailing 'strangeness', to use Bloom's term. Part of this is due to the depiction of Jews as mice, Germans as cats, Poles as pigs, and so on. This is what jolts most people who come to it for the first time, and still jolts me after several readings. It is such a *risky* artistic strategy, because it implies a suspect form of essentialism. Cats kill mice because they are cats, and that's what cats do. But is it really in the nature of Germans, as Germans, to kill Jews?

That question hangs over the whole work, and is never answered. Instead it is dispelled by the gradual gentle insistence that these characters might look like mice, or cats, or pigs, but what they are is people. They have the complexity and the surprisingness of human beings, and human beings are capable of anything. At the heart of the work is the tormented relationship between Art and his father Vladek, a survivor of Auschwitz, an obsessive, mean, doting, helpless, cantankerous, altogether impossible old man, whom we have come to know in two different worlds: the present-day world of penny-pinching retirement in New York and the Catskill mountains (names signify), and the remembered world of occupied Poland and the extermination camps. The work takes the form of a memoir by Art in which he tells us of his interviews with Vladek about Vladek's experiences under the Nazis. As Vladek tells him his story, the first-person past-tense captions in Art's voice give way to those in Vladek's, so the bulk of the story is technically a flashback.

The story is long, and takes nearly three hundred pages in two volumes to tell. But no one would wish it any shorter. For one thing, there is so much interesting stuff going on. There is the course of Art's growing obsession with getting the facts out of his initially doubtful father, his appalled discovery that Vladek has burnt Art's mother's diary of the time, his own doubts about the enterprise (Art worrying about art – names signifying again):

> I feel so inadequate trying to reconstruct a reality that was worse than my darkest dreams. And trying to do it as a **comic strip**! I guess I bit off more than I can chew.

Maybe I ought to forget the whole thing. There's so much I'll never be able to understand or visualize. I mean, reality is too **complex** for comics . . .'

There is the haunting legacy of the camps themselves, present in small details (the tattoo we see on Vladek's arm as he pedals his exercise cycle) and large (the later suicide of Art's mother Anja: like Bruno Bettelheim and Primo Levi, perhaps a victim many years later). There is the graphic poetry in such devices as the full-moon shape against which the characters are silhouetted at significant moments:

And most powerfully of all, there is the moment when Art discovers a photograph of Vladek, which is reproduced two pages from the end of the whole story. 'I passed once a photo place what had a **camp** uniform – a new and clean one – to make **souvenir** photos . . .', he says, and there he is, this character we have come, with Art, to hate and love and despair over in his old age, not a mouse any longer, but a man: a handsome man, a strong man, a proud and wary man in the prime of life who has survived appalling suffering, and survived in part because of the very qualities that make him so difficult to like and to live with: in short, a human being in all his urgent and demanding complexity. In Vladek's story, he sends the photograph with a letter to Anja, whom he last saw in Auschwitz, and she exclaims, 'And here's a **picture** of him! My God – Vladek is really alive!'

He is, in the same sense that King Lear is alive. I can never see that page except through tears. If there is a canon in this field, *Maus* certainly belongs at the heart of it.

Other developments

There has been no space in this chapter to look at other forms of graphic novels – Japanese Manga, recently introduced in English versions, for instance, or the more established European dimension. It must be said, however, that for all their huge popularity in English translation, *Asterix* and *Tintin* have had surprisingly little influence on British comic art. There are no British comic characters who appear in large-format hardback and paperback books, no teams of British comic artists and writers turning out full-colour titles that sell in respectable bookshops to informed adults. There seems to be an inborn resistance, among those who read comics at all in Britain, to respectability. Hence the popularity of VIZ, which has been well analysed by Roger Sabin.[20]

VIZ is certainly read by children, but it isn't published for them. In other words, the stories can be as rude as the writers like. One of the VIZ cartoonists, Steve Donald, has published a series of small-format 'graphic novel adventures' which are overtly for children, and thus have to mind their manners. *Orson Cart Comes Apart* (1993) and its sequels are robustly nonsensical in the VIZ manner, with drawings that look deliberately clumsy (and which are thus easy for comic-struck readers to imitate). Orson Cart has an accident with a radioactive lawnmower, which results in his being able to disassemble his body and for instance send his legs one way and his hands another. Donald has a great deal of fun with this notion, and so do readers; and that's what comics are for.

In the field of 'pure' graphic novels, a very recent event has been the publication of Doris Lessing's *Playing the Game* (1995), illustrated by Charlie Adlard. The publishers (HarperCollins) are not modest about this: the blurb hails it as, 'a revolutionary event in the world of graphic novels'. That is merely a blurb doing its job, but some reviewers have been equally excited: the *Financial Times* called it, 'a milestone: a significant achievement which deserves to promote wider acceptance of this neglected genre'.[21] The story suffers, it seems to me, from a consciousness of its own significance; the text, which rhymes, would work better as an opera libretto, and the pictures are not quite good enough to be admirable on their own account (unlike, for instance, Dave Gibbons's pictures in *Watchmen* (1987), which is a much more significant piece of work altogether, as I have pointed out elsewhere).[22] However, it is encouraging to see it at all. The *Financial Times* review quotes

Doris Lessing (though without giving a source) as saying, 'I am haunted by the vision of all those kids out there who are disqualified from the whole of culture, who perceive it as "not for us". It troubles me that they are unnecessarily excluded by those who don't even know they are doing it.'

Well, yes. But in order to reach the parts that solemnity alone cannot reach, earnest good intentions have to be wedded to narrative wit and artistic liveliness. *Eagle* showed that it could be done, briefly. It is good that a writer of Doris Lessing's calibre should take the graphic novel form seriously today; it would be a pity if anyone were to think that it wasn't worth taking seriously a long time ago.

References

1. W. Eisner (1978), *A Contract with God* (Princeton: Kitchen Sink Press; first UK edition published by Titan Books Ltd, 1989). The words *A Graphic Novel* occur on the cover, but not on the title page, which reads, *A Contract with God and other tenement stories*. Eisner's account of his method, contained in the Preface to *A Contract with God*, is worth quoting: 'The text and the balloons are interlocked with the art. I see all these as threads of a single fabric and exploit them as a language. If I have been successful in this, there will be no interruption in the flow of the narrative because the picture and the text are so totally dependent on each other as to be inseparable even for a moment.'
2. P. Pullman (1989), 'Invisible Pictures', in *Signal* no. 60, September, pp.167–8.
3. P. Vaughan (1995), *Something in Linoleum* (London: Sinclair-Stevenson), p.40.
4. Flyer advertising the facsimile reprint of *Rupert's Adventure Book*. Original edition published by Daily Express Publications, 1940; facsimile edition published under licence by Annual Concepts Ltd., Princes Risborough, 1992.
5. Figures quoted in K. Carpenter (1983), *Penny Dreadfuls and Comics: English periodicals for children from Victorian times to the present day*, a loan exhibition from the Library of Oldenburg University, West Germany at the Bethnal Green Museum of Childhood (London: Victoria and Albert Museum), pp.73–6.
6. L. Baxendale (revised edition, 1993), *On Comedy: The Beano and Ideology* (Stroud: Reaper Books), p.18.
7. Ibid., p.27.
8. Ibid., p.30.
9. Ibid.
10. Ibid., pp.20–21.
11. Ibid., p.41.
12. Carpenter, op.cit., p.101.
13. E.S. Turner (third edition, 1975), *Boys Will Be Boys* (London: Michael Joseph), p.291.
14. Interview with author, 16 August 1995.
15. Ibid.
16. Ibid.
17. Ibid.
18. Telephone interview with author, December 1995.
19. H. Bloom (1994, UK 1995), *The Western Canon* (New York: Harcourt Brace; UK edition London: Macmillan), p.4.
20. R. Sabin (1993), *Adult Comics: An Introduction* (London: Routledge), pp.116–26.

21.   M. Mulligan (1996), the *Financial Times*, 13 January.
22.   Pullman, op.cit., pp.13–14.

7   Different Worlds? Children's Books and the Media

Susanne Greenhalgh

With the first adaptations of children's books for radio, a long-term relation-ship was begun in which broadcasters made use of children's texts to add status and gravitas to their media, and in the process stimulated the reading of particular texts and authors. Despite the advantages to both books and broadcast media, this relationship has been and remains one of the most contentious areas in children's publishing. At its heart lies one question: do children's programmes and enactments of children's books promote reading, or do they contribute to a decline in the amount and quality of literature read by young people? But there is more to the relationship than this. For instance, it is important to understand the political uses to which broadcast versions of children's books (and children's programming generally) have been put; to consider the dynamic between viewing and listening; to be alert to the ways in which writing styles have been affected by children's viewing habits, and the effects of media on taste. In this chapter Susanne Greenhalgh addresses these issues, at the same time considering the changing nature of childhood in the worlds of text and performance, and the responsibilities placed on broadcasters who venture into the increasingly complex symbiosis between books, performances and merchandise.

Stories offered to children in book-form and those reaching them through the screen or the airwaves have often been regarded as the products of different, even rival worlds, drawing upon incompatible and competing skills. There are frequent laments that children's listening and reading skills, crucial to educational success, have given place to a hyper-stimulated visual sense without direction or discipline. More generally, public and political debate on children and the media in Britain, as elsewhere in the world, remains domi-nated by argument over whether television is 'good' or 'bad' for your kids, a 'plug-in-drug' or a home-based school-room, and by fears that filmed sex or violence disturb and corrupt the young viewer more powerfully than when represented in book-form. In the apocalyptic view of Neil Postman, childhood itself has disappeared in the twentieth century as the power invested in adulthood through command of print literacy has been overturned by the electronic media which give children a spurious equality of knowledge and information.[1] Similarly, according to Stephen C. Kline, the increasing dominance of promotional children's television series designed to market merchandise through tailor-made 'characters' has deprived children of the reference-points on 'real day-to-day experience' that childhood fantasy has traditionally helped develop, replacing 'healthy' narratives with 'an endless round of quasi-mythic stories which fascinate children as audiences and consumers'.[2] Others see television and print literacy, equally subject to historical change and development, as constantly shifting, mutually informing processes of social interaction.[3] Helen Bromley argues that, far from displacing books, videos should be acknowledged as a valuable form of 'literacy event' for the primary-school child, encouraging the skills needed to read ever-multiplying texts in a multimedia world;[4] whilst Maire Messenger Davies considers television 'good for your kids' precisely because it has introduced new narrative genres and forms of collective story-telling.[5]

Children today can be divided into a majority who are 'media-rich', moving freely between books, magazines, radio, audio-cassette players, terrestrial, satellite and cable television, VCRs, cinemas, and computers, and a much smaller number with restricted access who are 'media poor'.[6] Like children's literature, children's media narratives reflect the fantasies and desires of adults, not children, refiguring adulthood and its powers through their changing images of childhood, in an attempt to impose order and cohesion on the contradictions of subjectivity.[7] However, the representation of children's books in the British media is not simply a hall of mirror images. It is also one of the primary means by which radio and television originally established their legitimacy; a major focus for their implicit promise of 'quality' and public service, and this legacy continues to influence policy and practice in the present. Comparing the introduction of a daily children's hour on television in the 1950s with the approach taken by those who established the BBC's *Children's Hour* on radio in the 1920s, Mary Adams identified the same key questions needing to be addressed: 'First, and foremost, what is a child from the broadcasting point of view?' And then, 'What is a good programme in relation to Children's Hour?'[8]

Over the years both media have given varied and changing answers to these questions, some sharing the view of the child offered by children's book publishing together with its notions of what is 'good' for a young audience, while others arguably offer new and challenging images of children and their needs. Although programmes derived directly from children's books have always formed a relatively small part of the 'principled diversity'[9] which characterizes British broadcasting for children, they have had a status and visibility beyond their actual numbers. This output, from both the BBC and ITV, has helped to construct a 'great tradition' complete with its 'golden ages',[10] which provides a fascinating and revealing looking-glass world in which to trace changing images of children's books and childhood in twentieth-century Britain.

Radio

John Reith described the first *Children's Hour* as 'a new form of art, wholly novel, leaping into its permanent place in the scheme of popular life' and implicitly changing that life forever.[11] From the start the BBC took its child audience seriously, even if actual provision was at first haphazard and uncertain. Adopting its title from a Longfellow poem, the *Children's Hour*, in the words of Ian Hartley, 'provided amusement, excitement, wonder, and often a social focus with its Radio Circles of ardent young listeners';[12] it also relied heavily on a relationship with the book world that some feared it would displace.

In many ways the new broadcasting institution was set up like a publishing house, although in this case its editors were also often authors and even 'illustrators' when they acted as presenters or readers. One of the promises made by Radio Circle members was to 'look for beauty in books, pictures and in all things of our daily life'.[13] In the 1920s, BBC Standing Instructions, whilst laying down that the *Children's Hour* was for entertainment and recreation rather than for explicit instruction or moral improvement, suggested that it had a vital, if subliminal, role in moulding its audience's aesthetic development:

> If the organisers of the Children's Hour keep in mind the creation of the atmosphere of a good home, and the presentation of real beauty in song, story, music, and poetry, on a plane attractive to the young, they will inevitably, without self-conscious effort, raise the standard of culture in their young listeners, and the result will be educative in the best sense.[14]

This Arnoldian concept of children's radio as an 'ideal home' (presumably middle-class and in easy reach of art galleries, theatres and, above all, libraries), was sometimes overlaid by more overtly ideological goals. The first BBC-sponsored researchers, looking in 1939 at the social impact of broadcasting on the everyday life of a predominantly working-class community in Bristol, argued for its potential to dissolve class and cultural barriers and help create a more critical and knowledgable citizenry.[15] A characteristic BBC mixture of egalitarianism and paternalism informs the policy outlined in 1948 by Derek McCulloch, based on the conviction that 'nothing but the best is good enough for children, who are citizens of the future'.[16] Accordingly it was the programme's task to shape the listening tastes of those future citizens with the utmost responsibility, and, in particular, 'to stimulate their imagination, direct their reading, encourage their various interests, widen their outlook, and inculcate the Christian principles of love of God and their neighbour'. By providing a 'miniature' or 'microcosm' of adult broadcasting for a family audience notionally still gathered for five o'clock tea, children would gradually be admitted to a democratic 'common ground for listening and for discussion' with parents, enabling their gradual passage into a responsible maturity, for which it was the BBC's self-appointed role to provide them with models.[17]

Although a high-minded equation of good books with good works was to play a decisive part in this idealistic concept of children's radio programming during the first twenty-five years of broadcasting, there was, from the start, an alternative, infantilising approach. Ian Hartley terms this the ' "kiddiewinkie" attitude', offering spontaneous 'idiotic' backchat from jolly 'aunts' and 'uncles', or even 'animals'.[18] The first story told over the air fell into this category, when *Children's Hour* (only at certain periods was it actually a full hour) started broadcasting on 5 December 1922 with the tale of two dwarfs named Spick and Span.[19] During the 1920s and 1930s the programme, with its 'clean, wholesome humour',[20] became a fixed and significant part of the schedule, transmitted immediately before the 6.00 p.m. news bulletin, and listened to by many adults as well as children.[21] Striving to find both its audience and its own identity, the programme gradually moved away from 'babyish' items and the fairy tales that dominated airtime in the 1920s. A directive to studio directors insisted that 'the word "child" should be construed as the ordinary boy or girl of ten to twelve, living in a good middle-class home and attending a good school'.[22]

The quest to combine education and entertainment, and the stress on an intelligent, sensitive and sensible audience, deserving the 'best', ensured that adaptations of children's classics, in story-form or as plays, occupied much of the schedules; for instance, Browning's 'The Pied Piper' (read by Robert Donat) in 1929, *Treasure Island* (1936), *Alice in Wonderland* and *Through the Looking-Glass* (1937), and the first of several versions of *The Secret Garden* (1938). Presenters also wrote their own stories, which included retellings of Arthurian legends, Aesop's fables, Nordic sagas, and tales of British heritage, inspired by the Tower of London, or the roads, waterways, and castles of England. S.G. Hulme Beaman's *Tales of Toytown* (1928), discovered in a bookshop by May E. Jenkins in 1929, was the first example of a children's book given sustained exploitation by the media, generating many specially written stories of Larry the Lamb and Dennis the Dachshund for radio and, later, for television. But there was still a great deal of poor writing, condescending and anodyne, 'fairytale stuff',[23] designed to keep children in a mental nursery stocked with stories of Hepzibiah Hen and the farm-yard folk and narrated by talking-down adults, even if no longer specifically termed 'aunts' and 'uncles'.

Attempting as it did simultaneously to provide a 'fair share for everybody' and appeal above all to, 'the keen unspoiled mind of the child ... even the most precocious',[24] the programme often moved uneasily between elitism, populism and patronage. The BBC's first ventures into children's publishing,

Hullo Boys and *Hullo Girls* annuals in 1924, reflected this, offering unadventurous imitations of the established fare of the time, and displaying similar attitudes to empire and gender. *The Magic Doorway* (c. 1927), written by 'the BBC Aunts and Uncles' and based on its *Children's Hour* output, claimed to offer 'the treasures of the microphone . . . of the richest and rarest sort . . . a MAGIC DOORWAY such as the world has never before known', but only C.E. Hodges's 'Peeps Behind the Scenes' of *Children's Hour* hinted at the different perspectives made available by this new medium.[25]

When war broke out, the programme's role in maintaining a mood of normality, and even of national unity, was recognised.[26] Under wartime conditions it continued its self-appointed task of guarding the pristine innocence of its young audience. Directives from the highest level warned against any mention of the war in its stories and plays, jokes against Nazi leaders were forbidden, together with anything that might incite hatred of the enemy.[27] At first old favourites, such as *The Wind in the Willows* and *The Jungle Book* (1940), were scheduled to reassure an anxious public that traditional values remained intact, but later came more adventurous fare, such as a controversially colloquial *Life of Jesus*, scripted by the detective writer Dorothy L. Sayers (1941).

If the war could not to be addressed directly, there was room for stories of daring-do set safely in the past, such as *Kidnapped* and *Treasure Island* (1944), whilst the dramatization of John Masefield's *The Box of Delights* (1943) offered a comforting evocation of victory over the forces of evil. Writing in the BBC Handbook in 1945 McCulloch summed up the aims of the war-time *Children's Hour* as providing children with a sense of continuity in a world of chaos, a goal synonymous with giving them only the best in drama, music, and story.[28]

After the war adaptations of children's books continued as an important part of the schedules, perhaps compensating in some way for the stock made unavailable by bombing and shortages. Most of them still presented middle-class children and environments, whether in contemporary novels for young people such as Noel Streatfeild's own adaptation of *Ballet Shoes* (1947), Pamela Brown's *The Swish of the Curtain*, also adapted (and acted in) by the author, or the pre-war world of servants and suburban security of Richmal Crompton's William books (1946). Broadcasts of William stories were aired out of children's time, at 8.00 p.m.; they were so popular with all the family that a Sunday afternoon repeat was scheduled. As Ian Hartley observes, *William* was in effect an early situation comedy, and its success gave rise to further series based on Crompton's characters.[29] Another BBC commission which was subsequently published and now is best known in book form was also based around a hapless young male character: Anthony Buckeridge's Jennings.

In 1946 sound broadcasting's dominance of children's media was challenged when the BBC's television service offered its first children's programme, variously called *For the Children* and *Children's Hour*, followed in 1950 by *Watch with Mother. Children's Hour* on radio had received the accolade of Princess Elizabeth's first public broadcast in 1942; ironically the beginning of the end was signposted by the televising of her coronation in 1953. Once the coverage of the celebrations ended, twenty-six per cent of the adult population stayed switched on to watch its Children's Programme on a day which had seen much lower numbers listening to radio.[30]

By 1955, when Independent Television came on air, it was already clear that the BBC's sound output for children was reaching a declining audience, which had transferred its attention decisively to the new medium.[31] The children's slot finally disappeared in 1964, the same year that BBC2 was launched. Its last item, appropriately enough, was a reading of Oscar Wilde's story, 'The Selfish Giant', one moral of which is the need to be generous with beautiful possessions. As David Davis argued in a 1957 memorandum, it had sought to give children 'the things that sound alone can give: the freeing and setting to work of the child's imagination; active as opposed to passive participation'.[32]

Although its audience was down to 25000 (compared with four million at the start of the war), the place of children's radio in the national consciousness of an older generation was evident in the parliamentary motion criticizing its abolition, signed by sixty MPs.[33] Book dramatisations continued, but were now firmly aimed at a family audience, and were characterised by mainstream choices of material. For instance, two versions of *The Secret Garden* were broadcast in 1966 and 1975 respectively; *The Hobbit* in 1968, and *The Borrowers* and *The Borrowers Afield* in 1965 and 1966. Readings also found a place, notably in the late afternoon slot *Storytime*, which more enterprisingly included adaptations of Alan Garner's *Elidor* (1972) and *The Guizer* (1975) alongside such customary fare as Nesbit, Tolkien and Crompton.

Listen with Mother had proved an enduring success since its launch in 1950, with its soothing and repetitive diet of songs, nursery rhymes, and stories read by mainly female narrators to an audience 'sitting comfortably' after lunch, but by 1974 nearly half of two to four-year-olds 'watched with mother' compared with the 3 per cent who listened, and it too went off air in 1982 to be replaced by a five-minute *Listening Corner*.[34] As television hours (and channels) increased in the 1980s, and schedules extended into parts of the day traditionally regarded as radio-dominated – particularly the early morning – the child audience diminished further. With it went the last of radio's specialized children's programmes.

Radio Five: mission impossible

It took nearly thirty years for a dedicated children's radio strand to be reintroduced. In 1990, under the Controllership of Liz Forgan, BBC Radio Five was established with a special brief to serve child audiences, among other minorities, alongside an extensive range of sports coverage. Although designed to reach out to a very different kind of audience from that of *Children's Hour*, one at home in a multicultural, high-tech world for whom radio was only one option among the many leisure enticements on offer, the emphasis on literacy and literary tradition proved surprisingly durable. The following defensive statement formed part of a Programme Strategy Review in 1993, by which time the children's content was already under threat:

> Our aim is to provide entertainment for children and young people in their own time and in their own space. Readings and Drama help develop literacy, a love of literature and stimulate the imagination. Children, of all cultures, have always learnt about the world and their place in it through storytelling. Radio drama and stories can also teach them to listen and that is a valuable skill for life in general. . . . There is evidence also that many adults without a habit of listening may also find a new route back to an experience they missed as a child.[35]

Radio Five's emphasis on children's books complied with the guidelines for the BBC's new role contained in the 1993 policy document *Extending choice: The BBC's role in the new broadcasting age*. Its children's programmes, it was claimed, were crafted to reflect, 'insights and perspectives on the rest of the world'; mirror and nurture, 'the UK's rich cultural heritage'; portray a, 'multiracial, multicultural society', and respond to 'the diversity of cultures throughout the UK' In particular its readings and dramatisations were to provide, 'a planned output of classic literary adaptations, which over time will ensure frequent and regular exposure to the great works of writers', and, 'the work of our best living authors'.[36]

The yearly schedule included sixty hours of readings in the form of fifteen-minute slots each weekday night, aimed at seven to ten-year-olds, and covering a wide range of published material, from both the classic canon and current writing, including non-British literature in English or in translation. Frequent book dramatisations, mainly in serial form for either the child or family audience, occupied ninety-eight hours a year, on weekday evenings and Sunday mornings. This output included, 'longer-running socio-realistic serials that will also be enjoyed by other members of the family', and 'more compulsive' narratives of fantasy, detection and adventure.

Between 1990 and 1993 Radio Five transmitted or commissioned plays and readings based on a mixture of old favourites and new writing; for example, *Swallows and Amazons, Pippi Longstocking, Jennings, The Demon Headmaster, Emil and the Detectives, The Railway Children, The Secret Garden, The Adventures of Huckleberry Finn, The BFG, The Little House on the Prairie, Charlie and the Chocolate Factory, Tintin, Just William,* a collection of J.R.R. Tolkien's short stories, *Tales From the Perilous Realm,* Enid Blyton's *The Island of Adventure,* and Ghanaian storytelling. A statistical breakdown of its broadcast material revealed that its readings annually featured from 11 per cent to 17 per cent of newly published books, from 8 per cent to 31 per cent of classics, and from 5 per cent to 30 per cent of 'contemporary classics', all broadcast with the avowed intention of encouraging listeners to read the books, or others by the same author, for themselves.

In May 1991, in a notorious attack on the standard of children's broadcasting and its damaging impact on literacy and reading habits, the junior Minister for Education, Michael Fallon, praised Radio Five for showing, 'what can be done in intelligent programming to stimulate children's interests and help them read and love literature'. A year later the *Times Educational Supplement* noted the excellence of,

> dramas and stories [which] have been expertly produced with no feeling that second best will do. The mixture of classics with more modern writing, the willingness of storytellers and playwrights to tackle issues of importance, the readiness to embrace a variety of forms of spoken English, all these factors have combined to create a style of radio which is admirable and lively.[37]

The statistics for audiences were far less satisfactory, however. Although a new audience *was* attracted, rising from an average of 20,000 for readings in 1991 to 206,000 in 1993, and allowing the claim that, 'Radio Five delivers a "library book" (story) to one child for 0.7 pence', there was also evidence that that audience was mainly adult, with more children listening to the sports coverage than to the programmes made especially for them. By 1995, despite widespread critical acclaim and several awards for its children's output, Radio Five had been redesigned as primarily a continuous news service, and the BBC appeared to have more or less abandoned its public service commitment to quality speech radio for children.[38]

In the 1990s speech radio is perceived by its adult audience as an essentially personal medium, under individual control, demanding a positive commitment to listening, but also risking being used as 'background' sound to fill an empty room or help pass the motorway miles. But its drama and stories are also regarded as offering a luxurious prospect of 'time out' with the imagination, and overall the medium is seen as more honest and immediate, raising few of the concerns about representations of sex and violence that plague public debate on television.[39] For children, however, speech radio hardly exists as a medium, although many listen to commercial audio tapes of such broadcasts. Only 6 per cent listen to Radio Four, and at peak times, such as early morning, only 4 per cent of four to eleven-year-olds in 1991 were listening, mostly to music programmes on Independent Local Radio or Radio 1.[40] Even in education, where BBC Schools broadcasts are used by 68 per cent of infant teachers, the main demand is for dance and movement programmes. Despite emphasis on listening skills in the National Curriculum, teachers seem to accept that the decline in speech radio programmes made especially for children and the increase of visual stimuli in the home have irretrievably weakened the attractions of this form of media for children.[41] Certainly this is the view reflected in *Extending Choice*:

> By and large, the BBC should concentrate its investment in children's programming on television, which is the most likely way of reaching children. There should be rather less drama and other programming on radio aimed primarily at children, since it generally fails to reach its target audience. But the BBC should apply its creative skills to developing strands of speech based radio entertainment, including stories and adaptations that will be of interest to families and young people.[42]

In the mid-1990s, Children's BBC still retained a half-hour slot on Sunday evenings on Radio Four, in which dramatizations of books from many periods played an important part alongside specially commissioned children's series. Often such series made full use of the resources of the Radiophonic workshop to create fantastic worlds and creatures. They also seemed to be perceived as a way of presenting costume drama on the cheap – without the costumes. Many of these were originally transmitted or commissioned by Radio Five. Among those broadcast in 1995–96 were adaptations of Michelle Magorian's *Back Home*, set during the Second World War; C.S. Lewis's allegorical fantasy *Prince Caspian*; vocally and musically lavish versions of *The Jungle Book*, with Eartha Kitt as Kaa the snake, and a number of Asian actors; a spectacular *Peter Pan* by the producer of an earlier 'radio-cartoon' version of *Batman*; a thoughtful and aurally rich interpretation of Hadley Irwin's novel *We Are Mesquakie. We Are One*, about a Native American girl growing up amidst the destruction of her tribe (a repeat from Radio Five Live); and Alison Uttley's influential ghost-cum-period love story, *A Traveller in Time*. A particularly adventurous adaptation was made of Rosemary Sutcliff's historical novel, *The Eagle of the Ninth*, by Radio Scotland. It was recorded on location and skilfully and topically conveyed the colonial politics of the Roman attempt to subdue the Celts.

Like the Sunday classic serial on BBC1, such productions are targeted as much at adults as children, and in their pace and style often implicitly acknowledge that their listeners will draw on film and television images for their visualization of the series's aural imagery. Nor are the motives for this kind of continuing investment purely altruistic. BBC Enterprises (now subsumed into BBC Worldwide), the marketing arm of the BBC, boasts that its audiotapes, many of them derived from radio programmes (and, increasingly, from television), have the highest UK sales in this sector. *The Jungle Book*, *Peter Pan* and *Prince Caspian* are available as twin-cassette sets in the 'Children's Classic' series, as are *The Secret Garden*, *The Railway Children*, and *Tales of the Perilous Realm* from Radio Five. The list also contains tapes for the younger age-groups based on well-known TV animations, often complete with the voices and music of the original television series. These range from original creations such as *Postman Pat*, *Fireman Sam*, and *Pingu*, to those derived from existing books, such as Colin Dann's *The Animals of Farthing Wood*. Projects which may attract international sales and thus generate healthy profits have access to internal investment in the first instance.

Other television 'tie-ins' include new readings of Sunday serializations, sometimes narrated by actors from the screen version (for instance George Baker, who played the Duke in a 1996 television dramatization, reading *Little Lord Fauntleroy*). This recognition of the multiple ways in which media products now reach their audiences is a vital part of the 'revolution' which has swept through the BBC in the 1990s under the direction of John Birt in preparation for the new age of digital recording and multiple satellite and cable channels. 'The Children's Charter', devised by Anna Home, Head of

BBC-TV Children's Programmes, states that children's programmes, 'should be aired in regular slots at times when children are available to view *and/or distributed via other widely accessible media or technologies*' (my emphasis).[43]

This approach applies equally to radio. The BBC may have largely abandoned the quest for a young speech–radio audience, but by repackaging its programmes as audio-tapes it combines shrewd marketing with its accustomed reliance on a 'golden treasury' of classic children's literature, given extra gloss by the performances of well-known personalities – for instance, Joanna Lumley reading Dodie Smith's *One Hundred and One Dalmatians*. Children with Walkmans are not the only audience for 'talking books'. Listeners on the move, parents seeking an hour's peace and quiet, students studying set-books, foreigners in pursuit of British tradition, or older listeners reviving memories provide a growing market. In this sense at least the trend for audio-cassette versions could be viewed as a way of restoring children's books to an adult audience. However, if this is the case, that audience is no longer gathered with its children round the wireless at 5.00 p.m., but instead reflects the fragmentation of the traditional nuclear family, each member listening at a time and in a place of his or her 'extended' choice.

Television

A great adventure: BBC children's television, 1946–55

Children's television began in 1946, and as with children's publishing, women played an important role in its evolution (see Chapter 2). Mary Adams, Head of Talks, initiated live transmissions on Sunday afternoons.[44] Initially she was keen to retain the established values and even forms of radio's *Children's Hour* within the newer medium, as a memorandum of 1947 suggests:

> I believe story-telling (or even reading) good stories would hold interest without much additional visual support . . . We could simply show the illustrations while reading books like *Stuart Little* or *Babar* or *Orlando*. Or we could commission original stories by someone prepared to put in the necessary work.[45]

In 1950 she wrote of the, 'fundamental pleasures and immediate practical appeal of vision, as against the less direct and more sophisticated aural approach'. The image of the intelligent, sensitive young listener on the way to responsible citizenship through the exercise of considered programme choice was replaced by the spectre of the greedy, insatiable viewer, spellbound by 'magic in the living room', saturated in visual experience from films, picture magazines and visual aids in school, and part of a society which radio itself had helped to make more homogeneous.[46] Again, the BBC's approach required discrimination and judgement, 'to encourage initiative, applaud adventure, and translate into visual terms the widest range of emotional, aesthetic and intellectual experience', whilst also encouraging 'restraint in viewing'. This could be done by making distinctions between, 'the needs of boys and girls, town and country children, solitary and gregarious viewers'. More specialised programme content, made possible by the increase in viewing hours, was the way forward.[47]

A number of the first specialised posts went to women, some of whom had backgrounds in radio, theatre or even children's writing, Pamela Brown being a case in point. In her invaluable history of children's television, *Into the Box of Delights* (1992) – the title reflecting the affinity between children's reading and viewing – Anna Home, now Head of Children's BBC-TV, distinguishes two 'golden ages', both presided over by female Heads of Departments: Freda Lingstrom (known as 'Mum' by her staff) in the 1950s, and Monica Sims, formerly Head of Women's Programmes, in the late 1960s. It was no coincidence that these were also periods in which children's television made visible changing ideas of childhood and parenting under way in the society at large. One age-group, the youngest viewers, gained new prominence, due no doubt, to the impact of the work of child psychologists such as D.W. Winnicott and Melanie Klein, and popularizers of new modes of parenting such as Dr Spock. Despite 'young days' and occasional special items, after its early years radio's *Children's Hour* had often deliberately side-lined the 'tiny tots', whose attention span was regarded as too short for more than 'suitable short stories, fairy tales and fairy plays, nursery rhymes and so on'.[48] The prospect of specialised television programmes for pre-school children offered pioneering opportunities for meeting the needs of those still in the process of developing the language skills necessary for radio listening. Furthermore, the incentives of 'wholesome' entertainment and safeguards such as the 'toddler's truce' close-down between 6.00 and 7.00 p.m. were intended to be attractive to young families – vital for the expansion and renewal of the BBC's audience.

In the early 1950s, Lingstrom's partner, Maria Bird, created and developed *Watch with Mother*, which, it has been argued, through its narrative structure and use of female narrator, helped legitimize television for very young children in the sphere of the 'good enough mother', even when, in reality, some children listened alone, with the box in the corner acting as babysitter. The tradition of story-telling inherited from radio was also kept alive, illustrated by puppets (which Lingstrom loved), drawings, or latterly animation, in adaptations of existing picture books or specially commissioned series such as *Captain Pugwash* and *Noggin the Nog*, which were subsequently turned into publications.

For the much larger listening range from six or seven to the early teens, radio's adaptation of classic children's literature was transposed into live drama serials transmitted twice a week from a dedicated studio at Lime Grove, but especially associated with what became an established Sunday afternoon slot. Many of the chosen texts had already been dramatised for radio, indicating the emergence of a 'canon' of texts quality-sealed both by their literary status and their track-record in broadcasting. Given directors who often came originally from the theatre, there was a vested interest in expanding the range of children's drama, leading to charges of 'extravagance' from some quarters.[49] *Treasure Island* (1951), *Little Women* (1950–51), *The Railway Children, Five Children and It* (1951), *The Secret Garden* (1952), and *Huckleberry Finn* (1952) all received productions of varying success within the confines of studio conditions. There were also ventures into the bleaker territory of contemporary children's books dealing with the horrors endured during wartime, such as Ian Serrailier's *The Silver Sword* (1959), which traced the adventures of refugee Polish children searching for their parents. On a lighter note, 1952 saw the first of the highly successful *Billy Bunter* series. The tradition of children's annuals also continued, several edited by Lingstrom or Bird. As well as containing stories and extracts from scripts, they were now copiously illustrated with stills from children's drama to give the programmes, 'a more permanent existence'.[50]

In many ways the concept of the child viewer in these years echoed that of the child listener. Children were still seen as a 'lively audience', active not passive, 'thirsty for adventure', 'alert and eager' awaiting 'with an open mind this small separate part of his [*sic*] daily life'.[51] However, fears about the potential power of the new medium brought renewed anxieties about the nature of the experiences that might be encountered. Lingstrom's own portrait of the 'television child' has overtones of a modernist hero venturing into what might turn out to be as much a heart of darkness as of light:

> What does a child do when he watches so intently? Thousands of impressions fall lightly on his mind, some to sink deep and some to fade altogether or be so dimly remembered as only to be recalled if a set of similar circumstances presents itself. In his own time, consciously and unconsciously, he will distil from the multitude of sights and sounds an essence which must inevitably lead to his perpetually exchanging previously held values for new ones. Gradually there will emerge a character which will become recognisable to him as himself – his private, secret self which, beginning in childhood, a man must carry with him for his delight or torment to the end of his days. Who knows what chance comment may touch off the spark of ambition or whether some apparently harmless action may not put panic into his soul.[52]

Magic window or dark invader?: children's television in a competitive world, 1955–96

Although radio had always asked the question, 'can it harm children?' when making programming decisions,[53] a new mood of moral panic (prompted in part by the fear that post-war Britain was being 'Americanized' into a more violent and materialistic society) constructed the child as a particularly vulnerable member of the viewing public, especially after the advent of commercially-funded Independent Television in 1955. The next two decades were marked by increasing academic research and government reports on broadcasting and on education, many of which paid special attention to the child viewer. Labour amendments to the 1954 Television Bill imposed a public service duty on the new channels to provide suitable material for children, together with an over-seeing Committee of the Independent Television Authority (ITA), consisting of those with 'experience of and special interest in the welfare and education of young children', to advise on the 'principles' which should govern their practice.[54]

Despite this ethical pressure, and the presence of many ex-BBC staff in the new organizations, traditional literary materials for children were initially treated mostly as pretexts for adventure series rather than occasions for respectful adaptation. By 1958, when ITV was available to 76 per cent of the population, children could enjoy Robert Newton in a much parodied performance of the adventures of Long John Silver *before* he reached Treasure Island, as well as Robin Hood, Lancelot and Ivanhoe in a variety of action-packed, if unlikely, weekly exploits that owed little to their originals. In the same year the first public research on television and the child, sponsored by the Nuffield Foundation, was published. Hilde Himmelweit and her colleagues paid particular attention to the impact of television on reading and other childhood activities, concluding that, whilst television did displace books to some extent, mostly among the 'average' children, it was often material the researchers regarded as lightweight and dispensable (Enid Blyton, American-style comics) that was most affected. Lamenting the class-based pattern of reading found in the general population of children, they also welcomed evidence from teachers and librarians that serial dramatization of books stimulated interest in further reading and that familiarity with plots and characters of serials such as *Jane Eyre* enabled children to enjoy books beyond their reading age, although they noted that such classics could be as emotionally disturbing as modern crime thrillers.[55]

By now the BBC's child-viewing figures were under real attack by ITV, whose offerings remained dominated by adventure serials from America. As a generation began to emerge which had grown up with television, the BBC appeared briefly to suffer a crisis in the confidence that had marked its previous provision for children; perhaps because it was no longer so sure what a child was. Increased concern about audience size led to moves to attract a wider family audience. 'Family' became the BBC buzz word at a time when 'family values' appeared under particular threat from an emerging youth culture.[56] The phrase 'Children's Television' was dropped from programme schedules and announcements, the department lost its responsibility for drama and light entertainment, and in 1964 it was amalgamated with Women's Programmes to form Family Programmes. One result of these changes was a controversially violent version of *Oliver Twist* (1962) by the Drama Department, broadcast in the traditional safe haven of the Sunday classic serial slot, which, even when regained by the Children's Department in 1988, would in future be regarded as family viewing that was 'not unsuitable' for children.[57]

Joy Whitby's *Play School*, whose long run began with the launch of BBC 2 in 1964, also came under the auspices of Family Programmes, and marked a break with the 'soft-centre' attitudes to the very young inherited from radio.

Young people were viewed as more sophisticated, unsentimental and realistic than those in previous generations, demanding a 'hard-core' approach and programmes which made few concessions in their efforts to equip viewers with the knowledge they would need in a tough world. Even previously taboo content, such as violence, properly handled, was thought to enable a child to cope, through fantasy, with the harsh realities of life.[58] Throughout these changes, 'good' children's books remained the touchstone for 'good' television. New puppet-stories for *Watch with Mother*, combining fantasy and realism, would become the equivalent of 'the child's well-thumbed favourite story book', whilst the highest literary standards would be set to make *Play School* an effective vehicle

> for presenting a changing flow of music, poetry, stories, games, ideas, and infor-
> mation. Scripts are written carefully, logically, and with integrity. A cat is a cat and
> not a dressed-up pussy. Talking down by either word or voice tone is rigorously
> stamped on. Originality, wit, and quality of thought are at a premium. We believe
> the television screen should not be used for the dissemination of hack ideas, already
> available in the cheaper comics and books. For our programmes we are seeking
> out fresh views or using the best from the past whether they be the graphics used
> for an old story retold or the toys used to people the screen – whether it be those
> chosen to present the programmes or write the scripts.[59]

Judy Taylor, children's editor at The Bodley Head, advised on the fiction which was an important part of the daily programme. This led in due course to the establishment of a special graphics department which employed a wide range of styles and methods to translate picture-book illustrations to the screen with their original impact undiluted. Another spin-off from the programme was the famous *Jackanory*, which ran for thirty years, from 1965 to 1995. With its kaleidoscopic opening sequence and hypnotic whispered rhyme:

> I'll tell you a story of Jackanory
> And now my story's begun,
> I'll tell you another of Jack and his brother
> And now my story's done

the programme aimed 'to tell the best stories, of all kinds from all parts of the world, and to have them told by the best story tellers available'.[60] These ranged from established broadcasting favourites such as Alison Uttley's 'Little Grey Rabbit' stories, *Winnie-the-Pooh*, and *My Naughty Little Sister* to contemporary writing such as Ted Hughes's *The Iron Man*, Philippa Pearce's *A Dog so Small* and Roald Dahl's *George's Marvellous Medicine*. Readers included many distinguished actors, television personalities, and even the Prince of Wales, telling his own environmentally-concerned children's story *The Old Man of Lochnagar*. The shooting of dramatised inserts for some of the stories also preserved a tradition of children's drama made by specialists in children's television and broadened the range of content to include more contemporary children's writers, such as Lucy M. Boston, Nina Bawden, and Gillian Avery. According to Anna Home, who helped create the programme, its thinking was always governed by the certainty that watching television encouraged children to read and, together with *Play School*, the programme generated a constant stream of BBC publications in the form of records, audio-tapes, and videos, as well as books.[61] The assertion, in the 1995 policy document *People and Programmes*, that such traditional book-based story-telling was 'of only limited appeal to children' was not simply a nail in the coffin of one programme, but marked the declining power of an idea (or ideal) of childhood, 'as a time for developing literacy and propriety and a gradual induction into maturity'. According to Jay Blumler in his 1992 report on the future of children's television, this idea has been bound up with ideas of quality in children's broadcasting throughout its history.[62]

Such programmes and principles maintained the sense of distinctive tradition in BBC children's programmes during the interregnum until the Children's Department was re-established in 1967, under Monica Sims. She reclaimed drama production and developed a new genre of children's serials, such as *Grange Hill*, set in a comprehensive school, and *Byker Grove*, set in a youth club. In keeping with their soap-opera conventions, which required constant new cycles of engrossing narratives involving a wide range of characters, these programmes presented the experience of childhood in a society undergoing radical demographic, economic and political change as a period of frequent conflict and difficult choices, often centring on previously controversial topics such as drugs, teenage sex, and relationships between races. *Grange Hill* sparked off a paperback book series, as well as a storystrip in the BBC's youth magazine, *Beeb*, and both programmes encouraged a greater realism of tone and content in other areas of children's programming.

Technological advances, which have always influenced the development of television genres and styles, together with an increased emphasis on worldwide sales and international co-productions in the 1980s, made possible lavish 'flagship' dramatizations of stories set in fantastic worlds or peopled by strange creatures. Previously these had been considered impossible to make on television budgets. *The Box of Delights* (1984), with its then state-of-the-art animations and video frames-within-frames, provided an almost meta-televisual celebration of the 'wonder' of children's television. *The Chronicles of Narnia* (from 1988), based on the sequence of novels by C.S. Lewis, was a long-term project requiring extensive investment from BBC Enterprises and co-producers. It regained the Sunday serial slot for children's drama, and also attracted large audiences and high appreciation.[63] Although the genre continued with, for example, an updated version of Alan Garner's *Elidor* in 1996, which made computer games the magic doorway to a kingdom created by the latest digital technology, the introduction in the early 1990s of 'Producer Choice', which charges the real cost of production to programme budgets, makes it unlikely that children's series on the scale of *Narnia* will be attempted again.[64]

By the late 1960s ITV was approaching its children's output with increased seriousness. The Pilkington Report (1961) had led to the dismantling of the Children's Advisory Committee, and responsibility for children's programmes was now firmly with the broadcasters and the ITA (Independent Television Authority), which funded a five-year enquiry into the effects of television on young people. Within a network of independent regional companies, each with its own profit-making agendas, the arguments against the centralization of children's provision won the day, but in 1969 the Children's Sub-Committee was reconstituted and improved arrangements for network coordination of the planning and supply of children's programmes were put in place, leading also to a new weekday schedule which gave designated slots for drama, features, light entertainment and films.[65] The new concern for quality as well as audiences, and the increased space for drama, inevitably led to the same kind of reliance on the proven values of children's literature that had previously dominated BBC's children's provision. As early as 1963, Southern had made a studio version of C.S. Lewis's *The Lion, the Witch and the Wardrobe*, but the real upsurge came between 1969 and 1973 when there were networked productions of *The Owl Service* (Granada); *Redgauntlet* (STV); *Smith* and *Professor Branestawm* (Thames); *Catweazel* and *The Adventures of Black Beauty* (LWT); *The Black Arrow, Midnight is a Place, Worzel Gummidge, The Flocton Flyer* (Southern); *Follyfoot* (Yorkshire Television); *The Wind in the Willows* and *Treasure Island* (Anglia).

It was also an ITV company, Yorkshire Television, which introduced the first magazine programme dedicated to children's books, another original idea from Joy Whitby who, like many others from BBC children's television, had moved into the independent sector. *The Book Tower* (1979–89) was originally set in an actual tower, but latterly in different locations using guest presenters for each themed programme. These included episodes on football hosted by Bruce Grobelaar, romance with comedian Victoria Wood, and an award-winning programme on war, presented by Michael Rosen. Features on writers, interviews and dramatized book extracts provided a lively mix, but despite the weekly issue of a *Book Tower Watcher's Guide*, and the participation of publishers and booksellers, there was little evidence that books featured in the programme were widely read, let alone purchased.[66]

The strong BBC come-back, and the varied output of individual ITV companies resulted in nearly two decades of 'cosy competition', largely undisturbed by the advent of Channel Four in 1982, which chose not to give designated slots to children other than its daily lunchtime screenings of the American pre-school programme *Sesame Street*.[67] As broadcasting hours increased, the ITA drew up specialized afternoon, Saturday morning and Sunday schedules similar to those of the BBC. These were introduced from 1981 by a 'Children's ITV' logo and signature tune, and characterized by the same principles of diversity and balance, although the lack of a 'consistent and coherent policy'[68] meant that achievement rested on the vision and commitment of individual producers and programme bosses.

Particularly strong features of ITV's book-based output were the high-quality, innovative stop-frame and cell animations provided by companies such as Filmfair, a subsidiary of Central, and Cosgrave-Hall Productions

(Thames), which produced award-winning versions of *The Pied Piper of Hamelin* (1981), *The Wind in the Willows* (1983) and *The BFG* (1989).[69] Although very expensive at £2500–4000 a minute, animation, with its scope for character merchandizing and relative ease of dubbing for foreign distribution, can be profitable. The BBC was a major participant in a European Broadcasting Union co-production of Colin Dann's books about *The Animals of Farthing Wood*, with spin-offs including a magazine, and audio-tapes, as well as videos and books. Picture books usually require substantial additions if they are to be turned into even short feature films. In Raymond Briggs's *The Snowman*, music (including a chart-breaking theme song performed by a Welsh chorister) is a vital ingredient and additional flying and party sequences extend the pictures on the page. A less happy film-version by the same director is John Burningham's *Granpa* (1989, TVS and Channel 4), which, as discussed in Chapter 4, in its original book form invites the child reader actively to give meaning to the often cryptic snippets of conversation between a child and her grandfather. The film provides elaborate fantasy sequences of the pair's imaginary adventures, and both darkens and sentimentalizes the book's treatment of death with its emotional soundtrack, rain-drenched setting, and final image of Granpa as a boy dancing behind his granddaughter in a line of 'immortal' children.

In the 1980s, Conservative Government legislation aimed at strengthening competition in the market place moved the BBC, as well as the independent channels, closer to the practices of publishing, away from reliance on in-house programmes to the commissioning of more work from independent production companies. In this new climate a significant contribution to young children's broadcasting has come from the former teacher, Anne Wood, who founded Rag Doll Productions after publishing a magazine *Books For Your Children* (1965), setting up the Federation of Children's Book Groups, and working on YTV's *Book Tower*. Early commissions included *Storytime* for the BBC, which introduced story and picture books through live action. The company's most popular creations are probably *Rosie and Jim* (1990), whose secret adventures on a canal barge are juxtaposed with the stories about their imaginary doings, written by the boatman at the end of each episode, but the later *Tots TV* (1993), which includes a French speaker among its central puppet characters, is a more consciously 'book-aware' production. The Tots' house is full of carefully chosen books, and they are constantly seen reading to each other, or making up their own stories.

Rag Doll is also a publishing house, producing 'Rosie and Jim' and 'Tots TV' stories in a low-priced, 'Ladybird book' format, and selling these, along with tapes, videos, and magazines, from its own bookshop in Stratford-upon-Avon. Locating herself strongly within the dominant literary and broadcasting traditions of childhood, Wood believes that a good television programme, like a good book, provides a world into which children can imaginatively transpose themselves to learn through play. In her latest venture, a major early-learning series for the BBC called *Teletubbies* (1997), she deliberately seeks to push the viewer age-range as far back as eighteen months, replacing the Tots' language-play with the listening and interpreting of sounds from many sources to create a 'surreal' world of the infant imagination 'over the hills and far away', with influences that include Dr Seuss, children's radio, the Internet, and early television programmes such as *The Clangers*.[70] It will be interesting to see what kind of tie-in publications emerge from a series which makes television itself a main subject and, though retaining a narrator, uses relatively little dialogue and features very young child performers.

Conclusion: into the unknown

In 1992 Jay Blumler attempted to map out the future of British children's television. He praised its past achievements, based on committed and talented staff, a ring-fenced place in the schedules at times when children were able and wanting to watch, and a vibrant mix of information, entertainment and fantasy for a range of age groups. However, he saw cause for concern in the increased economic pressures faced by the commercial channels, by the creation of an internal market at the BBC resulting in greater reliance on international sales and cooperation. Another threat was posed by growing competition from a fifth terrestrial channel (from 1997) and from satellite and cable companies.[71] Children are always a minority audience, but one which regularly renews itself every three years, often bringing with it additional adult viewers, and in turn becoming the majority audience of the future. Research shows clearly that children's favourite programmes are in fact the 'family viewing' of soap operas and feature films, but there remains a substantial and highly appreciative audience for specially-made programmes.[72] Satellite and cable, including The Children's Channel (TCC), Nickelodeon, and Disney, are accessed by a higher percentage of families with children, but their share of the market and of the ratings remains relatively stable at 10 per cent, and to a large extent their output is dependent on cartoons, films and family 'sit coms' from America. However, there remains a real possibility that at some point children's television will disappear from the terrestrial channels, including the BBC, into 'niche' satellite subscription channels, perhaps targeted at different age-ranges.

An institutional and economic revolution of this kind would undoubtedly affect the types of material transmitted, as it has done in the past. Traditionally the children's media have created an image of the child attuned to changing British cultural assumptions, alongside bought-in foreign programmes. In a global market there will be increasing pressure (already dominating children's publishing) to choose material that will work in many national contexts, for instance *Little Lord Fauntleroy* (BBC1, 1995), with its American hero and heritage settings, or Elinor Brent-Dyer's 'Chalet School' series, with its scenic locations in the Tyrol, period detail, and international cast of characters. The international market also prefers long series, which can be shown over an extended time period. In place of the six-episode version of one book, there is a growing demand for longer series which, like *Toytown* and *William* years ago, can repay investment. *Five Children and It* (BBC1) was commissioned with a specially-written sequel, *The Return of the Psammead*, by Helen Cresswell, already in mind. One attraction of the hugely successful BBC version of *The Demon Headmaster* (BBC1, 1995) was the existence of a sequel, and the possibility for writing more.[73] Zenith North's version of Enid Blyton's *The Famous Five* (HTV/Tyne Tees), done as a period piece which evokes a never–never land of freedom and laughable villains: a relief perhaps for children growing up with knowledge of the Bulger case and the massacre at Dunblane. These qualities contributed to the decision to make a virtually unlimited series based on Enid Blyton's characters. On the other hand, the growth of the video market, much of it derived from television programmes of the past, offers an 'afterlife' to programmes that were previously ephemeral. Moreover, videos can be marketed – to schools and libraries as well as to homes – as products that are doubly 'classic', as books and as television drama. Although the impact on book sales of televisation only lasts a few weeks, no publisher can afford to ignore the chance to flash 'now a major TV serial' across a book cover, and new books based on programmes or 'character' soft toys proliferate on shop shelves.

Adaptations of children's books continue to find a place in the British media, especially when well-known and preferably out of copyright. Some contemporary authors, for instance, Anne Fine and Dick King-Smith, have hit the jackpot of purchased film rights and worldwide sales. Others see their work made into respectful, often nostalgic, tributes to a golden age of childhood. Such books are reviewed in the broadsheet papers, approved by politicians and educationists, available on video, or proffered as a slice of realism or anarchical release as part of a varied diet for the 'whole child'. If much of the adult schedules, as John Hartley has argued, are becoming 'paedocratised',[74] book dramatizations, for a family audience, still provide a reminder of how seriously the British broadcast media have taken children. Should they cease to do this, we would truly be in a new and different world.

Acknowledgement

I am grateful to the following for providing information and materials used in this chapter: Richard Callanan (Yorkshire Television), Carole Thomson (Rag Doll Productions), Paul Titley (Yorkshire Television), Leslie Oakden (Tyne Tees Television), Felicity Hayes McCoy, Fay Sinai (Blackwell's Children's Bookshop), Anne Wood (Rag Doll Productions).

References

1. Neil Postman (1985), *The Disappearance of Childhood* (London: W.H. Allen).
2. Stephen C. Kline (1995), 'The empire of play: emergent genres of product-based animations' in Cary Bazaigette and David Buckingham (eds), *In Front of the Children: Screen Entertainment and Young Audiences* (London: BFI), pp.162, 163.
3. David Buckingham (1993), *Children Talking Television: The Making of Television Literacy* (London and Washington DC: Falmer Press), p.34.
4. Helen Bromley (1996), ' "Did you know that there's no such thing as never land?": Working with video narratives in the early years' in Mary Hilton (ed.), *Potent Fictions: Children's Literacy and the Challenge of Popular Culture* (London: Routledge), pp.71–91.
5. Maire Messenger Davies (1989), *Television is Good for your Kids* (London: Hilary Shipman), pp.148–50.
6. Barrie Gunter and Jill McAleer (1990), *Children and Television: The One-Eyed Monster?* (London: Routledge), p.14.
7. David Buckingham (1995), 'On the impossibility of children's television: the case of Timothy Mallett' in Cary Bazaigette and David Buckingham (eds), op. cit., pp.47, 60.
8. Mary Adams (1950), 'Programmes for the young viewer', *BBC Quarterly*, vol. 5, no. 2, Summer, p.83. I am grateful to the BBC Written Archive, Caversham, for permission to quote from this article.
9. Jay G. Blumler (1992), *The Future of Children's Television in Britain: An Enquiry for the Broadcasting Standards Council* (London: Broadcasting Standards Council), p.22.
10. Ibid., p.34.
11. Adams, op. cit., p.81.
12. Ian Hartley (1983), *Goodnight Children . . . Everywhere: An Informal History of Children's Broadcasting* (Southborough, Kent: Midas Books), p.15.
13. Ibid., p.26.
14. Adams, op. cit., p.82.
15. Hilda Jennings and Winifred Gill (1939), *Broadcasting in Everyday Life: A Survey of the Social Effects of the Coming of Broadcasting* (London: BBC), pp.31, 39.
16. Derek McCulloch (1948), 'Entertaining the young listener', *BBC Quarterly*, vol. 2, no. 4, January, p.229. I am grateful to the BBC Written Archive, Caversham, for permission to quote from this article. (*Editors' note*: This motto was also associated with a number of children's publishers – see page 30.)
17. Ibid., pp.229–30.
18. Most of the presenters and contributors adopted the 'aunt' and 'uncle' sobriquets, but the staff of the Aberdeen station chose to call themselves after animals. As early as 1926 there was a concerted effort to remove these personas from the air, to the protests of children and parents. See Hartley, op. cit., p.17.
19. Hartley, op. cit., p.15.
20. John Reith, cited in Hartley, op. cit., p.16.
21. Asa Briggs (1995), *The History of Broadcasting in the United Kingdom, Vol. III: The War of Words*, rev. edn. (Oxford: Oxford University Press), p.105.
22. Cited in Hartley, op. cit., p.25. (*Editors' note*: This attitude is yet another reflection from the children's publishing world, as can be seen in the words of Eleanor Graham and Pam Royds, quoted on page 31.)
23. Roger Eckersley, memorandum to C.E. Hodges, February 1927, cited in Hartley, op. cit., p.24.

24. Editorials in *Radio Times*, 1934, *Children's Hour Annual*, 1936, cited in Asa Briggs (1985), *The BBC: The First 50 Years* (Oxford: Oxford University Press), p.122.
25. BBC 'Aunts and Uncles' (*c*.1927), *The Magic Doorway* (London: S.W. Partridge and Co.).
26. The programme went off air for four days in September 1939 but was soon transmitting again from its base in Bristol, and from the other regions. A closer link with the Religious department, which aired Bible-based stories and plays in an existing slot, 'For the Children' on Sunday afternoons, enabled an expansion into Sabbath broadcasting, to the alarm of those who feared a threat to Sunday School attendance, Briggs, (1995), op. cit., Vol. III, p.105.
27. Ibid. (*Editors' note*: Compare this to the treatment given to enemies in comics, discussed on page 3.)
28. Hartley, op. cit., p.32.
29. Ibid., p.63.
30. Briggs, (1995), op. cit., Vol. III, p.429.
31. Ibid., p.646.
32. Cited in Hartley, op. cit., p.64.
33. Briggs (1985), op. cit., p.335.
34. Anthologies of *Listen With Mother* stories were published by Hutchinson in 1982 and 1983.
35. BBC (1993), *Programme Strategy Review, BBC Radio 5 – Drama/Readings for Young People* (unpaginated).
36. Ibid., pp.32–3.
37. *Times Educational Supplement*, 3 April 1992.
38. See the article by Sarah McNeill, *The Independent*, 20 September 1995.
39. Andrea Millwood Hargrave (1994), *Radio and Audience Attitudes* (London: Broadcasting Standards Council), pp.23–8.
40. Sue Stoessl (1994), 'Children and radio' in Hargrave, op. cit., pp.46–7.
41. Caroline Sharp (1995), *Viewing, Listening, Learning: The Uses and Impact of School Broadcasts* (Slough: National Foundation for Educational Research for the BBC), pp.39, 45.
42. BBC (1992), *Extending Choice: the BBC's Role in the 1990s* (London: BBC), p.33.
43. BBC Press Service (1996), *Background Information for Governors' Seminar on the BBC and Children, June 1996*.
44. There was the usual opposition from those who feared competition with Sunday School attendance.
45. Memorandum from Mary Adams, 8 August 1947, cited in Anna Home (1993), *Into the Box of Delights: A History of Children's Television* (London: BBC Books), p.17.
46. Ibid., p.83.
47. Ibid., p.84.
48. McCulloch, op. cit., p.230.
49. Home, op. cit., p.28.
50. Maria Bird, 'Introduction', *BBC Children's Annual 1951* (London: Burke, by arrangement with the BBC).
51. Freda Lingstrom (1953), 'Children and television', *BBC Quarterly*, vol. 8, no. 2, Summer, p.99. I am grateful to the BBC Written Archive, Caversham, for permission to quote from this article.
52. Ibid., p.100.
53. Hartley, op. cit., p.25.
54. Cited in Bernard Sendall (1982), *Independent Television in Britain, Vol. 1: Origin and Foundation, 1946–62* (Basingstoke: Macmillan Press), p.104.

55. Hilde Himmelweit, A.N. Oppenheim and Pamela Vine (1958), *Television and the Child: An Empirical Study of the Effect of Television on the Young* (London: Oxford University Press), pp.23, 202, 321–2, 331.
56. Briggs (1995), op. cit., p.346.
57. Home, op. cit., pp.36, 89.
58. Doreen Stephens (1966), 'Television for children', *BBC Lunch-Time Lectures*, 5th series, 19 October, pp.8, 18, 4. I am grateful to the BBC Written Archive, Caversham for permission to quote from this article.
59. Ibid., p.9.
60. Home, op. cit., p.82.
61. Ibid., pp.85, 162.
62. Blumler, op. cit., p.4.
63. Samantha Beere, and Rosemary Newell (1990), 'Television and children', *BBC Annual Review* XVI (London: John Libbey for the BBC), pp.29–30.
64. See Roger Singleton-Turner (1994), *Television and Children* (Borehamwood: BBC Television Training), p.59.
65. Bernard Sendall (1983), *Independent Television in Britain, Vol. 2: Expansion and Change, 1958–68*, (Basingstoke: Macmillan Press), p.234; Jeremy Potter (1990), *Independent Television in Britain, Vol 4: Companies and Programmes, 1968-80* (Basingstoke: Macmillan Press), p.261.
66. Interviews with Patrick Titley, Tom Kingdon, and Anne Wood, August 1996.
67. The words 'cosy' or 'comfortable' competition were used by a number of those working in children's television in conversation with the author. However, the competition has taken on a sharper edge with the expansion of cable and satellite provision, increased programming for children on Channel 4, and the merger of BBC radio and television programme production in late 1996. It remains to be seen whether children's broadcasting will benefit or suffer from these changes and others still in progress at the time of writing.
68. Potter, op. cit., p.266.
69. See Allan Horrox, and John Hambley (1991), 'ITV's baby boom', *Guardian*, 15 April. This tradition continues; for instance, at the end of 1996 Channel 4 produced an animated version of *The Happy Prince*.
70. Interview with the author, 28 August 1996.
71. Blumler, op. cit., p.4; cf. note 69.
72. Beere and Newell, op. cit., pp.23–31.
73. Interview with Richard Callanan, 11 August 1996.
74. Hartley, John (1987), 'Invisible Fictions: Television Audience, Paedocracy, Pleasure', *Textual Practice*, vol. 1, no. 2.

Afterword
Nicholas Tucker

Much of the argument about children's literature in the last fifty years has concentrated on content. While only a few critics in 1945 were complaining about the narrow social range of characters in British children's books, many more were concerned with the bad influence on the young thought to arise from reading too many quickly produced stories of little literary merit, in particular those written by Enid Blyton, the post-war Pied Piper of children's literature. Arguments about social class and gender issues in fiction became more important in the 1960s, together with the whole topic of children's access to literature. Were public libraries too middle-class in outlook? Were too many bookshops concentrated in too few areas? Were most books still addressed to the good, motivated reader at the expense of children who needed something easier and more direct in order to win their initial interest?

During the 1970s, publishers reacted speedily and effectively to these concerns. New, popular paperbacks suddenly appeared written by authors unconstrained by some of the literary conventions and taboos that had once kept children's literature safe from most controversy and also occasionally more than a little dull. Characters of every class, colour and conviction swarmed on to the page, sometimes talking a brand of English owing little to the rules of formal grammar. For younger readers, picture books began to blaze with colour as never before, with contents often reaching into new dimensions of vigorous action and outspoken emotion. Social and gender issues, now well out into the open, were joined by newer concerns over the environment, health and disability. Critics who once accused children's literature of living in a cosy, unreal world could no longer find anything of this nature with which to take issue. More often the accusation was that children's literature, far from telling its young readers too little about real life, now often told them rather too much. Many adults found the new litany of near-hopelessness in some children's literature about subjects such as homelessness, unemployment, family break-up, bullying and dystopian visions of the future increasingly hard to take. Young readers themselves may have had fewer problems here; not for the first time, idealized adult images of children and their typical likes

155

and dislikes sometimes clash with what children often seem to want for themselves. Steven Andrew, producer of *Grange Hill*, still one of the BBC television's most successful drama series for the young, illustrated this point at a conference with the title 'What We Need to Know about the Child Audience', held at the London College of Printing on 28 June, 1996. According to him, it was child viewers who regularly suggested topics such as bullying or drug abuse for future inclusion. Far from gloomy adult producers foisting their pessimism on to a young audience, it seemed children themselves most wanted to hear about the darker side of life, whether their parents or teachers always approved or not.

Much other writing for children today has also come right back from the more sheltered visions of society it previously offered. Novelists such as Nina Bawden, Anne Fine, Jane Gardam, Alan Garner, Penelope Lively, Ian McEwan and Salman Rushdie have written books initially for children but which soon found a niche in the adult market as well. The problem that exists in the whole area of children's literature is no longer the content and style of children's books but their availability to young readers often less used to reading for enjoyment than was once the case. Censorship by the invisible forces of what were once considered conventional standards of good taste and form has been replaced by the censorship of market forces. Savage cuts in library provision in and out of school means fewer book purchases as well as fewer librarians to enthuse and inform young readers. Authors who relied on institutional as well as on popular sales are now sometimes losing their back-lists while facing an increasingly uncertain future.

Big publishing houses meanwhile are putting more resources instead into 'series' books, popular with readers but something of a strait-jacket for writers required to produce fiction to fit certain prescribed and narrow literary formulae. Some smaller publishers meanwhile, have also emerged offering new hope to new and old quality writers. Lower overheads and staffing costs can be an advantage here, plus the greater efficiency that can flow from an absence of complex and burgeoning internal hierarchies. But increasingly centralized book distribution through only a limited amount of retailing outlets remains a constant threat to all publishers, particularly those without the large financial assets necessary for launching new projects which may or may not be successful.

Society itself continues to turn towards electronic media for its main entertainment. Books are still sold in large numbers, but the habit of reading for pleasure can no longer be taken for granted, even among those who seem naturally good readers. In 1945 there were many such readers but a dearth of suitable material for them. In some ways there has now been a reversal of this picture: there are hosts of well-written, entertaining books but far fewer children for whom reading is still the main leisure-time pursuit. More changes can be expected in the future; whether these will be to the further advantage or disadvantage of children's literature remains an uncomfortably open question.

Bibliography

Adams, Mary (1950), 'Programmes for the Young Viewer', *BBC Quarterly*, vol. 5, no. 2, Summer.

Alderson, Valerie (1974), 'Paperback Review', *Children's Book Review*, vol. 4, no. 2, Summer.

Alderson, Brian (1986), *Sing a Song of Sixpence* (Cambridge: Cambridge University Press).

Background Information for Governors' Seminar on the BBC and Children, June 1996 (1996), (London: BBC).

Barker, Martin (1984), *A Haunt of Fears: The Strange History of the British Horror Comics Campaign* (London: Pluto Press).

Barnett, Steve (1991), 'The BBC After the Cold War', *Guardian*, 8 April.

Barr, John (1986), *Illustrated Children's Books* (London: British Library).

Barwise, P. and Ehrenberg, A. (1990), *Television and its Audience* (London: Sage).

Bawden, Nina (1994), *In My Own Time: Almost an Autobiography* (London: Virago).

Baxendale, Leo (1993), *On Comedy: The Beano and Ideology*, rev. edn (Stroud: Reaper Books).

Bazaigette, Cary and Buckingham, David (eds) (1995), *In Front of the Children: Screen Entertainment and Young Audiences* (London: BFI).

'BBC Aunts and Uncles' (*c.* 1927), *The Children's Hour Annual* (London: S.W. Partridge and Co.).

Beere, Samantha and Newell, Rosemary (1990), 'Television and Children', *BBC Annual Review* XVI (London: John Libby for the BBC).

Berry, Gordon, L. and Asamen, Joy (1993), *Children and Television: Images in a Changing Sociocultural World* (London and New York: Sage Publications).

Blumler, Jay, G. (1992), *The Future of Children's Television in Britain: An Enquiry for the Broadcasting Standards Council* (London: Broadcasting Standards Council).

Bonfield, G. and Hopkins, J. (1981), 'Carnegie Criteria', *Library Association Record*, vol. 83, no. 9, September.

Book Publishing (1992), (London: Key Note Publications Ltd).

Book Publishing in Britain (1995) (London: *Bookseller*).

Bradbury, Malcolm (1985), *Fifty Penguin Years* (Harmondsworth: Penguin).

Bradman, Tony (1983), 'The Awards Business', *Books for Keeps*, no. 20.

Bratton, J.S. (1981), *The Impact of Victorian Children's Fiction* (London: Croom Helm; Totowa, New Jersey: Barnes & Noble Books).

Briggs, Asa (1985), *The BBC: The First 50 Years* (Oxford: Oxford University Press).

Briggs, Asa (rev. edn, 1995), *The History of Broadcasting in the United Kingdom*, vols. I–V (Oxford: Oxford University Press).

Broadcasting and Youth (1979), (London: BBC).

Brown, Maggie (1996), 'The Square Window', *Guardian*, 5 June.

Buckingham, David (1993), *Children Talking Television: The Making of Television Literacy* (London and Washington DC: Falmer Press).

Buckingham, David (1995), *Moving Images: Understanding Children's Emotional Responses to Television* (Manchester: Manchester University Press).

Buckingham, David (1994), 'Television and the Definition of Childhood' in B. Mayall (ed.), *Children's Childhoods Observed and Experienced* (London: Falmer Press).

'Carnegie Awards' (1968), *Times Literary Supplement*, 20 June.

'Carnegie Medal' (1966), *Library Association Record*, vol. 68, no. 10, October.

Carpenter, Kevin (1983), *Penny Dreadfuls and Comics*, the catalogue of a loan exhibition at Bethnal Green Museum of Childhood (London: Victoria and Albert Museum).

Cecil, Mirabel (1996), *A Kind of Prospero: Sebastian Walker 1942–1991* (London: Walker Books).

Chambers, Aidan (1969), *The Reluctant Reader* (Oxford: Pergamon).

Children as Viewers and Listeners (1974) (London: BBC).

Children's Book Handbook (1996), (Edinburgh and London: Young Book Trust).

Clark, Margaret (1972), 'Eleanor Graham', *Signal* no. 9, September.

Clark, Margaret (ed.) (1993), *Signal* no. 70, January.

Clayre, Alasdair (1973), *The Impact of Broadcasting or Mr Buckle's Wall is Singing* (Salisbury, Wilts: Compton Russell by arrangement with the BBC).

Colwell, Eileen (1944), 'The L.A. Carnegie Medal', *Library Association Record*, vol. 46, no. 1, January.

Colwell, Eileen (1974), 'At the Beginning', *Signal* no. 13, January.

Crampton, Patricia (1984), 'The Hans Christian Andersen Award', *Books for Keeps*, no. 25.

Cristell, Andrew (1995), *Understanding Radio* (London: Routledge).

Crouch, Marcus (1957), *Chosen for Children* (London: Library Association).

Culf, Andrew (1995), 'BBC Ends Story of *Jackanory*', *Guardian*, 20 November.

Cusk, Rachel (1996), 'Books, Beer and Passion', *The Times*, 25 January.

Davies, Marie Messenger (1989), *Television is Good for Your Kids* (London: Hilary Shipman).

Davies, Marie Messenger and O'Malley, Kate (1996), *Children and Television Drama: A Review of the Literature* (London: School of Media, London College of Printing and Distributive Trade, The London Institute).

Dalley, Terrence (ed.) (1980), *The Complete Guide to Illustration and Design* (London: Phaidon).

Dent, J.M. (1938), *The House of Dent 1888–1938: The Memoirs of J.M. Dent* (London: J.M. Dent).

Doonan, Jane (1993), *Looking at Pictures in Picture Books* (Stroud: Thimble Press).

Dorr, Andrea (1986), *Children and Television: A Special Medium for a Special Audience* (London: Sage).

Duffy, Maureen (1989), *A Thousand Capricious Glances: A History of the Methuen List 1889–1989* (London: Methuen).

Dunn, G. (1977), *The Box in the Corner* (London: Macmillan).

Durell, Ann (1982), 'If There Is No Happy Ending: Children's Book Publishing–Past, Present, and Future', parts I and II, *The Horn Book Magazine*, February and April.

Duvoisin, Roger (1965), 'Children's Book Illustration: The Pleasures and Problems' reprinted in Virginia Haviland (ed.), *Children's Literature: Views and Reviews* (London: The Bodley Head).

Eccleshare, Julia (1995), 'We've got the treasure, but where's the confidence?', *Bookseller*, 8 December.

Editorial (1937), *Library Association Record*, vol. 39, no. 1, January.

Educational Television and Radio in Britain (1986) (London: BBC).

Elliott, David (1978), 'World's Work', *School Book Shop News*, no. 11, Autumn.

Ellis, Alec (1963), *A History of Children's Reading and Literature* (Oxford: Pergamon).

Ellis, Alec (1977), '40 Years of the Carnegie Medal: A Hallmark of Quality', *Library Association Record*, vol. 79, no. 2, February.

Eyre, Frank (1971), *British Children's Books in the Twentieth Century* (London: Longman).

Extending Choices: The BBC's Role in the 1990s (1992) (London: BBC).

Feaver, William (1977), *When We Were Young* (London: Thames and Hudson).

Flugge, Klaus (1994), 'Crossing the Divide', *Signal* no. 75, September.

Garrett, J. (1993), 'Far-away Wisdom: Three Nominees for the 1992 Andersen Prize', *The Reading Teacher*, vol. 46, no. 4.

Giblin, James Cross (1986), 'Children's Book Publishing in America: 1919 to Now', *Children's Literature in Education*, vol. 17, no. 3, Fall.

Goldthwaite, John (1990), 'Picking Up the Book', *Signal* no. 63, September.

Graham, Eleanor (1972), 'The Bumpus Years', *Signal* no. 9, September.

Graham, Eleanor (1973), 'The Puffin Years', *Signal* no. 12, September.

Graphic Account (Youth Libraries Group, 1993).

Greenfield, Patricia (1984), *Mind and Media* (London: Fontana).

Gritten, Sally (1991), *The Story of Puffin Books* (Harmondsworth: Penguin).

Gunter, Barrie and McAleer, Jill (1990), *Children and Television: The One-Eyed Monster?* (London: Routledge).

Hale, Kathleen (1994), *A Slender Reputation* (Harmondsworth: Frederick Warne & Co.).

Hall, Douglas (1982), *Listen with Mother* (London: Hutchinson in association with the BBC).

Hall, Douglas (1983), *More Stories from 'Listen with Mother'* (London: Hutchinson in association with the BBC).

Hardyment, Christina (1994), 'Slimy Jeremiads of a Serial Killer', *The Independent*, 16 July.

Hare, Steve (1995), *Allen Lane and the Penguin Editors 1935–1970* (Harmondsworth: Penguin).

Hargrove, Andrea Millwood (1994), *Radio and Audience Attitudes* (London: Broadcasting Standards Council Annual Review).

Hartley, Ian (1983), *Goodnight Children... Everywhere: An Informal History of Children's Broadcasting* (Southborough: Midas)

Hartley, John (1987), 'Invisible Fictions: Television Audience, Paedocracy, Pleasure', *Textual Practice*, vol. 1, no. 2.

Heeks, Peggy (1968), 'Looking for a Winner', *Times Literary Supplement*, 6 June.

Hill, Janet (1973), *Children Are People* (London: Hamish Hamilton).

Himmelweit, Hilde, Oppenheim, A.N. and Pamela Vine (1958), *Television and the Child: An empirical study of the effect of television on the young* (London: Oxford University Press).

Hodge, Robert and Tripp, D. (1986), *Children and Television* (Cambridge: Polity).

Hodges, Sheila (1978), *Gollancz: The Story of a Publishing House 1928–1978* (London: Victor Gollancz).

Hodgkin, M. (1985), 'A Personal Philosophy of Publishing for Children', *Signal* no. 46, January.

Hollindale, Peter (1974), *Choosing Books for Children* (London: Elek).

Holloway, Michael (1996), 'Why Small is Beautiful', *Y.B.T. News*, Summer.

Home, Anna (1993), *Into the Box of Delights: A History of Children's Television* (London: BBC Books).

Horne, Alan (1994), *Dictionary of Twentieth-Century British Book Illustration* (London: Antique).

Horrox, Allan and Hambley, John (1991), 'ITV's Baby Boom', *Guardian*, 15 April.

Howe, Michael (1977), *Learning from Television: Psychological and Educational Research* (London: Academic Press).

Howe, Michael (1977), *Television and Children* (London: New University Education).

Hunt, Peter (1995), *Children's Literature: An Illustrated History* (Oxford: Oxford University Press).

Jennings, Hilda and Gill, Winnifred (1939), *Broadcasting in Everyday Life: A Survey of the Social Effects of the Coming of Broadcasting* (London: BBC).

Jones, Harold (1993), in *The Box of Delights: Children's Book Illustrations by Twenty-One British Artists*, catalogue to the exhibition organised by Newport Museum and Art Gallery, Gwent.

Karl, Jean E. (1995), 'A History of Children's Book Publishing', *Journal of Youth Services in Libraries*, vol. 8, no. 3, Spring.

Karpf, Anne (1996), 'Sound off, Vision on', *Guardian*, 12 June.

King, Arthur and Stuart, A.F. (1965), *The House of Warne: One Hundred Years of Publishing* (London: Frederick Warne & Co.)

Kingsford, R.J.L. (1970), *The Publishers' Association 1896–1946 with an epilogue* (Cambridge: Cambridge University Press).

Lambert, J.W. and Ratcliffe, Michael (1987), *The Bodley Head 1887–1987* (London: The Bodley Head).

Leeson, Robert (1974), 'Boom', *Signal* no. 13, January.

Leeson, Robert (1986), 'The Way Ahead', *Children's Literature in Education*, vol. 17, no. 4, Winter.

Lewis, John (1984), *The Twentieth-Century Book: Its Illustrations and Design*, 2nd edition (London: Herbert).

Library Association (1956), Council minutes

Library Association (1978), *Study School and National Conference Proceedings* (London: Library Association).

Lingstrom, Freda (1953), 'Children and Television', *BBC Quarterly*, vol. 8, no. 2, Summer.

Lively, Penelope (1979), 'Winning Reflections', *Author*, vol. 90, no. 2.

McCulloch, Derek (1948), 'Entertaining the Young Listener', *BBC Quarterly*, vol. 2, no. 4, January.

Mann, Andrew (1975), 'The Other Award', *Signal* no. 18, September.

Manning, Andrew (1992), 'Satellite Viewing', *BBC Annual Report XVIII* (London: John Libby for the BBC).

Manning, Rosemary (1969), 'Whatever Happened to *Onion John?*', *Times Literary Supplement*, 4 December.

Martin, Douglas (1993), *Charles Keeping: An Illustrator's Life* (London: Julia MacRae).

Martin, Douglas (1989), *The Telling Line* (London: Julia MacRae).

Montanaro, Ann (1993), *Pop-Up and Movable Books: A Bibliography* (Metuchen, New Jersey and London: The Scarecrow Press).

Morpurgo, J.E. (1979), *Allen Lane: King Penguin* (London: Hutchinson).

Morpurgo, Michael (1992), 'When the Best is not Good Enough', *Times Educational Supplement*, 27 November.

Moss, Elaine (1973), 'Pat Hutchins: A Natural', *Signal* no. 10, January.

Moss, Elaine (1974), 'A Mirror in the Market Place', *Signal* no. 15, September.

Moss, Elaine (1975), 'Quentin Blake', *Signal* no. 16, January.

Moss, Elaine (1979), 'Raymond Briggs: On British attitudes to the strip cartoon and children's book illustration', *Signal* 28, January.

Murison, W.J. (1971), 'Carnegie Medal', *Library Association Record*, vol. 73, no. 8, August.

Noble, Grant (1975), *Children in Front of the Small Screen* (London: Sage/Constable).

Nodelman, Perry (1988), *Words About Pictures: The Narrative Art of Children's Picture Books* (Athens Georgia: University of Georgia Press).

'Notes from the Attic' (1973), *Junior Bookshelf*, vol. 1, no. 3, March.

Palmer, Patricia (1985), *The Lively Audience* (Sydney: Allen & Unwin).

Petrie, Duncan, and Willis, J. (1995), *Television and the Household* (London: BFI).

People and Programmes (1995) (London: BBC).

Philip, Neil (1985), 'The Smarties Prize for Children's Books', *British Book News – Children's Books*, December.

Postman, Neil (1985), *The Disappearance of Childhood* (London: W.H. Allen).

Powling, Chris (1994), *The Best of 'Books for Keeps'* (London: The Bodley Head).

Powling, Chris (1993), 'Contemplating Carnegie', *Books for Keeps*, no. 82.

Price, Susan (1991), *Books for Life* (Gondwanaland Press).

Pullman, Philip (1989), 'Invisible Pictures', *Signal* no. 60, September.

Rosen, Michael (1995), 'Raising the Issues', *Signal* no. 76, January.

Sabin, Roger (1993), *Adult Comics: An Introduction* (London: Routledge).

St John, John (1990), *William Heinemann: A Century of Publishing 1890–1990* (London: Heinemann).

Salway, Lance (1976), 'Kids' Oscars', *Times Literary Supplement*, 16 July.

Sayers, W.C. Berwick (1937), 'The Library Association Carnegie Medal and Mr Arthur Ransome', *Library Association Record*, vol. 39, no. 5, May.

Schramm, W., Lyle, J., and E.B. Parker (1961), *Television in the Lives of our Children* (London: Oxford University Press).

Sendak, Maurice (1989), *Caldecott & Co.* (New York: Reinhardt Books).

Sharp, Caroline (1995), *Viewing, Listening, Learning: The Uses and Impact of School Broadcasts* (Slough: National Foundation for Educational Research for the BBC).

Signal no. 78 (1995), September.

Silverstein, Roger (1994), *Television and Everyday Life* (London: BFI).

Singleton-Turner, Roger (1994), *Television and Children* (Borehamwood: BBC Television Training).

Sisson, Rosemary Anne (1994), 'What are we doing to our children?', *Daily Mail*, 15 July.

Snyman, Piet (1995), 'Towards a third golden age', *Bookseller*, 25 August.

'Straight Talk in the Library' (1995), *Bookseller*, 25 August.

Stephens, Doreen (1966), 'Television for Children', *BBC Lunch-Time Lectures*, 5th series, 19 October.

Stoessl, Sue (1994), 'Children and Radio' in Andrea Millwood Hargrave (ed.), *Radio and Audience Attitudes: Report for the Broadcasting Standards Council* (London: John Libbey).

Sutcliffe, Peter (1978), *The Oxford University Press: An Informal History* (Oxford: Clarendon).

Tait, Simon (1995), 'Children's Literature', *Times Educational Supplement*, 24 November.

Taylor, Jennifer (1981), 'Extraordinary', *Library Association Record*, vol. 81, no. 11, November.

Tebbel, John (1981), *A History of Book Publishing in the United States, Volume IV, The Great Change, 1940–1980* (New York and London: R.R. Bowker).

Townsend, John Rowe (1975), 'A Decade of Newbery Books in Perspective' in Lee Kingman (ed.), *Newbery and Caldecott Medal Books 1966–1975* (Boston: The Horn Book).

Townsend, John Rowe (1978), 'Ten Years of the Guardian Award', *Federation of Children's Book Groups Year Book* (Birmingham: Federation of Children's Book Groups).

Trease, Geoffrey (1983), 'Fifty Years On: A writer looks back', *Children's Literature in Education*, Autumn.

Tucker, W. (1991), 'Childhood in Puffins', *Signal* no. 65, May.

Turner, E.S. (1975), *Boys will be Boys: The story of Sweeney Todd, Deadwood Dick, Sexton Blake, Billy Bunter, Dick Barton, et al.*, 3rd edn (London: Michael Joseph).

Unwin, Sir Stanley (1976), *The Truth About Publishing*, 8th edn, revised and partly re-written by Philip Unwin (London: George Allen and Unwin).

Using Radio in the Primary School (1991) (London: BBC).

Walsh, Susan and Cassell, Catherine (1995), 'A Case of Covert Discrimination: Report of the Women into Management Study' (London: Bentinck Group).

Westall, Robert (1979), 'How Real do you want your Realism?', *Signal* no. 28.

Whalley, Irene and Chester, Tessa (1988), *A History of Children's Book Illustration* (London: John Murray).

'Whitbread Literary Awards' (1978), *Bookseller*, 9 December.

Young People and Broadcasting (1987) (London: BBC).

Index